D1061470

Unless

FROM THE SERIES EDITOR

The organization of students and their academic work in classrooms has been a problem confronting teachers for as long as there have been teachers and classrooms. Seeing to it that students are productive in classrooms is a challenge for any teacher. Add to this the formidable task of affording all students in a classroom an equal opportunity to learn and you have the pivotal practical dilemma that Cohen, Lotan, and their colleagues tackle in the series of studies brought together for the first time in this volume.

The studies in this collection illustrate the power of a strategy of applying and extending sociological knowledge. Beginning with a common understanding of interaction patterns in heterogeneous work groups derived from basic sociological theory, the authors of these chapters utilize this shared framework to guide analyses of student interaction in classrooms, particularly interaction around assigned learning tasks. Because the empirical studies reported here are all guided by a common theoretical framework, the entire body of work amounts to more than the sum of the parts, as each study builds upon the results of earlier studies to advance our understanding of how to modify classroom interaction patterns to achieve desired results. The theoretical framework of the studies also allows the authors to propose multiple approaches to addressing the same problem, such as status interventions and curricular changes to achieve greater equity and productivity in classroom groups. Moving beyond the classroom, the later chapters investigate problems of implementation by considering the organizational conditions necessary to support teachers who wish to employ these approaches.

The work collected here reveals the benefits to be derived from a sustained sociological research program that pursues solutions to an enduring practical problem. Cohen, Lotan, and the other researchers contributing to this volume have been able to bring their research to bear on a variety of classroom situations in which teachers find themselves, including elementary and secondary classrooms and classrooms with second language learners. Their efforts to address real problems faced by teachers in diverse circumstances signal their commitment to contributing to the improvement of educational practice. Furthermore, their work to develop knowledge in support of improved practice has resulted not only in knowledge of value to practitioners but also in a more robust empirical base for the further development of sociological theory.

Gary Natriello

WORKING
FOR EQUITY IN
HETEROGENEOUS
CLASSROOMS

Sociological Theory
in Practice

Elizabeth G. Cohen
Rachel A. Lotan
EDITORS

Teachers College
Columbia University
New York and London

Published by Teachers College Press, 1234 Amsterdam Avenue, New York, NY 10027

Library of Congress Cataloging-in-Publication Data

Working for equity in heterogeneous classrooms : sociological theory
  in practice / edited by Elizabeth G. Cohen, Rachel A. Lotan.
      p.   cm. — (Sociology of education series)
    Includes bibliographical references and index.
    ISBN 0-8077-3644-9 (cloth : alk. paper). — ISBN 0-8077-3643-0
  (pbk. : alk. paper)
    1. Mixed ability grouping in education.   2. Group work in
  education.   3. Educational equalization.   4. Educational sociology.
  I. Cohen, Elizabeth G., 1931–   .   II. Lotan, Rachel A.
  III. Series: Sociology of education series (New York, N.Y.)
  LB3061.3.W67   1997
  371.39'5—dc21   97-20465

ISBN 0-8077-3643-0 (paper)
ISBN 0-8077-3644-9 (cloth)

Printed on acid-free paper

Manufactured in the United States of America

04 03 02 01 00 99 98 97   8 7 6 5 4 3 2 1

Contents

**Part V: Effects of Complex Instruction on Academic Achievement,
Linguistic Proficiency, and Cognitive Development**

Part VI: Organizational Theory in Support of Teachers

Part VII: Conclusion

Preface

Developing a workable and equitable approach to instruction, one that reaches *all* children, is a challenge. The purpose of this book is to apply sociological theory and method to that challenge. Since 1979, my colleagues and I have been working on the solution to the problem of unequal status in heterogeneous classrooms: those without ability grouping; those that are bilingual, multilingual, or desegregated; and those in untracked middle and secondary schools. Studying interaction in small groups, we have documented the way high-status students talk more and learn more than low-status students.

Using expectation states theory, we have developed ways to help teachers produce equal-status interaction within small groups working in the classroom. Rachel Lotan and I have also used this theory to evaluate how well these strategies work to boost the participation of low-status students.

In addition to expectation states theory, sociology of education and organizational theory have played a critical role in producing equitable classrooms. We have called our approach complex instruction (CI); teachers in Europe and Israel as well as many in the United States are using this approach today.

Complex instruction permits teachers to teach at a high intellectual level while reaching a wide range of students. Students use each other as resources while completing challenging group tasks that require the use of multiple intellectual abilities. Teachers work to create equal-status interaction within the small groups. Studies of CI classrooms have documented gains on standardized achievement tests, on content-referenced tests, in learning to speak English, and in cognitive development.

Almost 20 years of painstaking research back the claims in this book. We have carefully studied the implementation of CI in classrooms with populations that are mixed ethnically, linguistically, and academically at the elementary and middle school levels. We have studied teachers working under differing organizational arrangements in order to test ideas about optimal organizational support for CI teachers.

Our initial hypotheses had a strong basis in theory. These propositions gained support as they were repeatedly tested in different settings with different age groups and various subject matters. Through this process of research, we gained confidence in the generalizations presented in this book. Because of this theory and research, the reader can apply what we have learned to a wide array of settings. For example, the application of organizational theory to the problem of classroom management when students are working in small groups is extremely useful for classroom researchers and educational developers.

The classroom as a field of research was long ago ceded to psychologists. This book illustrates how the concepts and theories of sociology can profoundly alter the social structure of classrooms. The work of this group of researchers is testimony to the exciting potential that sociological theory and research have for the field of education.

The audience for this volume is sociologists of education, educational researchers, researchers on cooperative learning, graduate students of education and sociology, scholars interested in multicultural and intercultural education, and a broad network of educators and scholars who want to examine the knowledge base for treating issues of equity in heterogeneous classes. The reader who does not wish to study the tables can follow the text with no difficulty. Some readers, after completing the first three parts of the book, may wish to select chapters according to particular interests. Because CI has a growing audience overseas, this book also is addressed to international educators. The issue of heterogeneity in classrooms is of growing importance in many parts of the world.

ABOUT GROUPWORK

Cooperative learning is the most widely accepted solution for the instructional challenges of heterogeneous classrooms. It is true that the use of small cooperative groups increases friendliness and trust among students from diverse ethnic, linguistic, and racial backgrounds. However, teachers find the use of groupwork a difficult strategy to manage. They worry about loss of control; they also are concerned with the failure of some students to participate while others do all the work. Parents of high achievers complain that their children are held back by the group and that they are working as "unpaid teaching assistants."

Groupwork in CI addresses these issues with intellectually demanding curricula and with extensive staff development for teachers. Teachers have been among the first to recognize the practical and powerful implications of this work. They ask: "Why didn't they ever teach me that children are supposed to talk to each other, or that teachers can delegate responsibility to students without losing control?" Parents easily can see that even "gifted" students develop skills demanding higher-order thinking and learn to accept help from other group members on aspects of a task.

In a CI classroom, students do not work in small groups all the time. Even within a CI lesson, the teacher alternates the use of small groups with whole class orientation and wrap-ups. CI is particularly effective in developing higher-order thinking skills. It combines well with techniques that are effective for teaching routine skills and supply background information.

ORGANIZATION OF THE BOOK

The first part of this book serves as an introduction to complex instruction and to the concept of an equitable classroom. The first chapter sets the research in the context of larger issues of stratification and the sociology of the classroom. The second chapter presents a detailed description of a classroom using complex instruction, its organization, and the nature of its activities.

Part II details the research on how the organization and management of the classroom yield interaction among students. Its two chapters present consistent evidence of the relationship between interaction and learning.

The third part focuses on status problems and their treatment. It starts with a chapter on the nature of status problems and their theoretical explanation. Following this is a chapter on specific interventions designed to treat status problems and another on the effects of gender as a potential source of status problems in the elementary classroom.

A central feature of complex instruction is the multiple-ability curriculum. Part IV contains the principles of creating multiple-ability tasks as well as a study of the effects of introducing multiple abilities in a secondary school curriculum.

Part V deals with the effects of CI on achievement. After summarizing the results of extensive achievement testing over the life of the program, we present a critique of achievement testing and offer an alternative mode of assessment. This is followed by a chapter on the effects of CI on English language acquisition among Spanish-speaking students and a chapter on the effects of CI on cognitive development among students in Israel.

Part VI contains four chapters reporting on research on organizational support and staff development for both experienced and preservice teachers. The concluding part discusses dissemination of the program and its impact on teachers.

Elizabeth G. Cohen

Acknowledgments

Various foundations have generously supported the work of the Program for Complex Instruction presented in this volume. We wish to thank the Walter S. Johnson Foundation, which supported the collection of data during the 1982–83 academic year. Since 1986, the Carnegie Corporation of New York has provided consistent support for the program. Anthony Jackson of the Carnegie Corporation, a strong advocate of middle grades reform, has made our work with middle schools possible. Also since 1986, the Stuart Foundations of San Francisco, through the skilled guidance of Ellen Hershey, have helped with the dissemination of complex instruction throughout California.

The Bilingual Consortium of San Jose, under the leadership of Aurora Quevedo, provided financial resources, access to districts and classrooms, connections to outstanding bilingual educators, and political support for the program. The strength of the program in linguistically heterogeneous classrooms grew out of this support.

Without Ed De Avila and Cecilia Navarrete, the program never would have started. Their pioneering work with the *Finding Out/Descubrimiento* (FO/D) curriculum and the preparation of teachers laid the foundation for complex instruction. Over the years, many staff members have contributed their expertise and experience in schools. In addition to those who have authored chapters in this volume, we would like to acknowledge the work of Maria Balderrama, Ronit Bogler, Lisa Catanzarite, Brenda Gentry-Norton, Chaub Leechor, Gerry LeTendre, Susana Mata and Charles Parchment. Joan Benton has had marked influence on the conceptualization of assigning competence to low-status students and on helping teachers to use status treatments.

We also would like to thank Gary Natriello and Susan Liddicoat for their invaluable editorial assistance. Ryo Shohara was of great importance in the preparation of the manuscript.

Most important, many teachers have made major contributions to the research and development of complex instruction. We will always be deeply grateful for their efforts, insights, feedback, and patience. No one of us is as smart as all of us together.

WORKING FOR EQUITY IN HETEROGENEOUS CLASSROOMS

Sociological Theory
in Practice

PART I

Introduction

CHAPTER 1

Equity in Heterogeneous Classrooms: A Challenge for Teachers and Sociologists

Elizabeth G. Cohen

Equity in classrooms is a highly valued goal for educators. Contemporary rhetoric idealizes classrooms where "all children can learn" and where "all children are seen as smart." To reach this goal, it is necessary to understand the forces outside and inside the classroom that create inequity among students. Such understanding is the traditional domain of sociologists of education. But sociologists can do much more than formulate and test hypotheses about the sources of inequity. Sociological theory and research are also critical in designing and evaluating interventions to promote equitable classrooms.

This book contains much of what has been learned over nearly 20 years in systematic attempts to understand and to intervene in classroom processes that create and maintain inequities among students. We report the results of a lengthy program of applied research that started with propositions concerning the phenomenon of status generalization. The early studies located status problems in the interaction of school-age children in mixed-status groups and tested interventions designed to produce equal-status interaction in an experimental setting (Cohen, 1993).

As my colleagues and I moved toward the production of equal-status interaction in classrooms, we became concerned with practical issues such as curriculum and with broader educational goals such as equity in racially, ethnically, and academically heterogeneous classrooms. The program we call "complex instruction" is a combination of strategies to treat problems of inequality within cooperative groups and a model of curriculum, instruction, and organizational support that is practical and workable in heterogeneous classrooms. The model has its roots in a sociological analysis of central features of classrooms, such as the nature of the tasks, the roles of students and teachers, and the patterns of interaction. These features can construct failure for students or, alternatively, can change the situation so that many more students can be successful. As the laboratory treatment entered the

3

arena of classrooms where learning outcomes are the major basis for legitimacy of any innovation, a shift in goals occurred. Although an applied sociologist may be content with having achieved equal-status behavior, most schools are unwilling to make time-consuming and costly changes unless they are convinced that the innovation will improve achievement scores. Thus the staff of the Program for Complex Instruction became concerned with the broader problem of increasing the academic achievement of low-status students.

EQUITABLE CLASSROOMS IN A CHANGING SOCIETY

What is an equitable classroom? Because equity is the bottom line of the interventions described in this volume, one must be clear about the observable features of the goal. In an equitable classroom, teachers and students view each student as capable of learning both basic skills and high-level concepts. All students have equal access to challenging learning materials; the teacher does not deprive certain students of tasks demanding higher-order thinking because they are not ready; classmates do not block access to instructional materials or prevent others from using manipulatives. Even students who cannot read or understand the language of instruction have opportunities to complete activities and to use materials. The interaction among students is "equal-status," that is, all students are active and influential participants and their opinions matter to their fellow students. Finally, the achievement of students does not vary widely between the academically stronger and weaker students. While the more successful students continue to do well, the less successful students are much more closely clustered around the mean achievement of the classroom rather than trailing far out on the failing end of the distribution.

Equity is a matter of degree; classrooms are more or less equitable. According to the definition we have posed, very few classrooms are highly equitable. Moreover, there is considerable concern among educators that classrooms are becoming increasingly inequitable. As national educational systems struggle to raise the standards of content coverage and level of difficulty, more students fail because they cannot meet the new standards. Compounding this problem is the fact that the demography of school populations has changed. There are many more students who do not respond to traditional educational methods and to demands for higher levels (as traditionally defined) of academic functioning.

More and more classrooms around the world contain racially, ethnically, and linguistically heterogeneous groups of students. This increase is a function of the growing heterogeneity of school populations. Areas that formerly contained culturally homogeneous middle-class residents have experienced significant in-migrations of economic and political refugees and migrant labor. In addition to these sources of migration, there has been a general increase in the transiency of world populations. Central-city areas have become increasingly polyglot in many countries featuring ethnic enclaves with distinctive languages and cultures.

Migrants from other countries are not the only source of diversity in the United States. Some minority families who have been concentrated in the inner cities are moving to the suburbs. In 1989 10% of students in metropolitan public schools outside of central cities were African-American, up from 6% in 1970 (National Center for Educational Statistics, 1992). Similarly, the percentage of Hispanic students in metropolitan areas outside of central cities went from 4.4% in 1972 to 10.2% in 1989. The fastest rate of growth in child poverty from 1973 to 1992 was in the suburbs, where the rate increased 76.4% (from 7.8 to 13.8%) (Cook & Brown, 1994). As a consequence of these changes, teachers who used to work with homogeneous middle-class populations now work with students from low-income households or from rural areas of other countries.

As a result of immigration, students may not be proficient in the language of instruction or may exhibit marked cultural differences from the majority group. In the United States, linguistic and cultural diversity are the currently preferred terms to describe the heterogeneity of school populations. The newcomers bring strengths and richness to the life of the school, particularly if school personnel know how to capitalize on the multicultural resources that these students represent.

Beyond the social fact of diversity, educators generally fail to face the implications of a hierarchical ranking of groups within the larger social system. School populations come from a larger system of social stratification. Immigrants often occupy places near the bottom of that system of social classes. Certain native-born racial, linguistic, and ethnic groups hold the same low ranks. With few economic or political resources, members of these groups may experience discrimination and exploitation by the dominant groups. Thus, teachers may face more than cultural and linguistic differences. They may face problems of dominance and inequality stemming from the larger society.

INEQUITIES OUTSIDE AND INSIDE THE CLASSROOM

Sociologists of education have documented the connection, in many industrialized societies, between differences in social class background of students and differences in educational success over long periods of time. In recent years, sociologists have advanced the argument that structural features of schools, such as ability grouping, streaming, laning, or tracking, play a role in ensuring that differences in social class become differences in school success. They argue that social class affects educational achievement and educational attainment partly because of structural features of schools. The lower-ability groups and tracks contain a disproportionate number of children from lower social classes (Braddock, 1990; Van Fossen, Jones, & Spade, 1987). Students in lower-ability groups and tracks do not do as well as those with similar early achievement scores who are in more heterogeneous settings (Van Fossen et al., 1987).

Educational Achievement and Inequity

In the sociological argument, achievement plays a pivotal role in mediating effects of social class differences on educational attainment. Class differences in achievement originate in the early grades.

The curriculum is a critical source of inequity even in the early elementary years. When children from parents with little formal education enter school, they do not come with the same repertoire of preliteracy and prenumeracy skills, or of other types of cultural capital, as children of parents with more years of schooling. The repertoire of middle-class students is a much closer match to the school's curriculum than the repertoire of lower-class students. These differences in repertoire translate into differential readiness to master reading and arithmetic. In the earliest grades, differential "readiness" becomes differential mastery of fundamentals in reading and arithmetic. Since the elementary curriculum relies so heavily on these skills, those who are slower to master them are seen as less able in schoolwork. Teachers do not expect them to be able to grasp more advanced concepts at the same pace as their classmates.

Another source of inequity arises from the response of educational decision makers to students whom they perceive as more and less "able." Once students from poorer backgrounds actually achieve at a lower level in the basic skills, teachers respond directly to the differences in academic achievement rather than to class, race, or ethnicity (Mercer, Iadacola, & Moore, 1980). Teachers and school administrators try to deal with the differences in achievement by dividing students into ability groups, streams, or tracks where they believe that a single instructional treatment will work for everyone in the group.

Once students are in different groups and tracks, they experience different curricula (Gamoran & Berends, 1987; Oakes, 1985). The lower groups receive a curriculum that is below grade level—a system of designed retardation. There is clear evidence that students in low-ability groups and tracks suffer negative consequences from that placement (Kerckhoff, 1986; Oakes, 1985; Van Fossen et al., 1987). Sociologists of education see these effects of school structure as a major mechanism by which schools reproduce in the next generation the inequalities in power and resources of the adult generation.

Sociological studies of status attainment show how school achievement mediates the effects of family background on years of schooling and occupational prestige. Entering variables of school achievement into a regression greatly weakens the effects of initial family characteristics on educational attainment. Similarly, ability grouping and tracking in the predictive equation further weaken the effects of initial differences in family background. Parental education continues to have some direct effects through the ability of better educated parents to negotiate the placement of their children in the higher tracks (Useem, 1992). However, the direct effects of parental education and income on educational attainment are small in comparison to those of the student's early achievement and placement in academic tracks or streams.

Educational reformers infer from this sociological literature that doing away with tracking and grouping will do much to solve the problems of inequity within schools. But even if one were to do away with tracking and grouping, there still would be differential responses to different levels of achievement *within* the heterogeneous classroom. One still would have a curriculum that handicapped those who were below grade level in basic skills. Social systems in heterogeneous classrooms have the potential to re-create a new status order that reflects, at least in part, the old status order of tracking and ability grouping.

Sources of Inequity in the Classroom

Just as sociologists argue that structural features of the school (such as tracking) mediate the effects of stratification on educational attainment, I argue that inequity in the larger society translates into inequality in the classroom, partly because of structural features of the classroom. Powerful social systems of the classroom can mediate direct effects of the outside society.

Classrooms vary in task structures, evaluation practices, and peer relationships; these features of classrooms can and do create their own orders of power, status, and sources of expectations for competence. Power and status differences within the classroom are a major source of inequity among students.

The task and evaluation practices of the classroom help to build inequity through a process of social comparison by which students see each other arrayed on a single dimension of ability in schoolwork. Social comparison shapes students' ideas about their own ability (Rosenholtz & Simpson, 1984). Students compare themselves with each other as they complete tasks and when they hear teachers make public evaluations. Standardized tasks encourage a process of social comparison in which students evaluate how well they are doing in completing assignments rapidly and successfully. Emphasis on marking and grading has the same effect, giving students objective grounds for deciding where each person stands on academic ability and achievement. The net result of this process of social comparison is an agreed-upon rank order by teachers and students on the relative "smartness" of each member of the class. The high level of agreement among peers and between students and teachers on ranking of reading ability or academic ability illustrates the consensual nature of this construct of intellectual ability (Rosenholtz & Wilson, 1980; Simpson, 1981).

Rosenholtz and Simpson stressed the "dimensionality" of classroom organization. Unidimensional organization of instruction establishes conditions that facilitate "ability formation." In unidimensional classrooms, daily activities encourage comparison and imply a single underlying dimension of comparison. When instruction and student performances imply few performance dimensions, students' perceptions of ability become one-dimensional.

The first feature of unidimensional classrooms is an undifferentiated academic task structure. All students work on similar tasks or with a narrow range of materials and methods. For example, unidimensional classes require reading for successful performance of most tasks and rely mostly on paper-and-pencil tasks. This task structure facilitates social comparison; students can easily tell how well they are doing in comparison to others. A second feature of unidimensional classrooms is a low level of student autonomy, reducing the variety of tasks and preventing students from using their own evaluations of performance. Third, unidimensional classrooms use whole class instruction or clear-cut ability groups. A final feature is the emphasis on grading to convey clear-cut, unidimensional evaluation by teachers.

In contrast, the multidimensional classroom has varied materials and methods, a higher degree of student autonomy, more individual tasks, varied grouping patterns, and less reliance on grading. In a comparison of these two types of classrooms, researchers have found that students' self-reported ability levels have a greater variance in unidimensional classrooms (Rosenholtz & Rosenholtz, 1981; Simpson, 1981). In multidimensional classrooms, fewer children define themselves as "below average," thus restricting the distribution of self-evaluations. Student reports of their peers' ability levels are also more dispersed and more consensual (as measured by a coefficient of concordance) in unidimensional classes, and perceptions of individual ability are much more closely related to ratings by teachers and peers.

There are also connections between classroom tasks and the creation of hierarchical peer status. Many classrooms exhibit an unequal number of sociometric choices; a few sociometric stars receive many choices, while social isolates receive few or no choices. The earlier sociometric studies claimed that this pattern was universal for elementary children. When students have more opportunity to walk around, to talk with others, to choose seats and activities, and to work in small groups, the pattern of peer status changes (Cohen, 1994a; Epstein & Karweit, 1983; Hallinan, 1976). There is a less hierarchical distribution of choices and fewer social isolates and sociometric leaders.

Thus, some task and evaluation structures help to create clear hierarchies of academic and peer status. In Chapter 5, I document how these status characteristics have the strongest influence on behavior within groups of students working together. Once the socially agreed-upon rank order has formed, it is a major source of inequity. There are high expectations of competence for those who hold high rank, and correspondingly low expectations of competence for those with low rank. These differential expectations can become self-fulfilling prophecies, producing differential effort and performance on the part of high- and low-ranking students.

Inequity in the outer society has no simple and direct reflection in heterogeneous classrooms. Although gender acts as a status characteristic in adult society, Leal-Idrogo reports in Chapter 7, that gender has no effect on interaction in elementary school classrooms using complex instruction. Classroom social systems generate their own inequities and can mediate the effects of the outer society. If Whites dominate African-Americans economically, politically, and socially in U.S. society, White students will not necessarily dominate African-American students in the classroom. If certain groups have low status in the larger society, one cannot expect that individual students from these groups will suffer from low self-esteem. Studies actually show that the self-esteem of minority students is either the same as or higher than that of majority students (Graham, 1994; Rosenberg & Simmons, 1971).

Insofar as differences in social background result in differences in achievement within a classroom, students from lower socioeconomic backgrounds are somewhat more likely to have low academic status than students from higher socioeconomic backgrounds. However, the severity of this effect depends on the task and evaluation structure of the classroom as well as on the range of academic achievement within the classroom. Moreover, peer status may have a life of its own that bears no relationship to academic status (see Chapter 5). If members of minority groups who do not do well academically have generally high standing among their peers, whatever inequities may occur in classrooms may have relatively little to do with minority status.

CHANGING THE CLASSROOM

Many educators have responded to the demands for increasing equity by taking the sociologists' advice and doing away with ability grouping and tracking. Sociologists, however, have not been particularly attentive to the tremendous technical challenge that newly heterogeneous classrooms represent for teachers. Given the heterogeneity of classrooms, teachers face several dilemmas. If they choose to work with a text at grade level, many students will not be able to read their assignments or do their written work. Some students who do not have proficiency in the language of instruction will not be able to follow oral presentations. If teachers decide to select materials that are easier to read and to give shorter, simpler assignments, the result is a curriculum that is less rigorous and less demanding. Middle-class parents will accuse the schools (with some justification) of "dumbing down" the curriculum and will demand the return of tracking and ability grouping.

Doing away with curriculum differentiation does not solve the problem of how to work with differences in prior achievement and skill level of students. Nor does it solve the problem of differences in family support that students receive that help them to succeed in the conventional curriculum.

Without substantial change in the social structure and in methods of instruction in the classroom, as well as in the learning activities, academic and peer status orders can simply replace grouping and tracking as a basis for ranking of students. Those students who have not achieved well in the past and those who are socially isolated take up the low-status positions within the heterogeneous classroom.

The sociologist must attack the issue of curriculum more directly. Because the curriculum of the school faithfully reflects the vigorous coaching that takes place in middle-class families, it becomes a major means of reproducing parental status. If one wants to greatly decrease the effects of social stratification on the school process, it is necessary to modify the curriculum.

Curriculum materials that reflect a wider range of human intellectual activity make it possible for different students to be seen as competent in different classroom activities. Intrinsically interesting and intellectually challenging activities can tap into the repertoire and motivation of students from lower social class and language minority backgrounds. In comparison to the traditional emphasis on routine learning, these multiple-ability activities more closely resemble the way adults use their intellectual capacity. Quite aside from considerations of equity, educational reformers are calling for similar changes in curriculum. There is a demand for more emphasis on problem solving, application of learning to life situations, representation of knowledge in multiple media, and creative and inventive thinking. Thus, a call for multiple-ability curricula by sociologists finds much support in educational circles.

In Chapter 8, Lotan describes the theory and practice of changing curriculum materials in order to foster equity while developing higher-order thinking. Bower (see Chapter 9) demonstrated in an experimental classroom study the positive effects on achievement of using multiple-ability tasks at the high school level.

In addition to changing the curriculum materials, it is necessary to change instruction so that the social system of the classroom does not generate and reinforce a single dimension of perceived intellectual ability. If task structure and evaluation practices help to create a unidimensional construct of ability, then it is necessary to develop practicable alternative task structures and assessment practices.

Complex instruction makes specific changes in the task structure and evaluation practices. For example, students use each other as resources in small groups. Since students have the right to ask for help and the duty to assist those who ask for help, the possibility of failure declines sharply. Since each group does a different task and because each task calls on multiple intellectual skills, the possibilities for invidious social comparison are few. Lotan presents an overview of these features of complex instruction in Chapter 2.

Interaction among students is the key to learning in this revised social structure. The teacher assigns specific roles to students that foster the desired level of interaction. In Chapter 4, Ehrlich and Zack report on research that documents the connection between student roles in groups, interaction, and learning.

It is also necessary to interfere with the process of expectations in which some students are seen as competent at a wide variety of intellectually important tasks and others are seen as generally incompetent. Modifying these expectations for competence is the only way to produce truly equal-status interaction within groups of students. If certain students have limited access to interaction, they will learn less, especially in the areas of higher-order thinking skills (see Chapter 3). Without modifying these expectations, only some of the students will be seen as "smart" and able to make important contributions.

Using expectation states theory (Berger, Cohen, & Zelditch, 1966), Cohen and Lotan have derived methods for modifying these expectations based on academic and peer status. They provide evidence, in Chapter 6, of the effectiveness of these treatments.

In review, creating equity in the heterogeneous classroom requires a change in curriculum materials, a change in instructional strategies, and a direct attempt to change differential expectations for competence that lead to status differences. Complex instruction is an attempt to produce equity in such classrooms. Program staff have developed all three kinds of change, have implemented them in many classrooms, and have studied both their implementation and their effectiveness. Complex instruction has favorable effects on standardized and content-referenced achievement tests at the elementary and middle school levels (Cohen et al., Chapter 10), on second language acquisition among Spanish-speaking students in California (Neves, Chapter 12), and on cognitive development among students in Israel (Ben-Ari, Chapter 13).

SOCIOLOGICAL THEORY AND METHODS AS TOOLS

The broad use of sociological theory and research methods in this program raises the general issue of application of sociology to practice. The design and evaluation of interventions for creating more equitable classrooms have used social psychological and organizational theories. Sociological tools of survey, experiment, and systematic observation have proved both necessary and useful in the design and evaluation of the equitable classroom.

Sociological theory has a powerful potential for improving the practice of education, but this potential is a well-kept secret within the discipline. Unlike psychologists, sociologists have been reluctant to carry out applied research. When they do so, the results often have been atheoretical policy research or methodological contributions. In the concluding section of this chapter, I briefly review the ways in which the researchers writing in this volume have used tools of the trade in conceptualizing and studying the classroom, the role of the teacher, and organizational support for the teacher.

From a sociological perspective, the classroom is more than a collection of 30 individuals and a teacher. It is a social system and a unit of a formal organization. The teacher is a supervisor of 30 workers who labor under crowded conditions. A heterogeneous classroom is an instance where the input has become highly uncertain and variable. No longer is it possible to use a large-batch treatment in which the teacher works only with the whole class. The early work of Perrow (1967) on the effectiveness of organizations in the face of increased uncertainty applies to the classroom as an organizational unit. When the task of teaching becomes more uncertain, one must delegate authority to students and one must increase lateral communication between those students.

In this application of organizational sociology, students are organizational workers. The use of the concept of worker does not mean that students are factory workers; they could be routine workers or they could be professional employees in research and development teams. The analogy is not a perfect one. For example, students don't get paid and one can't fire them for incompetence. However, the research on complex instruction has found much empirical support for propositions from Perrow, illustrating the utility of his early work.

The strategies of delegating authority and increasing lateral communication permit students to use each other as resources and to gain access to the meaning of the text or assigned activity. This is not simply a post hoc rationale for the use of cooperative learning that educators have recommended widely for heterogeneous classrooms. Sociological analysis of the role of the teacher and of the mechanisms of classroom control is different from the psychological analysis most common among the developers of cooperative learning.

Organizational theory is also useful in considering issues of support for teachers who attempt new and demanding technologies such as complex instruction. In order to master the new technology, teachers require evaluation and feedback that they perceive as soundly based. The adaptation of the work of Dornbusch and Scott (1975) on evaluation and authority permits the design and evaluation of such a feedback system. Ellis and Lotan (Chapter 14) examine the impact of this feedback on teacher learning and implementation. Because teachers are attempting a technology that is more complex and less routine, certain changes in work arrangements should take place. Teachers need the opportunity to talk and work together. Moreover, the presence of principals who are knowledgeable about the new technology and supportive of the teachers should have favorable effects on implementation of the innovation (see Chapter 15 by Lotan, Cohen, and Morphew). Dahl, in her work on factors that lead to continuation of the program (see Chapter 17), also makes strong use of the organizational concepts of coordination by the principal and perceived legitimacy of the program by district administrators.

Expectation states theory (Berger, Cohen, & Zelditch, 1966) provides a strong theoretical base for the modification of expectations based on status differences in the classroom. Because of the multiple sources of status in the classroom, it is necessary to evaluate the relative strength of different status orders before treating the problem. Inequity is a product of the classroom social system. Therefore, it is necessary to treat not only the "victim" of the system, the low-status student, but also the other members of the system who are part of the problem. One must modify not only the expectations held by the low-status students for themselves, but the expectations that fellow students hold for these low-status persons. Expectation states theory provides an explanation of the phenomenon of unequal-status interaction within cooperative groups (see Chapter 5). It also provides the basis for two inter-ventions designed to boost the participation of low-status students and to equalize the interaction between low- and high-status group members.

Social psychology as represented by the work of Bandura (1977) on modeling and social learning has also proved very useful to applied work in complex instruction. Bandura's theories about the importance of modeling prove to be an effective tool in helping preservice teachers learn how to implement status treatments (see Swanson, Chapter 16).

As the sociologist works with teachers and complex school settings, new problems of engineering arise. Research tools and a theoretical framework continue to be critical even as one deals with messy real-life situations. Having started down the road of making classrooms more equitable, the researcher must tackle one problem of innovation and schooling after another. Once the goals have expanded to include delivery of a different model of instruc-tion for students in a variety of classroom and school settings, the sociolo-gist must use every research tool and methodology. This is not a task for the narrow specialist or orthodox methodologist.

Complex instruction has evolved over 20 years of theory, research, and development. Filby (see Chapter 18), an educational psychologist from a regional laboratory, finds that it has had a unique impact on teachers. They respond to both the underlying theory and its role in development and test-ing of specific classroom practices. Although the many pieces of research each focus on different aspects of the program, Filby notes that these pieces depend on and support one another as part of a comprehensive and sys-temic model. Because of its theoretical and research base, the result is a body of knowledge that is applicable not only to complex instruction but to other complex and demanding innovations.

CHAPTER 2

Complex Instruction: An Overview

Rachel A. Lotan

Complex instruction is a pedagogical approach that enables teachers to teach at a high intellectual level in academically, linguistically, racially, ethnically, as well as socially heterogeneous classrooms. In many countries now, such diverse classrooms contain students who have a wide range of previous academic achievement. Some of these students may not be fully proficient in the language of instruction—be it English, Spanish, Dutch, Hebrew, Swedish, or German.

The above definition emphasizes two points: first, that in complex instruction, tasks are intellectually challenging for all students, even those who are academically more advanced than their peers; second, that in CI classrooms, most, if not all, students have access to these highly challenging tasks, and thus to academic achievement.

In the following chapters of this book, the authors present elaborate conceptualizations and empirical findings for complex instruction. They detail the theoretical principles of classroom organization in CI, including the roles of the teacher and students, problems of unequal participation in small groups and how to address them, features of the learning tasks, and the organizational conditions that support innovative teachers. In this chapter, I have chosen to illustrate these abstractions through a collage of vignettes for the benefit of those readers who would appreciate a more concrete description of what CI actually looks and sounds like in the classroom. Therefore, first I present a composite, yet realistic, portrayal of activities witnessed and conversations overheard in various CI classrooms. Then, while making the connection between these concrete examples and the theoretical principles, I summarize the dimensions of CI as a classroom technology. Finally, I provide a short synopsis of some typical queries about CI and the answers formulated by the staff of the Program for Complex Instruction.

COMPLEX INSTRUCTION IN ACTION

Let us visit Lakeview Middle School* in the San Francisco Bay Area. Located in a working-class neighborhood, the school has a diverse student popula-

---

*Names of persons and places are fictitious.

tion, increasingly typical of California. Like many other middle school educators, after much deliberation and somewhat hesitantly, the faculty and the
principal at Lakeview decided to untrack the school and to create academically heterogeneous classrooms. Soon, however, the teachers realized that
their traditional teaching strategies were no longer adequate—too many
absences, too many disruptions, too many unsettling questions: To which
level should teachers teach? How could they rely on the textbooks when
some students were reading at third- or fourth-grade level? What about the
15 (give or take a few) students in one classroom who were at various stages
of learning English, and who represented 10 different home languages? What
to tell parents who felt that their children were not being challenged academically? And finally, who was really paying the price of this misplaced
educational fad called untracking?

Gravely dissatisfied but resolute, the faculty and the principal thoughtfully researched various programs. They decided to invest time, money, and
effort in CI as the pedagogical tool to help them accomplish their goal: providing quality education to their students.

As we enter Ms. Knight's seventh-grade core (integrated language arts
and social studies) classroom, we are struck by the lively, contagiously spir-
ited environment. Undoubtedly the products of students' work, full-size drawings of samurai with fearsome swords, and elegant ladies in traditional, rich-
looking silk kimonos, adorn the walls. A map of Japan, posters of cherry
trees in blossom, lampshades of delicate paper, origami cranes on the win-
dow sills, and soft Japanese music in the background make us feel, for a
short moment, at another time, in another place.

At seven swarming learning stations, four or five students are working together, each group on a different task. At the station by the door,
students consult an ancient map of a castle town, carefully checking the
key to the map. They find out that housing patterns in Tokugawa, Japan,
closely replicated the social standing of the inhabitants. "Yeah," says LaToya,
one of the students, "that's like Beverly Hills, 90210, and East LA, right
here in California."

At the next station, students read and carefully interpret excerpts from
the legal codes of feudal Japan. "That's not fair!" Jimmy exclaims. "They can't
have different laws for different people!" "Obviously, they did," countered
Eddie. "That's like in feudal Europe, remember? Last quarter, remember?"

Ms. Knight overhears the conversation as she circulates among the
groups, clipboard in hand, jotting down notes. She smiles with satisfaction
and appreciation. "Aren't they great," she thinks proudly. "Listen to these
connections they are making! This is what social studies is all about."

We soon realize that at each of the stations, students explore the different aspects of social stratification and social barriers in the context of Tokugawa,

Japan. In the process, they read, write, build a three-dimensional map of a castle town, prepare a skit about law enforcement in feudal Japan, play a game with small bags of rice to illustrate the rise of the merchant class, or analyze a graph showing the frequency of peasant uprisings. These learning activities of the CI unit "Taking Your Proper Station: Life in Tokugawa Japan" were developed by the staff of the Program for Complex Instruction at Stanford. The unit incorporates many of the recommendations of the curricular frameworks adopted in California and frequently used as models by other states.

The classroom runs like a well-oiled machine. From time to time, students wearing a *Materials Manager* badge gather art supplies, shovels, baskets, umbrellas, poster boards, sticks, hats, or colorful gowns. Students designated as *Resource* bring dictionaries, books, and photo albums about Japan to their station. Much to their surprise, they sometimes even consult the textbook for additional information!

As we cruise from center to center, we can't help but listen to the conversations: "I can't do that, Tara," says Sam with the *Facilitator* badge. "Really, I can't let you copy my report. I have to make you understand first." Tara grows impatient. "But, it's not like I just want to copy it. I wasn't here yesterday. Come on, let me get on with it, because Ms. Knight is collecting the reports already, and you know the group can't go on if I don't have mine." "I know," Sam insists, "but I still have to explain it to you and make you understand." Tara seems resigned. "Okay, okay. Tell me what you did in the group yesterday." Sam describes how they planned and presented the fashion show: Kim was the shogun, and she wore the silk gown with all the special jewelry. Sam was the peasant. He wore simple clothes and a straw hat to shade his face from the sun while working in the rice field. "Guess what," he said, unable to resist interjecting a personal note, "Ms. Knight said that I was particularly good, because not only my costumes, but also my body posture showed how hard the peasants had to work in the fields. I had to look up what 'posture' means in the dictionary." Miguel, the merchant, was not allowed to wear silk, although he could trade in it. "Isn't that weird?" Sam concludes his explanation. "How come?" Tara asks with genuine curiosity. "No idea. Maybe we'll find out today, when the other group reports," says Sam.

We linger by the last group. This group doesn't seem to be working as harmoniously as most of the others. Dusty, the reporter, is frustrated.

> You guys, let's go. I can't keep doing everything by myself. I have to prepare the report, and we haven't even discussed the questions. We have to build the castle, and we have to complete the individual reports, and we have only 15 minutes left, and I've really had it! We'll never get it done in time!

Bobby dismisses her concerns.

> I know how to build the castle. I'll do it. Dusty, hand me that box.
> Go get me the scissors and the tape. Yeah, yeah, I know, I'm *Materials Manager*—but just do it! . . . I'll put the walls here. I'll build the
> moat here. I'll put towers here and here and here. You all do what I
> tell you.

Roberto, the third member of the group, seems lost, isolated at the far end
of the table. He remarks quietly: "Sure doesn't look like the Japanese castles
we saw on the slides last week!" But no one pays any attention to him. Roberto
smiles and shrugs his shoulders.

Ms. Knight watches the group intently. Roberto has just made an important comment—yet nobody listened! Bobby is building *his* castle, still
barking orders. Dusty's frustration is palpable. There is no discussion, no
problem solving together, no seeking out advice, just single-minded concentration to make a castle—any castle, as quickly as possible.

Finally, Ms. Knight intervenes.

> Time out, group! Roberto just noticed something crucial. He pointed
> out that this won't look anything like a Japanese castle town. He
> remembered the castles from the slides and he can probably describe
> them to you. You all need the information, so you better ask him for
> it. Roberto, you seem to have excellent visual memory, help'm out
> here!

Roberto nods, beamingly.

Later, Ms. Knight described Roberto in a narrative she wrote.

> Roberto entered this class at the beginning of second quarter from the bilingual core class after his bilingual teacher said his English skills were good
> enough for him to be in regular classes. Roberto certainly has some problems
> with reading and writing at grade level, but his general comprehension is pretty
> good, she said. Yet Roberto has done no work in six weeks and is failing in
> both English and social studies. He smiles and shrugs often, but his gray eyes
> are lively and he watches everything. Sometimes he can barely suppress his
> interest. (Kepner, 1995, p. 72)

Ms. Knight realizes that in this group, Roberto has low status: He seldom participates, is often ignored, and can rarely get his hands on the
materials. In contrast, Bobby dominates the group. Ms. Knight has recognized a status problem in the interactions of this group. To counteract the
problem, she assigned competence to Roberto. She will watch to see whether

Roberto's participation increases. "It should," she muses hopefully. "According to the theory, and if the Stanford folks deliver what they've promised."

Toward the end of the academic year, Ms. Kepner would comment:

> Roberto was one who had made much improvement. He spoke up more frequently, and, as I pointed out the value of his contributions, others in the class began to take his opinions more seriously. He was by no means a great student, but he was no longer failing. (Kepner, 1995, p. 74)

After about 35 minutes, it's time for wrap-up. Students get ready to present their day's work to the class. The reporter introduces his or her group, explains the task, and briefly summarizes the group's discussion. All members of the group participate in performing the skit, parading in the fashion show, or describing the castle town.

Ms. Knight sometimes interrupts the report to ask a clarifying question. Consulting her notes, she emphasizes what each group did particularly well and where students still needed to improve. She alerts students to interesting ideas that might come up as they rotate to the next task tomorrow. She challenges them to improve on the group products they saw today. She often refers to the idea of social stratification and social barriers, and probes for students' understanding.

When the bell rings, the teacher and her students are pleased. Most groups completed their assignments, worked well together, and presented adequate reports. They will finish their individual reports as homework. Next week, their tests will show that they have understood the main ideas of the unit and that they also know important facts about Tokugawa, Japan.

Four days ago, in her introduction to the CI unit, the teacher gave a brief orientation to the activities. She told students that they would be exploring a feudal society, where people held distinct and rigid social ranks. She also listed some of the intellectual abilities needed to be successful on these tasks: interpreting visuals (maps, graphs, pictures of people of the different ranks), reading and understanding a legal code, writing and performing a skit, acting with flair and expression, analyzing, explaining a difficult problem, examining alternatives, working attentively and patiently, building a model. Ms. Knight concluded: "No one has all these abilities, but each one of you has some. You need to work together and listen to everybody's contributions."

COMPLEX INSTRUCTION: A CLASSROOM TECHNOLOGY

Sociologists define technology as the materials, the procedures, and the knowledge of the participants used to carry out the work of the organization. When the classroom is the organizational unit, the technology consists of the curricular materials, the instructional practices, and the knowledge of the participants, all aimed at producing the expected educational outcomes.

To introduce complex instruction to the pedagogical repertoire of teachers like Ms. Knight, we describe to them three features of the classroom technology: (1) how to organize the classroom for productive groupwork, (2) how to assign learning tasks that are true group tasks, and (3) how to equalize participation of students of different status in the small groups.

Organizing the Classroom for Productive Groupwork

One of the most robust findings of the research on complex instruction is the positive relationship between student interaction in small groups and average learning gains. This finding holds at the classroom as well as at the individual level. At the classroom level, the proportion of students talking and working together is a positive predictor of average learning gains; at the individual level, the student's rate of participation in the small group is a significant predictor of his or her posttest scores, holding constant the pretest scores.

The findings at the classroom level have implications for the way the teacher manages the classroom, if he or she wants to maximize student learning. The findings at the individual level, coupled with further research that relates the student's rate of participation to his or her status in the classroom, have implications for the ways in which the teacher goes about weakening this detrimental connection between status and participation.

To enhance learning, then, teachers need to maximize student interaction in the small groups. Delegation of authority, a central concept in complex instruction, helps teachers to manage the classroom, by making students responsible for their own and their groupmates' learning. The teacher does so by holding students accountable for being on task, for keeping their groupmates on task, and for producing individual and group products as a result of their work. When students work at six to eight learning stations on six to eight different, open-ended tasks, as they do in CI, the teacher can no longer supervise students directly, telling them exactly how to proceed, how to manage their interactions, or how to solve the problem posed to them.

Many teachers fear that when they delegate authority, they might lose control and the classroom might deteriorate into chaos. To avert such an alarming scenario, a system of cooperative group norms and student roles aids teachers in their delegation of authority. This system supports the changed role of the teacher and of the students during small group instruction. Like the teachers, students need to learn how to adjust to delegation of authority. New ways of interacting with their peers require new norms of behavior.

The norms that teachers instill in students as they collaborate in small groups have to do with allowing students to serve as academic, linguistic, or any other kind of intellectual resources for one another. In traditional classrooms, when students use each other as resources, it is called "cheating" and is strictly prohibited. One of the first norms students learn in CI is, "You have the right to ask for help; you have the duty to assist when asked." Students also learn how to conduct constructive conversations in small groups by justifying their arguments and by explaining how, rather than by doing the work for someone else. The latter was the norm Sam acted upon in his interchange with Tara.

Also to support teachers as they delegate authority, students assume specific procedural roles. By playing these roles, students manage the groups and themselves; they take over the responsibility for some of the practical, yet mundane, functions and duties that traditionally have been the teacher's purview. Thus, in each group the facilitator sees to it that all members understand the instructions for the task and that they all get a turn. The facilitator also acts as the liaison between the teacher and the group. The reporter reports at the end of groupwork time what the group found out, introduces or describes the group product, and often evaluates how group members worked together. The materials manager collects the manipulatives, props, tools, and supplies as needed and oversees the cleanup. Depending on the task and the teacher's priorities, additional roles may be assigned: timer, harmonizer, safety officer, or resource person.

These roles are different from "content" roles such as theorist, questioner, or explainer that reflect metacognitive functions necessary for groupwork; they are also different from "professional" roles such as artist, musician, poet, and director—roles that potentially lead to a strict division of labor. Although division of labor is often an efficient way to get the job done, it also reduces interaction. In groupwork, when peer interaction is what we strive for, we need to achieve a healthy balance between division of labor and interdependence.

Each student in the group has a role to play, and roles rotate. In addition to participating fully in the content-specific, substantive work of the group, all students learn how to play all roles competently and develop important social skills highly relevant for adult life. Furthermore, acting as facilitator is also a potential status intervention that weakens the relationship between status and participation.

Working productively in small groups or assuming various roles usually does not come naturally to most students. At the beginning of the school year, during an initial period of skill building, the teacher introduces and reinforces these norms as students learn to recognize and to use them. It takes time and effort for both the teacher and the students to learn their respective new roles, become comfortable with them, and recognize the benefits of their use.

As teachers learn how to delegate authority effectively, they ask themselves poignant questions: When and how do I intervene? Do I let kids fail when groups clearly don't work out? Our research has shown that the teacher needs expert help in learning how to delegate authority, how to let go, and how to support the students while also holding them accountable. The teacher needs organizational help at the school level to manage the overall complexity of the technology. Such support and follow-up are an essential part of the professional development model for CI.

As they grow more comfortable with making students responsible for their own work, as they hover less over groups and rescue more and more infrequently, teachers find that they are free for the kind of teaching that attracted them to the profession in the first place: They ask questions to stimulate and extend their students' thinking. They push the students' understanding; make connections among ideas, situations, and events past and present; and elicit such connections from the students. They give feedback to the students on their work in the groups. In short, relieved from the burden of management, through feedback and questioning, teachers encourage the students to move beyond the procedural aspects of the task and to interact with one another at a higher conceptual level.

Developing Learning Tasks for Complex Instruction

Delegation of authority by the teacher and increased interaction among students represent working arrangements in the classroom that are different from traditional, whole class instruction. As educators (teachers, researchers, staff developers) aim to maximize interaction, and to provide equal access to this interaction and to the curricular materials for all students in small groups, they also need to design and develop learning tasks that match these different working arrangements. Most important, to further intellectual development and growth, learning tasks in CI are true group tasks: challenging, open-ended, and requiring many different intellectual abilities and resources. In true group tasks, students work interdependently; they are held accountable for a group product, but also for evidence of individual work. In addition to a final group product, each student completes an individual report that attests to his or her participation in the group discussion and gives the teacher a measure of the student's understanding and achievement.

Finally, group activities of a CI unit are organized around a big idea or a central concept of a discipline. As groups of students rotate through the activities, they have multiple opportunities to grapple with the concept, to understand the idea in different settings, and to recognize its multiple representations.

Equalizing Participation in Small Groups

At the heart of complex instruction are the interventions to equalize rates of participation in small groups. The features of the learning tasks and the management system for the classroom are designed to allow teachers to focus their attention on these interventions. Complex instruction offers two strategies to treat problems of status, that is, to weaken the relationship between status and participation: the multiple-ability orientation, and assigning competence to low-status students.

The Multiple-Ability Orientation. When using the multiple-ability orientation, teachers challenge traditional definitions of learning tasks and of what some students can or cannot contribute. When using multiple-ability tasks, they widen their own and their students' conception of "smarts." The multiple-ability orientation is grounded in the use and analysis of multiple-ability tasks and is based on the teacher's public recognition of the wealth of intellectual abilities that are relevant and valued in the classroom, just as they are in daily life.

A multiple-ability orientation usually occurs during the beginning of a unit or a day's work in groups. Teachers start by naming the different abilities necessary for successful completion of an activity, and then point out the relevance of each ability to the task. They convey the message to the students that no one person in the group will have all the abilities necessary to complete the task, but everyone will have some of the abilities. Teachers thus create a mixed set of expectations for competence. Herein lies the premise for CI: Each individual brings different abilities, an effective repertoire of problem-solving strategies, and valuable experiences to the task. All are needed to complete the task successfully.

Assigning Competence to Low-Status Students. While the multiple-ability orientation can help narrow the gap between rates of participation of high- and low-status students, the status order is deeply ingrained in the classroom. To boost even more the participation of low-status students, a second treatment is necessary.

Once the management system is in place and groupwork is proceeding smoothly, the teacher carefully observes the groups, asking probing questions and stimulating students' thinking. The teacher pays particular attention to low-status students and watches for those moments when they show how competent they are on some of the abilities previously identified in the orientation. He or she then tells these students what they did well and how their contributions are relevant to the group task. Often, the teacher also points out to the group how these students can serve as resources on similar multiple-ability tasks in the future.

PROFESSIONAL DEVELOPMENT FOR COMPLEX INSTRUCTION

Like a skillful juggler with countless balls in the air, the teacher attends to many dimensions of the classroom technology simultaneously. To understand and to master this complex technology, teachers require extensive professional development. It takes at least one full year for teachers to learn how to manage the classroom successfully, how to recognize and treat status problems. During this first year, teachers use as curriculum prototype units developed by the staff of the Program for Complex Instruction. After they grow comfortable with the instructional aspects, many teachers become interested in developing or adapting curricula for CI in their own classrooms.

Professional development for CI starts with an intensive, 2-week summer institute attended by teams of teachers from the same schools and often by administrators. During the first week, participants become knowledgeable about the theoretical base, the central principles and concept of complex instruction. They also practice the skill builders and examine the available curriculum. Sessions of the summer institute follow the CI format, so teachers not only read and hear about CI, but also actually experience it.

During the second week, teachers practice the new strategies with a group of students. As they teach in teams, staff developers or teacher trainers use systematic observations to give feedback to the teachers. They also videotape the lessons for more detailed analyses. The teachers themselves learn and practice how to conduct such systematic observations.

After the initial workshop, the year-long follow-up to provide sound feedback on implementation is an irreplaceable, nonnegotiable component of the professional development model. At least nine times during the year and often more frequently, the staff developer visits the teacher's classroom. The staff developer or a teacher trainer gathers systematic data on the students' activities and the teacher's practices during CI using the Whole Class Instrument (see Appendix A) and the Teacher Observation Instrument (see Appendix B), respectively. Periodically, after completing a full set of observations (six whole class observations, three observations of the teacher at learning stations, and three observations at orientation/wrap-up), the staff developer summarizes the data in bar graphs. These bar graphs provide the basis for a problem-solving session between the teacher and the staff developer. Three such feedback sessions are recommended during the year. During these meetings the teacher analyzes the graphs with the help of the staff developer. Together they identify problems and potential solutions.

This feedback to the teachers is soundly based: The teachers are clear on the criteria and the standards for the feedback because they have used the instruments themselves. There is adequate sampling of the teachers' implementation, so teachers perceive that the staff developer has an adequate picture of the implementation. Research has substantiated the relationship between such feedback and the quality of implementation.

Program developers have also specified the organizational conditions at the school level that contribute to the successful implementation of the program. In addition to support from the staff developer, teachers need to have the support of the principal and that of colleagues. Research evidence substantiates the call for such organizational support.

FREQUENTLY ASKED QUESTIONS ABOUT COMPLEX INSTRUCTION

Over the years, the staff of the Program for Complex Instruction has given countless presentations to various audiences in the United States and in other countries: to teachers, administrators, university faculty, staff developers, parents, foundation officers, and policy makers. Although members of these audiences have specific interests and concerns given their respective positions, many of their questions and comments are remarkably similar. Here are some of those questions and our answers.

How Do You Know a CI Classroom When You See One? The first clues are the messages on the walls of the classroom: posters that remind students of the cooperative norms, the role chart, and the poster with the ever-present, multiple-ability treatment: "No one is good at all the abilities. Everyone is good at some of the abilities." In many classrooms, students wear distinctive role badges. Although these are important signposts of the management system, what truly makes a classroom a CI classroom requires more systematic investigation: (1) Is a significant proportion (about 35–45%) of students talking and working together on intellectually challenging tasks? (2) Does the teacher use status treatments in efforts to treat status problems?

Although it has recognizable hallmarks, complex instruction is not a rigid mold. We do not use a fidelity model to disseminate the program. Many teachers have invented strategies for orientation and wrap-up, for improving and elevating student discourse, for making the organization of the materials work better. Some teachers insist more than others on detailed and formal plans from the groups. Teachers have made CI work for their own classrooms, with their own curricula. When they have mastered the underlying principles of complex instruction, teachers know how to keep interaction levels high and how to equalize participation without watering down the content.

With All the Multiple-Ability Curricula, What About Basic Skills? In CI, students constantly practice reading, writing, and calculating. They read the instructions to the task; they read historical documents, the textbook, and additional resources. They complete individual reports, summarizing their discussions in the groups, stating their own opinions, developing a personal argument, or presenting their own perspective. They gather numerical data, summarize the data, and devise ways to present the data graphically. Furthermore, they develop their language skills because they communicate extensively with their peers on pressing problems and issues. Contrasting conceptual learning and basic skills is a false dichotomy.

What About the High-Status Students? Because learning tasks in complex instruction are intellectually challenging, students with strong academic records (and often even adults) find that they need to work hard to complete them. Furthermore, they discover that they need to learn to rely on others to complete assignments on time—not an unnecessary lesson for adult life. Many academically high-achieving students have opportunities to explore and develop additional abilities. For example, many tasks require visual and spatial abilities, not necessarily the forte of students who might be excellent in reading, writing, and computing.

Some teachers and parents worry that raising the rate of participation of low-status students detracts from the participation of high-status ones. Participation, however, is not a zero-sum game. Status treatments have no effect on the participation of high-status students. In complex instruction, rates of participation increase for both high- and low-status students. In boosting the participation of low-status students, the gap in participation between students of different status is narrowed.

Where Is Complex Instruction Located in the Present Reform Movement? Many educators have recognized that because of its emphasis on the technology of the classroom, complex instruction occupies a central place in the current movement of school reform. To achieve many of the standards and the expectations that drive educational reform at present, change at the level of the classroom is inevitable. With the goal to provide educational equity and to increase opportunities to learn for racial, ethnic, and linguistic minority students, educators have identified CI as one of the most viable strategies. These educators also appreciate the solid theoretical foundation and research base of CI.

At present, educational reform promulgates a systemic approach and the restructuring of the school. Complex instruction relies on both: The change in the technology of the classroom matches a parallel change in the work arrangements at the school and the district levels. For example, commitment of financial resources at the district level legitimizes complex instruction in the eyes of parents and teachers and contributes to its long-term survival. At the school level, the principal needs to support teachers by coordinating resources and by providing organizational help with the logistics of implementation, such as acquiring manipulatives, or finding adequate furniture or storage space. Furthermore, teachers interact in collegial teams (by grade level or throughout departments) as they plan for implementation or work on developing additional units. Those are just some examples of how restructuring the school goes hand in hand with restructuring the classroom.

PART II

Organization and Management of the Classroom

CHAPTER 3

Organizing the Classroom for Learning

Elizabeth G. Cohen, Rachel A. Lotan, and Nicole C. Holthuis

Organizational theory has proved to be a powerful way to understand classroom arrangements that lead to learning in complex instruction. In this chapter, we review research findings on the relationship between the teacher's use of authority, the students' use of lateral relations, and learning gains. We report parallel findings across different subject matters in elementary and middle grades.

The detailed findings have been published elsewhere (Cohen, Lotan, & Holthuis, 1995; Cohen, Lotan, & Leechor, 1989). As noted in Chapter 1, a theoretical framework adapted from early work by Perrow (1967) on organizational structure and technology is of considerable utility in understanding classroom processes. Perrow related organizational arrangements to organizational effectiveness under conditions of complex technologies. In applying this theory, we define organizational effectiveness in terms of learning outcomes aggregated to the level of the classroom. In this chapter, we wish to illustrate the power of this theoretical view to explain classroom learning and to produce robust findings in a variety of classroom settings.

In this chapter we also illustrate an important substantive point: Learning in complex instruction is not merely a product of a special curriculum and cooperative groups. Rather, it is a product of a set of organizational arrangements that enable students to profit by engaging in group tasks. Organizational arrangements include the teacher's role and the ways in which students work together. Optimal learning outcomes are realized only when the teacher's role changes and students deal with the uncertainty of tasks by using each other as resources. In contrast to the bulk of the research on learning, we use the classroom as the unit of analysis. Individual characteristics are not explained, nor are they used as explanation. This level of conceptualization permits research on the connection between the operation of the classroom as an organization and learning outcomes of a class of students.

COMPLEX INSTRUCTION AS TECHNOLOGY

An organizational view of the classroom starts with the nature of work and moves to the organizational arrangements that make that work situation most productive. As pointed out in Chapter 2, sociologists define the nature of the work in an organization as its technology. Let us then start with a few examples of the nature of work in complex instruction. Imagine six different groups of three to five students each working at a different task. This technology is complex because it is highly differentiated, that is, different groups are carrying out different activities.

In an uncertain task, typical in *Finding Out/Descubrimiento* (De Avila & Duncan, 1982b), an elementary curriculum, the children measure the waist of an inflatable dinosaur. In addition to the dinosaur, materials include string and a metric ruler. The children first must decide where to locate the "waist" on the dinosaur. Then they must figure out how to measure a round object with an inflexible ruler. After much discussion and experimentation, they realize that they can put the string around the animal, mark off the circumference of the waist, and hold up the string to the ruler.

In a middle school social studies curriculum unit, "How Do Historians Know About the Crusades?" developed by CI staff (Program for Complex Instruction, Stanford University, n.d.), students must design a defensible castle for the Crusaders. They have pictures and floor plans of a ruined castle in the Middle East. The resource card provides some information about key features such as water supply. With a variety of materials to choose from, including cardboard, glue, and scissors, the group must construct a model and explain to the class what makes it defensible.

These are tasks with ill-structured solutions and a level of uncertainty that is challenging for both adults and youngsters. The answers do not lie in the resource cards or in some kind of routine procedure or algorithm. (See Chapter 8 for more on open-ended tasks.)

One person cannot complete these tasks alone. All students are important and necessary for the solution of problems, the building of a model, the creation and enactment of a role play, and so forth. Furthermore, students cannot easily divide the labor on such tasks. The roles that students play do not represent a division of labor. These are not substantive roles like those of artist and director, but procedural roles that move the students through the task, such as facilitator, harmonizer, and materials manager (see Chapters 2 and 4).

ORGANIZATIONAL ARRANGEMENTS AND EFFECTIVENESS

In his early work, Perrow (1967) stated that when workers face uncertain tasks two things must happen if the organization is to maintain its effectiveness. First, supervisors must shift from direct supervision to a delegation of authority to the workers. Second, to deal with the uncertainty of the tasks, there must be extensive use of lateral relations among the workers.

The management system used in complex instruction derives from this proposition. Teachers learn how to delegate authority to groups of students and to avoid taking on direct supervisory roles while students are working in groups. Students learn to work together to arrive at creative problem solutions and to make optimal use of the contributions of each group member.

Lateral Relations and Learning

Interaction in complex instruction is critical to the learning process. The following proposition, directly derived from Perrow, states this relationship:

> When classroom technology is uncertain, the extent to which students talk and work together will be related to organizational effectiveness.

Students help each other with reading and understanding the activity card (Leechor, 1988). Students also explain basic concepts and procedures to each other and give assistance on technical skills. This is the pattern of sequential interdependence that most people think of when they see students in small groups, that is, the outputs of one student become inputs for another. However, use of each other as resources includes more than asking for and receiving help. Because the tasks in complex instruction require multiple perspectives and varied input for creative problem solving, the students are not likely to achieve a satisfactory group product unless they exchange ideas. When there is mutual exchange, the pattern is one of reciprocal interdependence—each person's output is an important input for other persons in the group.

Teacher's Authority and Lateral Relations

If interaction is critical for achievement, then the job of the teacher is to foster and optimize this interaction. Unless the teacher delegates authority to groups while holding them accountable for performance, one may see little on-task interaction within the groups.

The extent to which the teacher applies direct supervision (the obverse of delegation of authority) will diminish the possibilities and opportunities for students communicating with each other. Within small groups, the self-directed nature of student talk tends to disappear when the teacher arrives (Harwood, 1989). If the teacher, as an authority figure, takes responsibility for their task engagement, students will not assume responsibility for solving problems related to the task. A teacher who uses direct supervision when students are working cooperatively, unwittingly sabotages the attainment of instructional objectives. By inhibiting the process of students' talking and working together, the teacher prevents them from developing a good grasp of concepts or from discovering things for themselves. Even a teacher who constantly interrupts the interaction of groups with higher-order questions runs the risk of depressing vital interaction among the students.

Moving beyond Perrow's statement, we argue that there is a causal connection between delegation of authority and lateral communication. Students cannot establish and maintain lateral relations in the face of direct supervision. Specifically, we propose the following:

> Given the uncertainty of the task from the students' point of view, the more frequently the teacher uses direct supervision, the lower will be the rate of lateral relations among students.

Differentiation and Direct Supervision

The uncertainty of the tasks and the sheer differentiation of the technology push teachers to use less direct supervision. A highly differentiated technology could lead to several alternative methods of supervision. The teacher could use direct supervision, managing and guiding the students' behavior through detailed rules and schedules. However, this solution assumes that workers are facing tasks that are relatively certain. When students face uncertain tasks as in complex instruction, direct supervision is impractical. Comstock and Scott (1977) summarized the argument for delegation of authority.

> But when work is not predictable, performance programs cannot be developed and individuals must be called upon to make the best judgments of which they are capable. When different groups of workers are carrying out different and uncertain tasks, it is more efficient if they have a clear sense of authority and can make their own decisions, and can learn from their own mistakes. (p. 177)

In the earliest version of complex instruction, where there were up to 12 learning centers, each with a different task, teachers sometimes tried to simplify the technology by reducing the number of groups so that they could use direct supervision. Some of them also simplified the technology by using fewer activities. It was then much easier to make sure that each group was solving the problem in a standardized fashion.

Even if teachers maintain a high level of differentiation, rather than delegating authority they may try to race from group to group to make sure that each task is being done properly and in the manner that they prefer. The sheer impracticality of trying to be everywhere at once when six groups are carrying out different tasks pushes teachers toward delegation of authority. Thus, both the theoretical analysis and observations of what teachers actually did in the earliest versions of complex instruction when they faced the enormous complexity of the technology lead us to the following proposition:

> Given uncertain group tasks, the number of different activities in simultaneous operation in a classroom will be negatively related to the use of direct supervision.

TESTING THE PROPOSITIONS

A simple diagram summarizes the theoretical framework we use to study implementation:

Differentiation → delegation of authority → lateral relations → effectiveness

The propositions in the preceding discussion pertain to each relationship in the framework. To test the propositions, we chose classroom indicators for each of these abstract sociological concepts.

Parallel Studies

Parallel studies of elementary and middle schools test the three propositions. We report two studies of elementary school classrooms, from 1982–83 and 1984–85, and one study of middle school social studies classrooms, from 1991–92. Despite differences in age and subject matter, all classrooms in these studies used complex instruction. Variability in teacher behavior among classrooms provides the opportunity to test the generalizability of the propositions.

We conducted systematic observations of each classroom using the Teacher Observation Instrument and the Whole Class Instrument. We describe these instruments in detail in the section on measurement later in this chapter. The measure of effectiveness consisted of gains in scores on standardized and content-referenced tests. The basic method of testing hypotheses was correlation of variation between classrooms in teacher behavior, differentiation of technology, observed interaction, and achievement gains.

In the elementary school sample, children were from lower socioeconomic family backgrounds; generally many of these children had little access to science and limited exposure to higher-order concepts in mathematics. Classes in the sample contained large percentages of students with limited proficiency in English. Test scores on reading and language arts averaged at the thirtieth percentile and below.

Data were drawn from classrooms in Grades 2–6. There were 15 class-rooms in 10 schools in the 1982–83 data set and 13 classrooms in 5 schools in the 1984–85 data set. Observers made 10 observations per teacher with the Teacher Observation Instrument in the first data set and 20 observations per teacher in the second set. In both data sets there were approximately 20 observations per classroom with the Whole Class Instrument.

Staff members collected middle school data during the 1991–92 school year in 5 middle schools, all in the process of untracking. The student popu-lation at all these schools was racially and ethnically mixed, a fair represen-tation of California's present demographics. There was a total of 42 class-rooms in the middle school analysis. The data for the analysis of achievement came from a subset of 22 classrooms, with a total of 246 teacher observa-tions and 502 observations with the Whole Class Instrument. Both teacher and student behavior varied sharply between classes taught by the same instructor. Therefore, we treated each set of observations on a classroom independently.

Measurement

As noted, we use two instruments for measuring technology of the class-room and the teacher's behavior throughout the studies in this volume: the Whole Class Instrument and the Teacher Observation Instrument. The gen-eral description here will serve as a reference for succeeding chapters as well.

Whole Class Instrument. The Whole Class Instrument (see Appendix A) provides a uniquely sociological view of the classroom that has proven invaluable in measuring implementation. Like a snapshot, the instrument yields information on the location and activities of each student and adult in the classroom at a given time.

Using a grid with each row representing a learning station or work group and each column representing a different type of activity, observers take about 5 minutes to fill out this instrument while students are working in groups. The observer accounts for each student in the classroom by placing a hash mark in one of the squares on the grid, indicating the student's group and activity. If the student is not at one of the work stations, the observer makes a mark in one of several categories at the bottom of the page, such as "in transition (on business)", "waiting for adult," or "disengaged and wan-dering around." The categories are exhaustive so that each student appears as doing one type of activity, even if that activity is wandering around the classroom. To summarize the results of an observation, the researcher totals the rows and columns and calculates percentages of students engaged in particular activities, for example, the percentage of students disengaged or in small groups.

A central category for the study of implementation is "talk or talk/manipulate." This is the major measure of lateral relations or student interaction. Students are in work groups and may be discussing the task, or manipulating materials and talking at the same time—discussion can be either substantive or procedural. If they are talking with the teacher, the observer inserts a symbol for the teacher. Other useful categories include "disengaged," "read/write," or "manipulating materials without talking."

Teacher Observation Instrument. The Teacher Observation Instrument (see Appendix B) is a measure of teacher role and the content of teacher talk in 10-minute samples. There are 10 categories of speech for the elementary version of the instrument and 11 categories for the middle school version. The categories are not exhaustive. A speech is counted once, regardless of its length until the teacher is interrupted or the talk changes category.

After 1983, we realized that teacher talk was very different when students were in small groups from when students were functioning as a whole class for orientation and wrap-up. As a result, research done after that date uses one set of teacher observations for groupwork and another for orientation and wrap-up. The 1982–83 data described in this chapter used teacher observations that were a mixture of these two settings.

Categories that measure direct supervision include "facilitates students' work," "disciplines," "informs/instructs/defines," and "asks factual questions." Facilitation includes telling students how to get through the task and procedural questions such as, "Have you read the activity card?" and "What do the instructions tell you to do next?" Two categories measure attempts to treat status problems: "assigns competence" and "talks about multiple abilities." Other nonroutine teacher behavior includes the categories "stimulates higher-order thinking" (e.g., extends students' thinking, generalizes concepts and relationships), "makes connections," and "gives specific feedback to individuals or groups."

Reliability. Assessment of reliability of these observation instruments was the percentage agreement between an observer and a criterion observer on each category of student or teacher behavior. In the elementary studies, the overall average reliability for all categories on the Whole Class Instrument was 90% in 1982–83 and 95.54% in 1984–85. The reliability on the Teacher Observation Instrument was 91% in 1982–83 and 91.48% in 1984–85. For the middle school study, the reliability for Whole Class Instrument was 94.42%. The reliability for the Teacher Observation Instrument was 93.64%.

Target Student Instrument. For the analysis of data from the elementary school, we made some use of the Target Student Instrument (see Appendix C). This instrument is described in detail in Chapter 5. For the purposes of this analysis it is sufficient to know that a subset of approximately 10 target children in each classroom was observed for 3 minutes at a time, approximately 10 times while the children were working at the learning stations. Observers scored these children for the frequency of all task-related talk with their peers, as well as for the number of times they worked together with their peers. We calculated the average total frequency of these behaviors. The overall reliability for this instrument was 92.9%.

Indicators of Major Concepts. The number of different learning stations in operation is an indicator of *differentiation* derived from the Whole Class Instrument. In the elementary studies, we calculated a ratio of learning centers to students. There were typically five students to a center, but sometimes teachers used fewer centers and larger groups, or more centers and smaller groups. In the middle school study, the indicator of differentiation was the number of different activities in simultaneous operation. None of the middle school teachers used very large groups. However, some of them reduced the number of different activities in simultaneous operation.

The instruments do not provide a direct measure of *delegation of authority* because it is a difficult concept to observe. Because they look alike, it is difficult to distinguish delegation of authority from a laissez-faire teacher style. However, if a teacher engages in direct supervision of students, he or she is *not* delegating authority, but is carrying out the obverse of that role.

The index of direct supervision for those studies where we had separate measures of the teacher while the students were in groups was the average rate per 10 minutes of "facilitates," "instructs," and "disciplines." Since there were multiple observations of each teacher, the rates were calculated on an average frequency per 10 minutes across a number of observations.

The 1982–83 elementary school study did not have separate data for teachers' behavior while students were at learning centers. The only indicator of direct supervision that was much more likely to occur while students were in small groups was facilitation. Therefore, we selected this variable as the closest approximation to direct supervision while students were in groups.

The standard indicator of *lateral communication* in all of this research was the average percentage of students scored as talking or talking/manipulating from the Whole Class Instrument. We often refer to this as the rate of talking and working together. The early elementary study (1982–83) and the middle school study (1991–92) used this measure.

In the 1984–85 data set, despite a high reliability on the instrument as a whole, the observations for the number of students talking and working together were unreliable. After the data collection, we found statistically significant differences among observers on this variable. Therefore, for the 1984–85 data set, lateral communication was measured by the average rate of talking and working together for all target children in a classroom. This figure was derived from the Target Student Instrument, briefly described above.

The indicators of *effectiveness* were gain scores taken from achievement tests administered in the fall and spring. For the elementary studies, gain scores on the math concepts and applications and computation subscales of the California Test of Basic Skills (CTBS) (1982) achievement tests served as the indicator of achievement. The 1982–83 data has percentile gains from fall to spring. The 1984–85 data set includes gains in scale scores standardized by grade. To examine achievement at the classroom level, we calculated a grand mean of the average gain scores for each student for whom we had a fall and spring test score. For the middle school, we used gain scores on a multiple-choice, content-referenced test of the social studies units developed by the CI staff. Chapter 10 describes these tests in detail. For purposes of this analysis, we constructed a gain score for each student and calculated the average gain score per classroom based on individual gain scores.

RESULTS

Detailed results and analysis are available in two reports of this research: For the elementary school results, see Cohen, Lotan, and Leechor (1989); for the middle school results, see Cohen, Lotan, and Holthuis (1995). Both of these publications include path models. In this chapter, we present simple correlations between the variables specified in the propositions.

Table 3.1 summarizes the results for all three data sets. The correlations were all statistically significant and were in the direction predicted by the theoretical propositions. There were very strong relationships between the measure of lateral relations and the measure of effectiveness. At the elementary school level, the more that students in a classroom talked and worked together, the higher were their gains on the standardized achievement test in mathematics ($r = .72$, $p < .05$ for 1982–83 and $r = .52$, $p < .05$ for 1984–85). At the middle school level, the higher the percentage of students talking and working together, the greater were the gain scores on the social studies test ($r = .50$, $p < .01$).

The more the teacher used direct supervision while students were working in groups, the more infrequent were lateral relations. In each case

Table 3.1: Correlations Between Differentiation, Direct Supervision, Lateral Relations, and Gain Scores: Elementary and Middle School Classrooms

Variables	Elementary School		Middle School
	1982–1983	1984–1985	1991–1992
Differentiation/ Direct Supervision	-.50*	-.55*	-.40**
	(n = 15)	(n = 12)	(n = 42)
Direct Supervision/ Lateral Relations	-.43*	-.49*	-.44**
	(n = 15)	(n = 12)	(n = 42)
Lateral Relations/ Av. Gain Scores[a]	.72*	.52*	.50**
	(n = 11)	(n = 12)	(n = 42)

[a]For elementary schools gain scores on CTBS Concepts and Applications subscale; for middle school gains scores on social studies tests.
* $p<.05$ ** $p<.01$

there were negative correlations between these two variables ($r = -.43$, $p < .05$ and $r = -.49$, $p < .05$ for the two elementary school data sets and $r = -.44, p < .01$ for the middle school). In other words, the more the teacher tried to direct behavior while students were working in groups, the less they talked and worked together.

The more highly differentiated classrooms had less direct supervision than the less highly differentiated classrooms. In the case of the elementary data, teachers who used larger groups and fewer learning centers were more likely to tell the students what to do directly. Middle school teachers who used fewer different activities were more likely to facilitate, instruct, and discipline than teachers who had up to six different activities in simultaneous operation.

These findings are at the classroom level, but the relationship between lateral communication and achievement also holds at the individual level. Leechor (1988) combined the elementary school data for 1982–83 and 1984–85 to assess the effects of talking with peers on individual learning. He found that the student's average rate of task-related talk was a significant predictor of posttest score, holding constant pretest score and student status (Leechor, 1988). In a study of 56 students in sixth-grade science classes using complex instruction (Bianchini, 1995), the correlation between the average rate of talk and a gain score summed over several unit tests was $r = .453$ ($p < .001$).

DISCUSSION

Organizational arrangements of the classroom predict learning outcomes. Interaction is a strong and consistent predictor of achievement gains across subject areas and grade levels in three separate studies of complex instruction. Ruth Cossey (1996) conducted a fourth study of 10 complex instruction classrooms in mathematics. She also found a strong relationship between talking and working together and the average classroom gains on a test of mathematical communication (Spearman $r = .77$). The proposition also holds at the individual level.

However, this robust relationship between interaction and achievement will not hold under all conditions. In her studies of collaborative seatwork in mathematics, Webb (1983, 1991) has never found a consistent relationship between interaction and achievement. In an analysis of productivity of research and development (R & D) teams in industry and groups of children working together in classrooms, Cohen and Cohen (1991) conclude that it is *only* under the conditions of a true group task and an ill-structured problem that interaction is vital to productivity. The collaborative seatwork used in the Webb studies meets neither of these conditions. In contrast, complex instruction tasks fit the definition of a true group task. They require resources (information, knowledge, heuristic problem-solving strategies, materials, and skills) that no single individual possesses so that no single individual is likely to solve the problem or accomplish the task objectives without at least some input from others (Cohen & Arechavala-Vargas, 1987). Complex instruction tasks are also ill-structured problems in that they are open-ended, nonroutine problems for which there are no standard procedures. In contrast, the tasks in Webb's studies are computational or require the application of an algorithm. Thus, the importance of interaction for learning holds only for specified kinds of tasks.

Perrow's proposition on delegation of authority in the face of uncertain tasks is a powerful one for classrooms. Although we did not have a direct measure of delegation of authority, its obverse—direct supervision—had a negative effect on lateral relations consistently documented in the three different data sets. Perrow's proposition implies that both delegation of authority and lateral relations are direct antecedents of effectiveness. Our study of the relationship of the three variables suggests a different pattern in which direct supervision is a precursor of lateral relations, which are, in turn, a precursor of effectiveness. In a regression of achievement gains on both of these variables, direct supervision does not have a direct impact on achievement. Thus, we conclude that a better theoretical model is one that poses an indirect relationship between delegation of authority and productivity.

The results of differentiation of classroom technology suggest that a variety of activities and groups that are smaller than five push the teacher to limit the use of direct supervision. The pattern of correlations in the middle school data suggests that the use of fewer activities allows the teacher to do more direct supervision. When middle school groups were very small (e.g., pairs), there was also more direct supervision (Cohen, Lotan, & Holthuis, 1995). The maintenance of groups of four or five and a highly differentiated task structure helps the teacher delegate authority.

PRACTICAL IMPLICATIONS

These three strong and generalizable propositions provide powerful tools for the teacher and for professional development. Teachers who study complex instruction understand that whatever adaptations they must make because of the nature of their classrooms, they must minimize changes that will decrease the level of interaction or increase their level of direct supervision while students are working in groups. Although intervening in the work of a group is sometimes unavoidable, high levels of direct instruction will lead to low levels of interaction among students. Therefore, while students are working in groups, teachers would do well to observe groups that are having difficulty, waiting to intervene until they are sure the group will not solve the problem for itself. The negative impact of direct supervision on student interaction does not imply that there is no role for direct instruction. Particularly at the middle school level, students must acquire the background for the topic prior to carrying out multiple-ability groupwork.

Another interesting example of use of these general principles comes from the adaptation of complex instruction in Israel. Here classes are large (40), and there are 9 to 10 groups in simultaneous operation. Without resources for materials for 6 different tasks, the teachers produced differentiation by having each group report to the class on answers to a different set of questions.

Another set of practical implications arises from the relationships of organizational arrangements in the classroom to productive discourse in student groups. Educators today emphasize the capacity of students to construct their own knowledge in group discourse. Constructivist theories of learning and teaching stress discourse, debate, and dialogue as means of gaining conceptual understanding. Contructivists almost unanimously recommend small cooperative groups as settings in which students have the opportunity for such discourse (Linn & Burbules, 1993; Noddings, 1990; Tobin & Tippins, 1993; von Glaserfeld, 1991; Wheatley, 1991).

There is, however, little understanding among these researchers and curriculum developers of changes in conventional classrooms necessary for productive discourse to take place in small groups. If the constructivist curricula have poorly engineered group tasks, they will not produce the required interdependence for interaction. Nothing is said about having different groups carry out different tasks. Moreover, the teacher cannot simply let the students work in groups, adopting a laissez-faire role. Rather, he or she must clearly delegate authority to the groups. If not, results can be chaotic and the discourse of students disappointing. Thus, multiple-ability curricula as well as these constructivist curricula require the changes in organizational arrangements we have described.

CONCLUSION

Using organizational sociology, we have been able to develop and test conditionalized propositions that relate the type of differentiation in the technology, the nature of the teacher's supervision, and work arrangements among the students to gains in achievement at the classroom level. These results dramatize the possibilities for sociologists of education to achieve a different level of understanding of educational achievement. These propositions also provide practical insights for instruction—insights that are relevant to current trends in classroom practice. The results are sufficiently robust to conclude that the sociology of education is a strong potential contributor to the improvement of classroom practice.

CHAPTER 4

The Power in Playing the Part

Dey E. Ehrlich and Marcia B. Zack

While there has been some controversy among practitioners of cooperative learning over the utility of roles in groupwork, they are an important feature of complex instruction. Far from being superfluous or distracting, roles not only encourage learning by facilitating groupwork processes, but they encourage it through their very implementation as well.

WHAT ARE "ROLES"?

The term *role* is used in sociology to denote that "conduct adheres to certain 'parts' (or positions) rather than to the players who read or recite them" (Sarbin & Allen, 1968, p. 489). A set of activities, including interactions, characterizes the role of the individual occupying the position (Pfeffer, 1982). Roles can be procedural and formalized. Procedural roles help the group accomplish the task by giving group members rules for interacting according to a set of expectations placed on each member's role. Formalization is important, since when roles are formally assigned, it is easier to accept the behavior associated with them. Formalization is also a way to clarify role expectations, and this clarification has been related to group productivity (Sarbin & Allen, 1968). Roles also can foster interaction or lateral relations, which are especially effective and productive. As Cohen (1986) states, "In groups where members have different roles and jobs to do, they feel very satisfied with their part in the group process" (p. 65).

Types of Roles

The types of roles used in the classroom are dependent on the age of the students (for example, in middle schools the role of harmonizer is used to help keep the peace among group members) and the tasks they are expected to perform (for example, a safety officer is necessary when the task has elements of danger, such as a heating component or the use of sharp objects). All groupwork can benefit from a facilitator, a reporter, and a materials manager; other roles might include a timer, a cleanup organizer, a checker, and

44

a resource person to bring dictionaries and so forth to the group. The facilitator is responsible for making certain that everyone in the group gets the help needed, as well as for identifying resources to resolve problems that may come up within the group. The reporter tells the class about the work accomplished by the group, often describing the task and its results, as well as relating any problems or interesting things that happened to the group.

Why Use Roles?

As suggested in previous chapters, classroom heterogeneity and organizational complexity require nontraditional management strategies. While implementing complex instruction, the teacher must be a resource for information rather than a direct supervisor. By delegating authority through the use of roles, the teacher shifts administrative duties such as checking for understanding and for work completion to the students; by assigning students duties such as making sure that all students are involved in the activity, the teacher enhances interdependence within the group. Each person in the group has a task necessary for the success of the entire group. Assigning administrative duties to the students has the added benefit of creating a situation where children must verbalize their ideas (in sociological terms, an increase in lateral relations), and this helps students serve as resources in problem solving for one another.

During successful cooperative groupwork, a diverse group of students should be able to understand and complete nonroutine tasks, interact with one another (thus developing their verbal skills and reinforcing their learning), and increase their interpersonal skills. The use of roles is a strategy that simplifies the maintenance of order and allows for high levels of on-task behavior even though many different activities and groups are in operation in the classroom. Role usage also serves to encourage behaviors associated with higher-order thinking skills. In both of the studies that are described in the remainder of this chapter, roles were found to foster the interaction that leads to conceptual gains.

THE POTENTIAL OF A WELL-PLAYED ROLE: THE ROLE OF FACILITATOR

A study by Zack in 1988 looked at the effect of the facilitator role in classrooms implementing complex instruction. This study examined whether increased use of the role resulted in more frequent talking and working together among the students, and whether its use actually reduced student need for teacher supervision while maintaining high levels of on-task performance.

Delegation and Facilitation

Zack (1988) tested the power of student facilitation in contrast to teacher facilitation in a path model that was closely related to the hypotheses concerning teacher supervision, lateral relations, and learning outcomes described in Chapter 3. She introduced to the 1984–85 data set her variable of student facilitative talk, contrasting its power to predict lateral relations to that of teacher facilitative talk. She also introduced the variable of the percentage of students waiting for the teacher as a way to test the undesirable effects of teachers trying to facilitate student work while groups are in operation.

In this path model, Zack hypothesized that when teachers did less facilitating for the students while more students simultaneously facilitated for one another, there would be an increase in the amount of students' talking and working together. Student facilitation was a positive indicator of the theoretical concept of delegation of authority, while teacher facilitation was a negative measure. Zack argued that student facilitation is an indicator of delegation of authority because the teacher gives to students a role that the teacher ordinarily plays. Teacher and student facilitation should have opposite effects on lateral relations, and lateral relations are the critical feature in predicting learning outcomes (Cohen, Lotan, & Leechor, 1989). The extent of students' talking and working together, as discussed in Chapter 3, is an indicator of the concept of lateral relations.

In Zack's view, teacher facilitation should lead to a higher percentage of students waiting for the teacher. If the only way students can get information is from the teacher, then there will be greater pressure on hierarchical channels of communication. To the extent that the teacher tells students how to do their task, students will believe that the teacher is the only source of authoritative knowledge. To the extent that the group becomes an alternative source of knowledge, there should be less use of hierarchical channels. Therefore, it was also predicted that the rate at which students acted as facilitator would have a negative effect on the same variable (percentage of students waiting for the teacher).

Path Model

Zack's analysis was at the classroom level with the 13 classrooms in the 1984–85 data set. The inclusion of a measure of learning gains for this data set necessitated the use of the control variable of percentage of students working alone. (For a discussion of the effect of this variable, see Cohen, Lotan, & Leechor, 1989.)

Data on teacher behavior came from the Teacher Observation Instrument. As described in Chapter 3, data on the average rate of student task-related talk and working together came from the Target Child Instrument.

Zack developed a special measure of rate of student facilitative talk for the Target Child Instrument. Procedural interactions by students that were relevant for completion of assignments made up the measure of student facilitative talk. This measure included directing others what to do, asking one person to help another, making general announcements to the group, and asking questions regarding members' progress. Observers scored any of these interactions as facilitator talk, regardless of whether the speaker held the official role of facilitator. Facilitator talk was excluded from the task-related talk measure that constituted the measure of lateral relations.

The percentage of students waiting for the teacher is a coding category on the Whole Class Instrument. Table 4.1 lists the indicators used, grouped by concept.

Results

Figure 4.1 presents Zack's path model of implementation and productivity. The regression of target children talking and working together on teacher facilitation and student facilitation shows the predicted contrasting relation-

Table 4.1: Concepts, Indicators, and Sources of Data for Zack's Study of Facilitators

Concept	Indicator	Source
Delegation of authority	Rate of student facilitative talk	Target Child Instrument
	Rate of teacher facilitative talk while at learning centers—negative measure	Teacher Observation Instrument
Productivity	Rate of student task-related talk	Target Child Instrument
	Rate of students working together	Target Child Instrument
	% of students waiting for teacher—negative measure	Whole Class Instrument
	Average learning gains—math computation	(CTBS/English)

Figure 4.1: Teacher and Student Facilitation, Implementation, and Productivity (Zack, 1988).

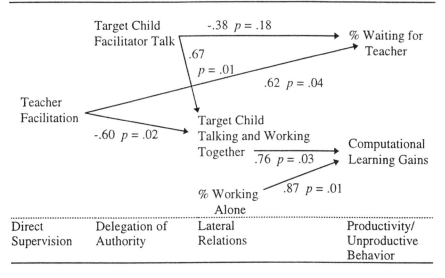

ships. There is a strong negative effect of teacher facilitation (path coefficient of $-.60, p = .02$) and an equally strong positive effect of student facilitation (path coefficient of $.67, p = .01$) on the average rate of target children talking and working together. Also, as hypothesized, the teacher's facilitation has the effect of increasing the percentage of students waiting for the teacher (path coefficient of $.62, p = .04$). Simultaneously, student facilitative talk has a negative effect on the percentage waiting for the teacher, but the path coefficient is not statistically significant. As described in Chapter 3, the measure of lateral relations has a strong positive effect on learning gains. In this analysis, Zack chose the computation subscale of the standardized achievement score to measure learning gains.

Importance of the Student Facilitator

The teacher's use of the facilitator role and the student's use of this role had opposing impacts on both unproductive behavior and the extent of lateral relations. This supports the value of delegating authority to students in the form of structured roles. When the teacher cuts down on the amount of teacher supervision, it is necessary for the students to take up the slack. Assigning students to facilitate for one another ensures the effectiveness of lateral relations. The facilitator role serves as a mechanism within the group that helps members to stay focused on the task. It keeps the group members functioning as a unit and increases interdependence.

THE POWER OF ROLE MODIFICATION: CHANGING THE ROLE OF REPORTER

We have seen how a well-played role can make a major difference in the functioning of the classroom system, thereby influencing student outcomes. But it is not only an established role that can make a difference in student achievement—rather, roles are such powerful tools that teachers can modify them to influence student behavior to such an extent as to modify student outcomes as well. For example, the reporter role in CI normally is implemented by having the reporter talk to the entire class at the end of the group's activity about how the task went. Ehrlich (1991) modified the standard implementation of the reporter role by developing reporter forms that required the reporter to work with the entire group in order to complete the forms. The result of Ehrlich's intervention was to motivate elementary school students to do their group task in a more thoughtful, systematic way, engaging in behaviors such as observing, inferring, sharing their findings, predicting, and hypothesizing. This served to specifically increase those interactions associated with analytical processes.

The Application of Organizational Theory to the Group

Borrowing from organizational theory, Fry (1982) conceptualized structure and technology within the smaller organization of the group working together to accomplish their task. The degree of interdependence of the group is one of the analytic dimensions within the organization of the small group. Interdependence has to do with the interrelatedness of the work processes and group members; an organization is composed of interdependent parts when each unit must perform well so as not to jeopardize the success of the group (Thompson, 1967).

When the outputs of all units of the group become the inputs for other units, such that each unit is penetrated by the others, these are the conditions for reciprocal interdependence. Reciprocal interdependence places "increasingly heavy burdens on communication and decisions" (Thompson, 1967, p. 56). This implies that within a reciprocally interdependent task group, group members have a greater need to communicate and interact, which is particularly useful when their task is complex and uncertain. Cohen and Arechavala-Vargas (1987) found that high levels of reciprocal interdependence were associated with high levels of unit productivity and interaction when an R&D team was involved with innovative, nonroutine work. Ehrlich (1991) proposed that if reciprocal interdependence were heightened, task group interaction (lateral communication) would be greater and unit productivity (achievement) would increase as well.

To increase reciprocal interdependence, the group must have a task that demands input from everyone in order for the group to be successful. The group could include a role that, when played, required all group members to interact with one another in order to complete a task that demanded input from everyone. Formalizing a role associated with that task clarifies expectations and stimulates lateral communication. Ehrlich hypothesized that the presence of a role that fosters reciprocal interdependence will be associated with greater interaction than the absence of such a role.

Once interaction was increased, however, the problem would remain to secure a higher-order level of interaction. If a subtask was created to be accomplished alongside the group task—a subtask that required the group to engage in science thinking behaviors (STBs)—the group would have the opportunity to practice higher-order skills. STBs include observing, asking thinking questions, requesting justification, identifying concepts, making analogies, controlling variables, predicting/hypothesizing, and inferring/concluding. The group member who played the new role would have the job of seeing to it that the subtask was accomplished. The more opportunities the group would have to perform this special subtask, the more practice the group would have with the science thinking behaviors. Engaging in these thinking processes would become learned behaviors, exhibited even when the new role and the particular subtask were not required of the group.

Ehrlich's second hypothesis was that when a small task group included a role encouraging science thinking behaviors, there would be a relationship between the opportunities to practice the role, with its expectations for the behavior of others, and the frequency of STBs observed in the absence of the role. Because of the paucity of literature on the effects of task group processes on task group effectiveness, however, the question of whether a relationship exists between STBs and achievement/group effectiveness remained an exploratory one.

The Research Design

In CI, the reporters play their roles at the end of the time at the learning centers. Often, as the students are told to clean up, the reporter scrambles to figure out what to say to the class. To stimulate greater interaction throughout the activity, the task groups learned a new set of behaviors for the reporter role that included filling out special reporter forms—one for science activities and a different one for activities based on mathematics. The enhanced reporter's job was to encourage the group to think and talk together and to come up with answers to the questions on the special forms as a group. The group was required to complete the reporter forms during the time the students were working on their activity. The questions on the forms prompted the entire group to respond interdependently (theoretically increasing interaction within the task groups) and were constructed in such a way as to stimulate science behaviors; for example,"What does your GROUP predict will happen in your SCIENCE EXPERIMENT? Explain WHY the group made this prediction." "Were the GROUP's predictions supported by your observations? Explain."

Timing was very important for the success of the new role and forms. At the start of the activity, the reporter initiated a group discussion to answer the first question on the forms. Later on, the reporter was signaled to stop the group's actions and to initiate a group discussion to answer another question. Finally, the reporter pulled the group together to answer the last question at the end of their activity.

The Population and Setting of the Study. The data for Ehrlich's study were collected in 1990 independently of any other data collection described in this volume. The students in the study were from fourth- and fifth-grade academically heterogeneous classrooms from the greater San Francisco Bay Area. The majority were Latino children, with Black, Southeast Asian, and Anglo children also represented. Parental background was mostly working class to lower middle class. The 16 teachers who agreed to take part in this study were all implementing CI using *Finding Out/Descubrimiento* (*FO/D*) (De Avila & Duncan, 1982b).

Treatment Groups and Testing for Achievement. Two sets of classrooms, both of which were implementing CI, received differing treatments. In the first set of classrooms (Treatment I), CI was implemented in the usual manner. The other set of classrooms (Treatment II) used CI as well, but, through use of the enhanced reporter role and forms, the students had additional opportunities to engage in science behaviors in the task groups. Both treatment groups were fairly evenly matched in terms of teacher experience with CI. Quality control of implementation of CI was monitored using the Whole Class Instrument. Ehrlich collected all the reporter forms at the end of the year and scored them on the completeness and quality of the responses. This score was an indicator of the determinants of the quality of implementation of the treatment. Finally, all students in both treatment groups were given a science pretest and posttest based on the *FO/D* science curriculum (referred to as the *FO/D* test). The test is criterion-referenced, based on the entire *FO/D* curriculum of 17 units. It is administered orally in English and in Spanish, so that neither a student's reading ability nor level of English proficiency (at least for the Spanish-speaking students) interferes with the student's ability to express understanding of the scientific concepts being tested.

Testing for Understanding and Science Behaviors. After having studied a minimum of four *FO/D* units, both sets of classrooms studied the same unit on electricity with the same series of orientation lessons. When they finished the electricity unit, the students were presented with the Electricity Test, a criterion-referenced task intended to measure their science knowledge on the unit. The 40-minute test was similar to a standard *FO/D* activity in that all the regular *FO/D* norms and roles were in place. It consisted of a hands-on task that required experimentation and a worksheet with questions about the experiments. The task groups needed to use their knowledge of conductors, resistors, and circuits to solve four experiments that they had never been exposed to, transferring their knowledge of how they made a bulb light up (from the electricity unit) to figure out how to make a buzzer sound (for the test). Only enough materials were provided so that the activity had to be done as a group with everyone sharing. As with regular *FO/D*, even though the test was taken by the group, each group member was responsible for a personal worksheet, and procedural roles were randomly assigned. Groups from both treatments were tested in exactly the same way, and no reporter form was given to either group during the test.

Observation of group members during the test provided a comparison of science behaviors by students in each treatment. Ehrlich selected task groups from each classroom for videotaping using several criteria: student acquiescence to being videotaped, parental consent, and control for status differences within the group.

Classifying the Science Behaviors. Once the videotapes were collected, they were transcribed and scored depending on the type of statements made and their context. For example, in the conceptual category "interprets/concludes," context differentiated predictions from conclusions. If a student said, "The square battery is the loudest!" before having tried any of the batteries, it was scored as a prediction. But if after having tried three batteries in turn the student said, "The square one is the loudest!" it was scored as a conclusion. In scoring the transcribed videotapes, intercoder reliability was 95% using the formula found in Miles and Huberman (1984).

Measurement and Results

A list of the variables and how they were operationalized is found in Table 4.2.

The first hypothesis proposed that when a small task group was working under conditions of uncertainty, the presence of a role that fostered

Table 4.2: Variables and Measures for Ehrlich's Study of Reporters

Variable	Measure
Implementation of intervention	Quantity/quality of reporter forms found by sum of scores on the following items: Teacher's use of both reporter forms # of units implemented with reporter forms # of reporter forms used Quality of responses on representative sample of forms
Interaction	% of students talking, talking and working, and working alone, while using reporter forms (Whole Class Instrument)
Science thinking behaviors	% of incidents of STBs expressed by each group member
Group success at the Electricity Test	Group points for success with four experiments plus average Electricity Worksheet score
Achievement on *FO/D* science test	Gain scores aggregated to group level, for total test and subset of science questions

reciprocal interdependence would be associated with greater interaction than when the group was working without such a role. The tests for this hypothesis came from Treatment II's classroom level data (using the Whole Class Instrument): the percentage of students marked as working in groups when they were using the STB reporter forms versus when they were not using the forms. Observers also recorded when students were talking; talking, manipulating, and reading; and working alone. Table 4.3 shows the results of these analyses.

The results support the first hypothesis. When reciprocal interdependence increased, that is, when the students were working on the STB re-

Table 4.3: *t*-Tests of Percentages of Students Talking in Groups, Working Together in Groups, and Working Alone, With and Without the STB Form in Hand (Paired samples *t*-test with 50 cases)

Variable	Mean Difference	t	p	SD Diff	DF
Students talking together	9.405	2.156	.036	30.846	49
Students talking, reading and manipulating materials together	10.158	2.070	.044	34.706	49
Students working alone	-13.525	-2.852	.006	33.536	49

porter forms, interaction was higher than when they were not using the forms, whether the students were talking or doing other on-task activities, such as reading, writing, and manipulating materials. The converse is also true: When the students were actually working with the reporter forms in hand, they were less likely to be working alone. All three *t*-tests are significant at the $p < .05$ level, providing consistent support for this hypothesis.

The second hypothesis stated that there would be a relationship between the opportunities to practice a role that encourages reciprocal interdependence and the frequency of STBs seen even when the role was not being played. In testing this hypothesis, the unit of analysis is the task group, rather than classroom observations. *T*-tests determined whether there was a difference between the two treatment groups in the average number of STBs that the groups exhibited during the Electricity Test. Each of the five relevant STBs was tested separately, and three of the behaviors showed significant differences between treatments ($p < .05$), as seen in Table 4.4.

Of the two behaviors without significant differences, one (observing) was exhibited so frequently by all students in both treatments that it lost

Table 4.4: *t*-Tests for Differences in Means of STBs Between Treatment Groups I and II

STB	*n*	Mean	SD	*t* value	*p*
1. *Observing* *DF = 21.9*					
Treatment I	18	4.08[a]	0.77	-0.578	.569
Treatment II	14	4.28[a]	1.13		
2. *Asking Thinking Questions/Requesting* *Justification* *DF = 25.6*					
Treatment I	18	4.94	42.73	-2.717	.012
Treatment II	14	7.86	3.21		
3. *Using Concepts/Analogies/Controlling* *Variables* *DF = 20.8*					
Treatment I	18	3.28	2.65	-1.343	.194
Treatment II	14	5.00	4.19		
4. *Predicting/Hypothesizing* *DF = 20*					
Treatment I	18	3.89	2.47	-2.652	.015
Treatment II	14	7.21	4.15		
5. *Inferring/Concluding* *DF = 17.7*					
Treatment I	18	5.22	2.98	-2.898	.010
Treatment II	14	10.43	6.19		

[a]These values are squared means. Groups' scores for this behavior were mostly clustered around the mean; because of the skewed distribution, *t*-tests were conducted on the square root of the variable.

importance, and the definition of the other (using concepts/analogies/controlling variables) was so general that it became somewhat of a catch-all variable and the individual science behaviors were indistinguishable.

To ascertain whether the use of science thinking behaviors led to greater achievement (the exploratory question), *t*-tests were run to compare the average gains on the *FO/D* test between treatment groups. Treatment II groups started out significantly behind Treatment I groups on all three tests; however, after experiencing the intervention, they had greater gains on all three tests, although none of the differences were significant.

To test the relationship between achievement on the *FO/D* science test and the use of STBs exhibited by a science task group, an analysis was carried out at the group level using multiple regressions. English proficiency was a control variable in the regressions. For each regression, the dependent variable was one of the posttests: the total test, or the subsets of science or electricity questions. In each case, the respective pretest was held constant. The independent variable in each case was "Use of STBs," a score of the total number of the five relevant STBs exhibited by each videotaped group. The equation was: Posttest = Constant + Pretest + Use of STBs + English Proficiency. The results of this series of regressions are shown in Table 4.5.

Table 4.5: Regressions of *FO/D* Posttests (Mean Group Score) on Group's Use of STBs

Variable	Coefficient	Standardized Coefficient	*t*-value	*p* (two-tailed)
Both Subtests				
Constant	24.295	0.000	4.554	0.000
Total Pretest	0.701	0.788	7.715	0.000
Use of STBs	0.987	0.199	1.934	0.063
English Proficiency	3.188	0.131	1.240	0.225
$n = 32$ $R^2 = .847$ $F = 51.574$ $(p < .000)$				
Science Subtest				
Constant	12.965	0.000	2.257	0.032
Science Pretest	0.603	0.695	5.506	0.000
Use of STBs	1.003	0.294	2.312	0.028
English Proficiency	2.026	0.121	0.925	0.363
$n = 32$ $R^2 = .754$ $F = 28.588$ $(p < .000)$				
Electricity Subtest				
Constant	0.943	0.000	1.439	0.161
Electricity Pretest	0.376	0.440	2.449	0.021
Use of STBs	0.087	0.371	2.150	0.040
English Proficiency	0.125	0.109	0.556	0.583
$n = 32$ $R^2 = .319$ $F = 4.380$ $(p < .05)$				

These regressions show that while the use of STBs is not a significant predictor of scores on the total *FO/D* test, there is a significant relationship between STB use and two of the subsets of the test: the science questions and the electricity questions.

Implications

The results of these analyses indicate that the intervention had considerable success. There was a greater incidence of students interacting with one another when they used the reporter forms. Those students who were given the opportunity to practice science thinking behaviors used that specialized language more often. This was true even though these students had significantly lower levels of English proficiency.

The findings on the exploratory question suggest that students who were observed using science thinking behaviors were more proficient at answering the questions related to science and electricity. If Ehrlich's reporter forms can promote the internalization of STBs, then using them can indirectly benefit students studying science. It may be that because the students had a new, enhanced way of thinking about their experiments and communicating about them with each other, they were able to learn more of the science being taught to them. Teachers who used the reporter forms in their classrooms cited increased benefits in improved writing skills and oral communication, and expressed their delight in seeing students improve in organizing their thinking, increasing their abilities to reason out a problem, and using science vocabulary and science methods to help them experiment and understand the "why" of a problem.

CONCLUSION

Both of these studies serve the important purpose of illustrating that a classroom's management system, as represented by rules and expectations for behavior, can be selected and developed in such a way as to improve classroom processes and student achievement. Formalized roles have a large, important part to play in group dynamics. The literature on role theory has been negligible in this area, but the results of these studies point to a way to add strength and cohesiveness to task groups.

Zack found that use of the facilitator role results in increased lateral relations. This suggests that it would be useful for others interested in cooperative learning to consider including this role as part of a cooperative management system. It should not be assumed that everyone in the group can completely depend on the facilitator, since if the facilitator did not play that role well, it would be essential for other group members to have the cooperative skills to keep the group functioning. However, the important and unique role of the facilitator should be acknowledged.

The analyses showed that lateral relations influenced measures of productivity in desirable ways in the form of students waiting for the teacher and learning gains. The results strongly imply that instead of a direct connection between the use of roles and the teacher's use of authority, both of these variables have an impact on the process of lateral relations, and that they serve to enhance the ability of students to deal with uncertainty. The theory could be reformulated to state that the use of procedural roles will promote lateral relations that deal with uncertainty, while direct supervision will deter the occurrence of lateral relations. These findings suggest that as teachers withdraw from the facilitator role and let students function independently, students become more successful in the role.

Ehrlich's study showed a strong relationship between the enhanced reporter role and task and science behaviors. The reporter forms offered a means to encourage students to use the scientific method for problem solving by making them practice it, both orally and in writing. By changing the work arrangements in the classroom, teachers also changed the way students talked with one another, suggesting that learning outcomes can be affected by work arrangements.

While the reporter forms used in this study were developed for elementary students and were subject specific, similar reporter forms could be developed that would be suitable for other ages and subjects. There is no reason why teachers cannot prod students who are assigned group tasks in other subjects and other grades to think more profoundly about their work. Students also need to consider the "why" of what they are doing, instead of just looking for the most expedient way to get through the task.

Roles have the potential to increase the value of groupwork for students and teachers. Skills such as problem solving, analyzing, and higher-order thinking remain with students long after they have left the classroom. These are the skills we should take every opportunity to teach and reinforce.

Presently, groupwork in the elementary classroom is used mostly as a method to teach cooperation, but its value can be far greater. It can be made more valuable for the students and more useful for the teacher. Roles such as that of facilitator and reporter can strengthen groupwork by increasing interaction; with some manipulation, the interaction can be focused to emphasize thinking and reasoning skills, essential for all students.

PART III

Status Problems and Their Treatment

CHAPTER 5

Understanding Status Problems: Sources and Consequences

Elizabeth G. Cohen

Miguel was a shy and withdrawn child who spoke no English and who stuttered when he spoke Spanish. His Spanish reading and writing skills were very low, and although math was his strength, nobody seemed to notice. Recently arrived from a small community in Mexico, Miguel lived with relatives—more than 10 adults and three children in a two bedroom apartment. He came to school hungry and tired, wearing dirty clothes. Shunned by his classmates, who said he had the "cooties," Miguel was left out of group activities. Even when he had a specific role, other members of the group would take over and tell him what to do. Miguel was obviously a low-status student. When I observed Miguel's group I saw that the other members simply wouldn't give him a chance. Cooperative learning was not helping him at all. Miguel grew more isolated by the day. Students increasingly teased him and he was getting into fights and becoming a behavior problem. (Shulman, Lotan, & Whitcomb, 1995, pp. 59–60)

Teachers who have tried cooperative learning are asking for help with problems of social and intellectual isolation such as those Miguel experienced. They also worry about the student who "does all the work" in the small group or the student who dominates the interaction, talking much more than anyone else, telling others what they must do while reserving the right to make final decisions.

The student who dominates the group and the student who fails to participate or to whom no one ever listens represent two sides of the same coin—a status problem in the group. This problem is not due simply to the individual characteristics of a student such as Miguel or to those of the dominant student. Other members of the group have decided that Miguel has nothing to contribute and actively shut him out. Similarly, participants often agree that the dominant member has the best ideas and evaluate that person as the most competent in the group.

Teachers attempt to treat the problem of unequal interaction by changing the composition of the groups. However, within another group, the dominant student is still likely to dominate, and the nonparticipating stu-

61

dent is still unlikely to speak up. Alternatively, a new pattern of inequality arises in which someone fails to participate while someone else does too much talking.

Status characteristic theory has proved to be an invaluable tool in understanding and treating these problems. Studies of the earliest version of complex instruction in 1979 (Cohen, 1984) documented status problems before status treatments became a major focus of staff development. Following the introduction of status treatments, Cohen, Lotan, and Catanzarite (1988) found interaction to be significantly more equal-status. Moreover, status was no longer a direct predictor of learning gains. It is, however, naive to expect the status gap to disappear in all complex instruction classrooms; status problems represent a powerful and persistent phenomenon.

In this chapter, I examine the persistence of status problems in some complex instruction classrooms. Further evidence for the effectiveness of status interventions appears in Chapter 6. Status problems in the middle school classroom are more complex than those in the elementary school. In middle grades, peer popularity is a powerful basis for status and may operate quite independently of the academic status order. The last part of this chapter presents post hoc analyses of middle school data on the effects of the relationship of peer and academic status and on effects of race and gender.

THE PROCESS OF STATUS GENERALIZATION

Status generalization (Berger, Cohen, & Zelditch, 1966, 1972) is the process by which status characteristics come to affect interaction and influence so that the prestige and power order of the group reflects the initial differences in status. (For a full description of this process, see Berger, Rosenholtz, & Zelditch, 1980.) The process of status generalization has three important components: status characteristics on which individuals in the group differ; expectation states that are determined by status information; and behavioral inequalities that are the end product of the operation of differential expectations for competence on the task. The behavioral inequalities observable in cooperative groups are a function of the differences in expectations for competence at the assigned task.

Observe Miguel and four other members of his class at work on a group task in which students discover what makes structures strong. They are creating structures from straws. Miguel and the members of his group base the expectations they hold for themselves and for the other members of the group on any and all differences in status that existed before the formation of the group. In Miguel's case, cues that can activate expectations for competence or incompetence might include inability to speak English, poor reading and writing skills, darker skin color, dirty clothes (indicating low socioeconomic status), plus superior math skills.

Theoretically, all this status information becomes *salient* or *activated* in the situation of the cooperative task and is used to form *specific performance expectations* about how well Miguel will do in the new assignment. Even if discovering what makes a structure strong by building bridges out of straws has no rational connection to any of the status information, the members of the group *will act as if the information were relevant to the task.* Miguel's classmates combine the one item of positive status information (his math ability) with all the negative information. Therefore, as his teacher reports, math skills have little impact on expectations for his competence.

A Self-Fulfilling Prophecy

Performance expectations are not directly observable, but they have observable consequences for behavior. Among these consequences are a higher rate of interaction and influence for those members of the group for whom there are positive performance expectations. Miguel works quietly and effectively, carefully following the diagram on the activity card, while other members of the group hold an animated discussion in English (all but one speak both English and Spanish). They are quite confused about the task, partly because they have paid no attention to the diagram or the instructions on the activity card. The person who talks the most in the group is mistaken about what makes the structures stronger, but the group treats her opinions as very important and follows her lead. Miguel is all but invisible. If no one intervenes, the net result in this group will be a self-fulfilling prophecy. Neither Miguel nor the other group members will see him as competent on the task or as having made an important contribution. Even though the group, as a group, is not successful on the task, members see the dominant girl as having had the best ideas and as having done the most to lead the group. Thus, the prestige and power order of the group at the end of the task will reflect the initial status differences in the group. If the same group goes on to another learning station, the perceptions of relative competence and incompetence at the bridge-building task will act as still another bit of status information that will become salient in the next task. Performance expectations in the next task will therefore reflect all the initial status differences plus the new status difference in ability to understand what makes a structure strong.

The process of status generalization (Webster & Foschi, 1988) has several important features. First, the infection of new situations by status distinctions is a powerful process for both low- and high-status individuals. In the above example, the expectations for competence held for Miguel are parallel to those he holds for himself. Second, although behavioral inequalities in the group are directly observable, the expectations are not. They are not necessarily represented in conscious cognition and researchers cannot ask about them on a questionnaire. Third, expectations for competence are always relative to expectations held for other members of the group. In status characteristic theory, one speaks of having high expectations for a particular group member *relative* to the expectations held for other persons engaged in a collective task.

Status Characteristics and Expectations

In describing the status information that becomes salient in Miguel's case, I have included a variety of bases for status distinctions. Theoretically, these are all status characteristics with high and low states. Status characteristics are agreed-upon social rankings where people believe that it is better to be in the high than in the low state. Attached to the high and low states of the status characteristic are performance expectations—high expectations for those in the high state and low expectations for those in the low state.

Different types of status characteristics can activate the process of status generalization. Some characteristics, such as minority group membership, social class, or linguistic status, are *diffuse status characteristics*. Diffuse status characteristics have general expectations for superior and inferior competence that are without limit or scope (Webster & Foschi, 1988). For example, both men and women expect men to have superior competence on a wide range of valued tasks. The origin of these sexist beliefs, as with other beliefs about general competence of people of different races or social classes, lies in the culture. In contrast, *specific status characteristics* include occupation, skill, and training; they give specific and limited information about individuals (Webster & Foschi, 1988) and have only specific performance expectations attached to high and low states of the characteristic. Examples of specific status characteristics in the classroom are skill in using the computer or ability in adding numbers.

Peer and academic status are *local status characteristics*; these characteristics have a local character that distinguishes them from diffuse status characteristics. Like diffuse status characteristics, there are general expectations for competence attached to high and low states of the characteristics. However, unlike diffuse status characteristics, the beliefs underlying these expectations for competence do not stem from the general culture. Rather, the definitions of high and low states on these characteristics and their accompanying expectations come from local school culture—beliefs about what it means to be "smart" in school and what it means to be popular and socially desirable. This set of beliefs can and does vary from school to school and from class to class (Cohen & Lotan, 1997).

All these different kinds of status characteristics become salient when a task meets the scope conditions of the theory. Unless the actors know for sure that a salient status characteristic is irrelevant, they will treat it as if it were relevant to success or failure on the task. As the "burden of proof assumption" states, "the burden of proof rests on someone who would claim that a status characteristic is irrelevant" (Webster & Foschi, 1988, p. 10). Once members have aggregated all the status information and have developed matching performance expectations, the prestige and power position of individual members will be a direct function of the expectation advantage that actors have over one another. In the case of Miguel's group, the student who can speak English well, who receives top grades in the class, and who is very popular will have a significant expectation advantage over Miguel.

Scope Conditions

Miguel will not be an uninfluential nonparticipant under all conditions. His behavior is a product of a social situation that meets the scope conditions of status characteristic theory. Scope conditions specify that at least one status characteristic differentiates the actors. The participants are engaged in a collective task and believe that they can either succeed or fail as a group. Furthermore, they view the task as requiring some specific skill or skills; they do not view success or failure as a matter of luck or as a product of forces beyond their control. Lastly, the participants are involved in the task and perceive the situation as one requiring them to act as a collective. Scope conditions represent *sufficient conditions*; in other words, at least under these conditions one may expect to observe the process. There may well be other conditions that will also trigger the process.

Evidence of Effects on Behavior

An extensive literature of laboratory studies documents the effects of diffuse and specific status characteristics on behavior (Berger, Rosenholtz, & Zelditch, 1980). In addition, Webster and Foschi (1988) review the empirical evidence for the propositions concerning the nature of the process of status generalization.

My first step from the highly controlled setting of the laboratory toward the complex field setting of the classroom was to study more open interaction in mixed-status groups of schoolchildren as they worked on a collective task under controlled conditions. The earliest studies of this genre documented the effects of race, ethnicity, and gender among students playing a standardized game that required the group to make collective decisions as to which way they would proceed on a game board (for a review of this early literature, see Cohen, 1982, 1993).

Rosenholtz (1985) and Tammivaara (1982) documented the effects of perceived reading ability as a status characteristic on interaction. Even though the collective tasks of these two studies required no reading, those students having higher perceived reading ability were more active and influential than those perceived as having lower reading ability. Hoffman (1973) had similar findings for students seen as better at schoolwork.

True differences in ability do not explain the observed differences in behavior among students varying in academic status. Perceived ability differences affected interaction in groups working on math problems, but measures of actual ability had no such effects (Webb & Kenderski, 1984). Dembo and McAuliffe (1987) used a bogus test of problem-solving ability to create a status characteristic that produced the predicted pattern of domination by high-status students, who were more likely to be perceived as leaders than were low-status students.

STATUS PROCESSES IN THE CLASSROOM

According to status characteristic theory, the importance of a particular status characteristic in predicting behavioral outcomes in a group depends on its relevance to the task (Berger & Fisek, 1974). Academic status is of central importance because of its direct relevance to the work of schooling.

Once an academic-status order has formed, teachers appear to use it as a basis for their expectations for performance more than race or ethnicity (Mercer, Iadacola, & Moore, 1980). In many cases, states of the diffuse status characteristic are positively correlated with academic status. For example, White students may be more likely than African-American or Latino students to have high academic status. Working with data from intact classrooms, it is not always possible for the data analyst to pull these status characteristics apart and analyze their effects separately.

Differences in perceived attractiveness or popularity (i.e., peer status) also can act as bases for status generalization (Maruyama & Miller, 1981; Webster & Driskell, 1983). If a group contains some popular class members who are seen as poor students and some socially isolated members who are seen as excellent students, the result will be equal-status behavior (Cohen, 1993). Equal-status interaction occurs because everyone in the situation combines all the status information into an aggregated expectation state

(Webster & Foschi, 1988). The combining principle is a key to treatment of status problems discussed in Chapter 6.

STATUS AND INTERACTION WITHIN COMPLEX INSTRUCTION

Although the tasks in complex instruction require multiple intellectual abilities, they meet the scope conditions of status characteristic theory. The students work with each other in a collective fashion, and any single group will have students who differ in status. The mixed-status character of the groups arises because of the heterogeneous nature of the classrooms and because ability grouping is not used with complex instruction. Thus, unless something such as a status treatment intervenes, students will use all the status information available to decide who will be good at a new task. *Nothing about the rich character of the task will prevent them from doing so.*

The extensive training in cooperative norms in connection with complex instruction raises the level of interaction and leads to more sharing of materials and more asking for and giving assistance (Cohen, Lotan, & Catanzarite, 1988). However, the introduction of cooperative norms will not, by itself, change expectations for competence (Morris, 1979). This research and theoretical reasoning leads to the following hypothesis:

> High-status students will be more active than low-status students within small groups engaged in collective tasks.

A restatement of the above hypothesis applies more specifically to complex instruction and to other uses of cooperative learning that employ similar open-ended tasks.

> When working in groups on open-ended tasks, students who are seen as good in the subject matter and those who are popular will be more active than those who are not popular or not seen as good in subject matter.

Design of the Status Studies

Rachel Lotan and I have tested this basic hypothesis in elementary (1982–83) and in middle school classrooms (1991–92) using complex instruction (Cohen & Lotan, 1994; Cohen, Lotan, & Catanzarite, 1988). The basic design of these studies was the same. We selected a sample of target students with varying positions in the status structure of the classroom. Observers collected systematic data while learning stations were in operation and scored the frequency of task-related interaction for these target students for a 3-minute period. There were five or more observations of each student on different occasions on which the task and the membership of the group varied. Since there was no ability grouping and the classrooms contained a wide range of academic achievement, we assumed that low-status target students would interact with students who had higher status. By taking multiple observations, we estimated a stable rate of interaction. If status generalization occurred, students of higher status should talk more than students of lower status, and rates of participation should correlate with the relative status of the student.

By 1982–83, the classroom management system of complex instruction was fully developed (see Chapter 2). Thus, any status problems observed were not a function of weak preparation for cooperation or inadequate attention to group accountability. Nor were inequalities in participation between high- and low-status students a result of uninteresting and unsuitable tasks. According to the Whole Class Instrument, very few students were disengaged from the group tasks, although the average percentage disengaged was somewhat higher in the middle school than in the elementary school. Staff development, by 1982, included training in one status treatment, the multiple-ability orientation. In 1992, middle school teachers learned to carry out an additional status treatment, assigning competence to low-status students (see Chapter 6).

Measurement

Because status is an agreed-upon social perception, we measured the independent variable with a sociometric instrument prior to observing behavior. Elementary school students circled the names of those in their class who were "best at math and science" (academic status) and those who were their "best friends" (peer status). After standardizing the percentage of choices received according to quintiles of the classroom distribution, each student was given a score of 5 (high) to 1 (low), indicating the relative percentage of choices received for each of the two status characteristics. For a single measure of status, we added the two scores together to create a "costatus score" ranging from 2 to 10 (see Cohen & Lotan, 1994). Scores for the two status characteristics were combined because, according to the theory, participants aggregate status information (Berger & Conner, 1974).

For middle school students, we measured academic status by asking students, "In your opinion, which students are the best at the subject in this class?" To measure peer status, we asked, "If your class had a popularity contest and you could vote for as many students as you wanted, who would you vote for?" Costatus scores were calculated in the same way as for younger students.

At both levels of schooling we used the Target Student Instrument (Appendix C). The observers recorded the frequency of task-related talk and nontask-related talk. Procedural talk about cooperation and roles was a separate category of speech. Observers also scored talking like a facilitator, for example, "Does everybody understand?" as well as behaving like a facilitator (pointing or directing others how to behave). The observation instrument was divided into six 30-second intervals, so that if a student were talking about the task continuously during the observation, he or she would be scored six times. If a student shifted from task-related talk to talking like a facilitator and back to task-related talk within a 30-second interval, he or she could receive more than one score for task-related talk per time interval. An instance of talk or behavior in any of the categories earned a single check as long as another student did not interrupt the speech or the speaker did not change speech category. Interobserver agreement for task-related talk was 90% for the elementary school and 94.69% for the middle school.

To calculate an average rate of talking or behaving across observations, we divided the total frequency of these speeches and behaviors by the number of observations for each student. Before aggregating observations in an average rate for each student, we conducted analyses of variance to ensure that there was less variation within the observations of a given student than between observations of different students. The rate of peer task talk at both levels of schooling yielded a significant F value for classrooms from the elementary school ($F = 1.28, p < .033$) and from the middle school ($F = 10.2, p < .001$).

The elementary school sample consisted of 131 target students drawn from 10 classrooms, Grades 2–5. We selected 47 high-status target students with costatus scores of 8–10, 40 medium-status students with scores of 5–7, and 44 low-status target students with costatus scores of 2–4. The student populations were from working-class backgrounds with a large percentage of Latinos.

The middle school sample was drawn from 19 social studies classrooms. The classroom populations were racially, ethnically, and academically mixed; the schools were all in the process of untracking. From each classroom we selected five high-status (costatus scores of 2, 3, and 4) and five low-status (costatus scores of 8, 9, and 10) target students. If there were not five students available with scores in these two categories, we selected students from the closest middle category to complete the sample of the total of 146 target students. There were 58 low-status, 71 high-status, and 17 middle-status students.

Results

The high-status students, on average, talked more than the low-status students. In the elementary school sample, the high-status students had an average rate of talk of 4.27 per 3 minutes, the rate for the medium-status students was 4.05, and the rate for the low-status students was 3.66. None of the differences among the three groups were statistically significant as they had been in earlier work. Cohen, Lotan, and Catanzarite (1988) attributed this softening of status differences partly to the introduction of status treatments in 1982. For the middle school students, the rate of participation for high-status students was significantly higher than that for low-status students ($t = -2.42, p < .027$), although the average difference between the two groups was only .36. The rate of participation in peer task-related talk was markedly higher for both low- and high-status students (6.48 and 7.84 per 3 minutes, respectively) in the middle school than in the elementary school. The standard deviation of these statistics was also much higher. For example, the range of talk by low-status students ran from .6 per 3 minutes to 17 per 3 minutes (which was slightly higher than that by the most talkative high-status student), yielding a standard deviation of 3.66 for low-status students. The comparable standard deviation for low-status students in the elementary school was 1.61.

There is a linear relationship between the costatus variable and the rate of talk at both levels of schooling. The correlation is .165 ($p = .06$) at the elementary school level and .362 ($p < .001$) for middle school students. Table 5.1 presents regressions of task-related talk on the costatus variable for the two studies. (For the intercorrelations of variables in these regressions, see

Table 5.1: Effect of Status on Task-Related Talk to Peers: Regressions for Elementary and Middle School

Predictors	Elementary School ($n = 131$)		Middle School ($n = 146$)	
	Beta	S.E.	Beta	S.E.
Costatus	.178*	.003	.213**	.101
Multiple Ability Status Treatment	.205*	.067	—	—
% Students Talk	.028	.007	.325*	.043
% Work Alone	.114	.006	—	—
Gender	—	—	-.023	.546
Race/Ethnicity	—	—	.105	.564
	$R^2 = .293$		$R^2 = .425$	

*p=<.05; **p<.01; ***p<.001

Note: Dependent variable for elementary regression used square root of all values of peer talk variable in order to normalize the distribution.

Cohen & Lotan, 1997; Cohen, Lotan & Catanzarite, 1988). The costatus variable had a significant impact on the rate of participation at the elementary and middle school level, that is, the higher the status of the students, the more they talked.

The most important control in these regressions is the general rate of interaction in the classroom as measured by the percentage of students talking and working together, taken from the Whole Class Instrument. This statistic indicates the extent to which the teacher was able to foster peer interaction in the groups; if the teacher had difficulty in delegating authority, then both low- and high-status students talked less (see Chapter 3). This general rate of interaction and interdependence for each classroom had no effect on the rate of participation of individual target students at the elementary level (Beta = .028, p = .393). In contrast, the same variable had a significant impact on participation at the middle school level (Beta = .325, p < .05).

In the elementary school regression, we also controlled on the rate of the teacher's use of a treatment designed to reduce status problems (multiple-ability treatment) and on the percentage of students working alone. The frequency of the teacher's use of the multiple-ability treatment tended to boost the participation rate of all target students (Beta = .205, p < .05). In Chapter 6, we describe status treatments and their effects in detail. In the 1982–83 data set we had to control on the percentage of students working alone because of the tendency of this variable to mask hypothesized effects.

The control variables in the middle school regression included gender and race/ethnicity. The diffuse status characteristics in the middle school regression did not have a significant impact; the next section will present more detail on the interrelationship of costatus and the diffuse status characteristics.

Interpretation

Status effects are persistent despite excellent preparation for cooperation, a role for each student to play, and status treatments that increased the participation of low-status students. As we will see in Chapter 6, it is possible to modify, but very difficult to eliminate, status problems. From a strictly theoretical perspective, this should not be surprising. *It is not possible to prevent expectations from status differences from forming expectations for a collective task.* However, one can add new bases for expectations to the situation.

The effect of status on interaction would not in itself be worrisome to most educators if it were not for the effects of interaction on learning gains (see Chapter 3). In the setting of complex instruction and in other classrooms where cooperative learning is used for open-ended tasks, the operation of status generalization means that low-status students learn less than they would if they had equal access to interaction. Status has an indirect effect on learning outcomes mediated by interaction. The regressions of achievement test scores on interaction show no direct effects of status in either the middle or the elementary school data. This contrasts with the earliest work in 1979–80 (Cohen, Lotan, & Catanzarite, 1988, Table 4, p. 41) before cooperative norms and roles were introduced, where there were additional direct effects of status on learning outcomes.

COMPLEXITIES OF STATUS IN THE MIDDLE SCHOOL

This section presents two post hoc analyses of the middle school data. The first examines the effects of gender and race/ethnicity on interaction within the small groups in social studies classrooms. The second looks at the contextual effects of the relationship of peer and academic status at the classroom level on the observable severity of status problems.

Effects of Diffuse Status Characteristics

Although sociologists see class, race, and ethnicity as the most powerful status characteristics, they are not the most directly relevant to classroom tasks. In the middle school study, Cohen and Lotan (1997) attempted to tease out the effects of diffuse status characteristics from the effects of academic and peer status.

The first diffuse status characteristic examined was gender. There is ample evidence that gender operates as a status characteristic by the time students reach puberty (Lockheed, Harris, & Nemceff, 1983). Analysis of means of task-related talk for boys and girls indicates that there were no overall differences by gender. When high- and low-status groups were examined separately, boys were somewhat more active than girls in both status groups, but the differences were not statistically significant.

In more controlled laboratory settings, there is considerable evidence that African-American or Mexican-American students will be less active and influential on a collective task than White or Anglo students (Cohen, 1982). In these data, Whites and Asians were classified as high on the race/ethnicity status characteristic, and African-Americans, Mexican-Americans and Central Americans, and "other" as low on this status characteristic. Teachers categorized students as to race and ethnicity; their categorization is necessarily a rough one and might well differ from categories based on self-identification.

White/Asian students have a significantly higher mean rate of task-related talk (7.70 acts per 3 minutes) among peers than African-American and Latino students (6.69 acts per 3 minutes) ($t = -1.68, p < .05$). When the sample is divided according to status, the difference between Whites and Asians and other racial/ethnic groups is in the same direction as that for the whole sample, but in neither case are the mean differences statistically significant.

For the sample as a whole, the regression reported in Table 5.1 also shows no effects of gender or race/ethnicity on task-related talk, even when the effects of costatus and classroom implementation are controlled. However, when separate regressions are calculated for high- and low-status students, an interaction effect appears. Table 5.2 gives the effects of gender and ethnicity in a separate regression for low-status students. This regression contains an additional control variable: the rate at which the target student talks and behaves like a facilitator. This kind of talk was scored separately from task-related talk.

The results in Table 5.2 demonstrate that for low-status students, both gender and race/ethnicity are significant predictors of interaction. Among the low-status students, boys were more active than girls, and Whites or Asians were more active than African-Americans, Latinos, or those classified as "other."

In addition, playing the role of facilitator had a strong and significant positive effect on the rate of task-related talk. The effect was far stronger than any observed for the elementary students.

Neither gender nor race/ethnicity had a significant effect on rate of interaction of high-status students (not shown in tables). Only the variables measuring quality of implementation (% talk/work) and playing the role of facilitator had a significant positive effect on rate of task-related talk.

Table 5.2: Regression of Task-Related Talk on Gender and Ethnicity: Middle School Low-Status Students ($n = 57$)

Predictor	B	Beta	t	p (one-tailed)
Constant	-4.463	.000	-1.670	.055
Facilitator Talk/Behavior	4.134	.585 (.682)[a]	6.064	.000
% Talk/Work	.227	.394 (.058)	3.879	.000
Gender	-2.074	-.278 (.765)	-2.711	.005
Race/Ethnicity	1.511	.203 (.743)	2.032	.024
$R^2 = .721$				

[a]Standard error in parentheses

Contextual Effects on Status Problems

The relationship of peer status to academic status is a structural feature
that varies among classrooms; the two dimensions can be positively or
negatively related or they can be independent of one another. In elementary classrooms below the sixth-grade level, we found that peer and academic status were positively related, that is, those who were high in academic status were also highly chosen as friends (Cohen, Lotan, &
Catanzarite, 1988). With older students, peer status becomes increasingly
powerful as an independent source of prestige. Wilson's (1979) study of
sixth graders was the first to show that these dimensions may be negatively related or unrelated.

When the two dimensions are independent, the overall impact of status
on interaction may be lessened because there are not many students who
are in the high state on both characteristics. The chances of consistently high-
status students interacting with consistently low-status students are smaller.
Thus, the overall relationship of status to interaction should be reduced in
such a setting. In the middle school study, Cohen and Lotan (1997) explored
the impact of variation in this structural feature of the classroom on the
severity of observed status problems.

Index of Status Congruence. Incongruent classrooms are classrooms
where peer and academic status are *unrelated* or *negatively related* to each
other. Congruent classrooms are those where peer and academic status are
positively related. The index of status congruence is the correlation of these
two variables in a classroom. On the average, the correlation between the
two dimensions in these classrooms was .04. Thus, on the average, these were
incongruent classrooms. The index value, however, ranged from –.26 to +.60.

Status Problems at the Classroom Level. The correlation of the
costatus score of target students with their observed rate of task-related talk
is the measure of status problems at the classroom level. The index of status
problems ranged from –.23 to +.79. There were three classrooms with a negative index value below –.10. In these classrooms, there was a tendency for
low-status students to be more active on the task than high-status students.
In contrast, there were nine classrooms with an index value of .50 or higher,
indicating a statistically significant association between being higher status
and talking more.

A regression analysis on all 19 classrooms (see Table 5.3) evaluates the
effects of structural factors on the index of status problems. The effects of
congruence in the classroom were not clear in the regression analysis until

the percentage of low-status students in the classroom was entered as a control variable. The power of status congruence in predicting status problems was not observable in a simple correlation matrix where status congruence was uncorrelated with the index of status problems. (See Cohen & Lotan, 1997, for the intercorrelation of variables in this regression and for a detailed discussion of the percentage of low-status students.)

Another variable of interest in this regression is the presence or absence of "mainstreaming" in the classroom. (Mainstreaming refers to combining students who are classified as having learning disabilities with respect to the ordinary school program with more typical students.) There were two mainstreamed classes among the 19 in the study. They were both taught by highly experienced and skilled teachers who had a thorough understanding of status problems and how to treat them. Nonetheless, both of these classrooms exhibited more severe status problems than anything studied in the elementary school.

Table 5.3 presents the results of regressing the index of status problems on the index of status congruence, mainstreaming, and the proportion of low-status students. The index of status congruence was a statistically significant predictor of status problems. Looking at this result another way, the incongruent classrooms had less severe status problems. Mainstream classrooms had more severe status problems, holding constant status congruence and the proportion of low-status students. Finally, those classrooms with a higher proportion of low-status students had less severe status problems.

Discussion of Middle School Complexity

The differential impact of diffuse status characteristics for high- and low-status students indicates an interaction effect between costatus and the two status characteristics of gender and race/ethnicity. If the student was high

Table 5.3: Regression of Index of Status Problems on Status Congruence, Mainstreaming, and Percentage of Middle School Low-Status Students: Classroom Level (n = 19)

Predictor	B	Beta	t	p (one-tailed)
Constant	.213	.000 (.334)[a]	.636	.267
Mainstream	.670	.597 (.237)	2.829	.007
% Low-Status	-.024	-.577 (.011)	-2.259	.010
Status Congruence	.726	.495 (.382)	1.899	.039
R^2 = .641				

[a]Standard error in parentheses

on academic or peer status, then these two status characteristics did not matter. If, however, the student was low on peer or academic status, then being male or being White/Asian predicted higher rates of interaction than being female or African-American/Latino. According to this analysis, the student who suffered the most from effects of status problems was the minority female who was neither particularly popular nor seen as a good student. In math and science classrooms, where there are stereotypical beliefs about competence in these subjects for Whites and Asians and for males, the effects of gender and race/ethnicity may well be visible regardless of academic and peer status.

The finding of less severe status problems in status incongruent classrooms suggests that something may be reducing the severity of status problems that is quite independent of what the teacher is doing. When students create an alternative status characteristic that is unrelated to the official school value on academics, it is almost as if they are creating a natural status treatment. They are creating a situation in which they are not dependent on the school as the only channel for gaining status with their peers.

The combination of status characteristics with inconsistent states for many individuals can lead to equal-status interaction. The presence of status incongruence may produce this desirable effect. In Chapter 6, we will turn to deliberate interventions designed to produce equal-status interaction.

Raising Expectations for Competence: The Effectiveness of Status Interventions

Elizabeth G. Cohen and Rachel A. Lotan

Chapter 5 documented the persistence of status generalization in some classrooms using complex instruction. Some status generalization occurred despite the introduction of a multiple-abilities curriculum, training in cooperative norms, and the use of rules and roles designed to increase participation. The introduction of these strategies most certainly helped to raise the level of interaction of all students and to avoid gross discrimination such as denying low-status students access to materials. As a result of their cooperative experiences, students were more prosocial and cooperative, and there was a marked increase in friendliness (Cohen, Lotan, & Catanzarite, 1988). Yet, status was still a significant predictor of participation for the sample of target students.

If the sources of this tough and persistent problem are differential expectations for competence, then one cannot produce equal-status interaction without doing something about those expectations for competence. Teachers can modify status processes by altering the expectations for competence that students hold for themselves as well as the expectations that students hold for one another. "Status treatments" is the shorthand term for interventions designed to create equal-status interaction. In this chapter we describe the theoretical and practical nature of the two status treatments used by hundreds of teachers in heterogeneous classrooms. We review evidence for the effectiveness of these treatments in the elementary school and present evidence on the challenge of measuring effectiveness in middle school classrooms.

TWO STATUS TREATMENTS

Cohen has worked on the problem of altering expectations in the laboratory and in classrooms since 1970 (see Cohen, 1993). She and her colleagues have derived ways to modify the operation of expectations for competence.

The theoretical basis of the interventions includes the initial version of status characteristic theory and the more advanced versions of expectation states theory developed through an extensive research program.

Multiple-Ability Treatment

In a multicharacteristic situation such as a classroom, actors combine all salient units of status information to form aggregated expectation states for themselves and others. If the information is inconsistent, so that there are both positive and negative expectations for the competence of actors in a given status state, and if they are of equal relevance to the task at hand, then these can average with each other (Berger, Fisek, Norman, & Zelditch, 1977; Humphreys & Berger, 1981). Using this combining principle, it is possible to introduce specific status characteristics on which high- and low-status individuals receive inconsistent assignments. Because people combine these high and low expectations, the net effect is to reduce the expectation advantage of the high-status person. Theoretically, the new status characteristics combine with the older status characteristics. In other words, it is not possible to *eliminate* expectations based on academic and peer status. One can, however, *modify* their effects by diluting them with a new, inconsistent set of expectations based on specific status characteristics.

In a multiple-ability treatment, teachers and students discuss the many different intellectual abilities relevant to the collective tasks in the unit they are about to study (e.g., spatial ability, creativity, reasoning). Moreover, the teacher explains that no one student will be "good on all these abilities" and that each student will be "good on at least one."

These different intellectual abilities are specific status characteristics with direct relevance to the group tasks. The objective of the treatment is to convince students that no one is in the high state on all these characteristics and that each person is in the high state on some of them. If the treatment is successful, the students will assign to themselves and others both high and low states on the new characteristics. When these expectations combine with expectations based on pre-existing status characteristics, there will be less of an expectation advantage for the high-status students than would be the case without this treatment. Because of their direct relevance to the success of the group, the new set of specific status characteristics will have an especially strong impact on expectations for the group tasks.

The multiple-ability treatment proved effective in weakening status effects in a laboratory study (Tammivaara, 1982) and in a controlled classroom experiment (Rosenholtz, 1985). In the elementary school data described in Chapter 5, the status effects were not as severe as those in the pilot version of complex instruction in 1979–80. We attributed this improvement to the introduction of the multiple-ability treatment in 1982–83 (Cohen, Lotan, & Catanzarite, 1988).

Assigning Competence to Low-Status Students

In 1984, we introduced a new status treatment, assigning competence to low-status students. In this intervention, teachers assign low-status students the high state on a new specific status characteristic that is directly relevant to the assigned group task. This treatment derives from expectation states theory and from source theory (Webster & Sobieszek, 1974). In the language of source theory, the higher the status of an individual, the greater is the likelihood of that individual becoming a source of important evaluations. The high-status individual can thus influence one person's self-evaluations relative to another. If the teacher, as a high-status source, positively evaluates a student's performance, that student will come to believe that his or her ability is consistent with the teacher's evaluation. That belief in turn will affect the student's expectations for competence in classroom tasks. In a classroom experiment designed to test this proposition, Entwisle and Webster (1974) found that students who had received positive evaluations from the teacher were more likely to raise their hands to volunteer a response than students who had not received positive evaluations from the teacher.

Teachers who use this treatment in complex instruction watch for instances of low-status students performing well on various intellectual abilities that are relevant to success on the assigned group task. These are often, although not necessarily, the same multiple abilities that the teacher has discussed in the multiple-ability treatment. The teacher then provides the student with *specific, favorable, and public evaluation*. For example, on observing the neglect of Luis, similar to Miguel in Chapter 5, the teacher said:

> Luis is really looking at the [activity] card when he is building this structure and following the diagram on the card. He puts one straw across like this to make it stronger. He's really doing that by following the diagram. You know, that is a great ability to have because he could be an architect. So he's a great resource here in this group because you guys can rely on him to make your structure much stronger. [She repeated the treatment in Spanish for Luis's benefit.] You need to tell Luis what you want to do because he is the one who is a resource here, but he has to understand. Otherwise he can't help you. (Cohen, 1994b)

In a successful treatment, the student and his or her peers accept the teacher's evaluation of the low-status student as competent on an impressive and relevant ability. Expectations for competence on this specific status characteristic then combine with other expectations for competence (both high and low) held by and for the individual. Note that the teacher strengthened the power of her assignment on the new specific status characteristic by telling the group that they could not succeed without Luis's competence, that is, the specific characteristic had a direct path of relevance to successful completion of the task. The net result of successful treatment will be more participation and influence by low-status group members relative to high-status group members. Research has shown the power of these newly assigned expectations for competence to transfer to new task situations (Berger, Rosenholtz, & Zelditch, 1980; Webster & Foschi, 1988). The transfer of successfully treated expectations to new situations means that the teacher does not have to continually treat the same low-status individuals.

EVALUATION OF EFFECTIVENESS

Using similar research designs, we evaluated the effectiveness of these status treatments in the elementary school (1984–85) and in the middle school (1991–92). We related the frequency with which teachers used status treatments to measures of status problems at the individual and classroom levels. There was considerable variation among teachers in their observed rate of using either of the two status treatments, the independent variable. As in the studies described in Chapter 5, we selected a sample of target students from each classroom, based on a sociometric questionnaire. Target students consisted mainly of high- and low-status students. They were observed with the Target Student Instrument (see Chapter 5 for description). The dependent variables were the observed rate of interaction of the low-status target students at the individual level, and an index of status problems at the classroom level. Observers took measures of the behavior of the target students in any group in which they found them. We assumed that the highest-status students in the class would be in groups where some others were of lower status. Likewise, we assumed that the lowest-status students in the class would be working in groups where most other members were of higher status.

The effectiveness of the status treatments should hold in classrooms that meet two conditions. One is the use of a multiple-ability curriculum. Students will not find status interventions believable if reading, writing, and computing are the only skills required in the curriculum. The second condition is a high rate of interaction among the students. Interaction is important to the success of these interventions because it allows peers to recognize the competence of low-status classmates. In addition, a series of interactive tasks provides opportunities for low-status students to continue to exhibit competence. Because of these conditions, the research design called for classrooms with complex instruction and teachers who had learned to carry out these two interventions.

Measurement

The Teacher Observation Instrument, described in Chapter 3, provided data for measuring the rate at which teachers used status treatments. For 10 minutes during each observation period, observers tallied the frequency with which teachers talked about multiple abilities and assigned competence. The 1984–85 data set collected in elementary schools included 285 observations, with an average of 21.9 observations per teacher. There were at least 17 observations for each teacher. Tests of reliability yielded an average of 91.48% agreement between observers.

The data set from middle schools also included observations on the teacher and target students. There were at least 10 observations for each teacher. When the teacher taught more than one class, we calculated rates separately for observations on the different classes. The agreement between observers using the Teacher Observation Instrument (see Chapter 3) was 93.64%. Because there was considerable variation in the total amount of teacher talk in all categories, especially in the middle school, we calculated the proportion of teacher talk about multiple abilities and teacher assignment of competence relative to total talk in all categories of the observation instrument.

We use two critical measures of status problems in the analyses reported in Chapter 5 and this chapter: (1) the rates of task-related participation by high- and low-status target students (Target Student Instrument, Chapter 5), and (2) the correlation of the costatus variable with the rate of talk for target students in each classroom (the classroom index of status problems). (See Chapter 5 for the calculation of these measures.)

It was necessary to control several variables when using rate of participation as a dependent variable. One of these controls was the general rate of interaction among students in the classroom, a measure of the success of the teacher in fostering interaction. Another control variable was the rate of acting and behaving like a facilitator. The enactment of the role of facilitator has a very positive effect on rates of interaction (see Chapter 4).

In the elementary data, we found it necessary to control the standard deviation of the achievement scores. If the achievement scores showed wide variation in a classroom, status problems were more severe. As explained in Chapter 5, there were special features of middle school social structure that had major effects on the severity of status problems. These included the degree of congruence between academic and peer status, the percentage of low-status students, and whether the class contained mainstreamed students from special education.

Elementary School Data: 1984–85

The data set for 1984–85 consisted of 13 classrooms, Grades 2–6, from 3 schools in the San Francisco Bay Area. Large proportions of these students were from language minority and/or low-income backgrounds. Students in two classrooms were Southeast Asian immigrants and in 9 classrooms were predominantly Latino. Despite the similarity in socioeconomic status and ethnicity within 11 of these classrooms, there was heterogeneity in academic skills, ranging from grade level performance to an inability to read or write in any language.

In each classroom, we selected 7 target students from the upper and 7 students from the lower end of the distribution of choices. Because of the high transiency rates at some of these schools, we were not able to collect a complete set of observations on all the selected students. The target sample included 61 low-status students and 67 high-status students, with at least six observations for all 128 children in the study, using the Target Student Instrument.

Results. Here we review the key features of the results (for a full description of the analysis, see Cohen & Lotan, 1995). Table 6.1 presents the means and standard deviations for the variables of the study. Target students talked about the task, on the average, more than 4 times per 3 minutes. On the average, high-status students participated at a significantly greater rate than low-status students ($t = 1.81$, $p < .05$). Although all students had an equal chance to play the role of facilitator, high-status students were much more likely to behave and talk like a facilitator ($t = 2.67$, $p < .01$).

For teachers, the average rate of using each of the status treatments was quite low—less than one-third of an instance per 10-minute observation period. Some teachers had scores of "0" on one or both treatments. Others did a status treatment as often as once per 10 minutes. Because the rates for these two treatments correlated so highly with one another ($r = .78$, $p < .001$), we added them together for purposes of data analysis.

The overall means comparing high- and low-status students hide important variability in the severity of status problems among classrooms. The average value for the index of status problems was .32. However, the index ranged from –.10 to +.59. Among treated classrooms, only two showed a positive and statistically significant correlation between costatus and rate of talk. In all the other classrooms, the correlation was not statistically significant; in two classrooms, the value of the index was close to zero.

In both studies, we hypothesized that the rate of status treatments would have a positive effect on the participation of low-status students. To test this hypothesis, we used a regression to hold constant the effects of facilitator

Table 6.1: Means, Ranges, and Standard Deviations of Variables for
Elementary School: Individual and Classroom Level

	n	Mean	Range	SD
Individual Level Variables				
Rate of Participation				
Low Status	61	4.09	1.00–8.57	1.82
High Status	67	4.63	1.50–8.63	1.55
All Target Students	128	4.37	1.00–8.63	1.69
Facilitator Talk/Behavior				
Low Status	61	.69	.00–2.86	.75
High Status	67	1.08	.00–4.13	.88
All Target Students	128	.89	.00–4.13	.84
Classroom Level Variables				
Teacher Use of Status Treatments				
Multiple Abilities	13	.29	.00–.88	.31
Assigning Competence	13	.25	.00–1.00	.31
Status Treatments	13	.53	.00–1.88	.57

talk and behavior and the general rate of interaction in the classroom (measured by the percentage talking and working together). Table 6.2 presents this regression. (See Cohen & Lotan, 1995, for intercorrelation of predictor variables for all regressions.)

The frequency of status treatments had a statistically significant positive effect on the participation rate of the low-status students. In other words, in the classrooms of those teachers who used status treatments more frequently,

Table 6.2: Regression of Participation of Low-Status Students on Frequency of
Status Treatment, Classroom Level of Talk/Work, and Individual Rate of
Facilitator Talk and Behavior: Elementary School ($n = 61$)

Predictor	B	Beta	t	p (one-tailed)
Constant	-.582	.000	-.67	.254
		(.873)[b]		
Facilitator Talk/Behavior	.423	.175	1.54	.065
		(.276)		
Classroom Level Talk/Work[a]	.526	.562	4.83	.000
		(.109)		
Status Treatments	.246	.194	1.80	.039
		(.137)		

[a]Does not include Facilitator Talk
[b]Standard Error in parentheses
$R^2 = .359$ (adjusted)

low-status students talked more in their groups. The rate at which the low-status students talked or behaved like a facilitator also had a positive effect on their participation rates, albeit not a statistically significant effect. In this equation, the strongest predictor of the individual's participation rate was the average rate of interaction in the classroom. As predicted, a parallel regression for high-status students showed no effect of status treatments.

The specific prediction for classrooms was that the percentage of teacher talk pertaining to status treatments would be *negatively associated* with the index of status problems. There were 11 classrooms in this regression. One teacher was never seen assigning competence and had a relatively low rate of talking about multiple abilities. Nonetheless, her classroom provided no evidence of status problems ($r = -.103$). Using a SYSTAT technique for identifying outliers, we omitted this classroom because the observations had an undue influence on the correlation (Wilkinson, 1988). We also omitted one classroom because we did not have pretest scores on reading.

Results, given in Table 6.3, show that the status treatments were a statistically significant *negative* predictor of the correlations between status and interaction in the classroom. This means that the teachers' use of the two status treatments reduced the incidence of status problems. In classrooms with a lower value of the index of status problems, high-status students did not participate more than low-status students. The variability in reading pretest scores was also a powerful positive predictor of status problems. This regression equation accounts for more than 69.20% of the variance.

Discussion of the Elementary School Study. Teachers' use of status treatments can lessen significantly the effect of status on small group interaction. Eleven out of 13 classrooms showed no significant relationship between the measure of student status and the rate of task-related talk. More-

Table 6.3: Regression of Index of Classroom Status Problems on Teachers' Rate of Status Treatment and Standard Deviations of Reading Pretest Scores: Elementary School ($n = 11$)

Predictor	B	Beta	t	p (one-tailed)
Constant	-.08	.00	-.70	.252
		(.12)[a]		
Status Treatments	-.12	-.49	-2.38	.023
		(.05)		
SD Reading Pretest	.58	.83	4.04	.002
		(.14)		

[a]Standard Error in parentheses
$R^2 = .69$ (adjusted)

over, the interventions boosted the participation of low-status students, but did not suppress the participation of high-status students. Because the sample included some of the most attractive and academically successful students in the class and some of the weakest and most socially isolated students, achieving equal-status interaction was especially significant.

The overall frequency of teachers' use of status treatments was low. Field experiments with status treatments have shown that it is not the number of times but rather the fact that particular groups of students receive treatment, that counts (Cohen, Lockheed, & Lohman, 1976). One status treatment can be enough to modify competence expectations for a particular student in ways that will persist over a series of collective tasks.

In the only previously published study in which teachers attempted to raise student expectations for competence, teachers simply reinforced contributions by low-status students (Entwisle & Webster, 1974). Regardless of the child's response, teachers systematically reinforced and praised the child in the experimental group. From an educational perspective, unconditional reinforcement of students is not desirable. From a theoretical perspective, assigning competence to low-status students represents a significant advance over this early experimental version. In the first place, this treatment manipulates expectations of classmates as well as those of the low-status student. In the second place, making competence relevant to the task helps the low-status student to become a valued resource for the group.

One interesting result in these data was the suggestion that talking and behaving like a facilitator had a positive effect on participation of the low-status students. Although the beta coefficient did not quite reach statistical significance, this was the first evidence of a potential alternative treatment. The role of facilitator involves legitimate leadership. Telling other people what to do can serve as a *task cue* in the interaction of the group (Berger, Wagner, & Zelditch, 1985). Task cues, such as speech rates, fluency, tone, and eye gaze, provide information that is relevant to the task characteristic possessed by the actors in the situation. Members of the group will take these cues as indicators of competence or a high state on a specific status characteristic. In this way, group members may conclude that the low-status student playing the facilitator role is competent on a skill that is relevant to the success of the group. If this occurs, then playing the facilitator role will result in raised expectations for competence of low-status students.

Limitations of This Research. Despite the considerable number of students and observations, regressions on a sample of 11 raise issues of reliability of the results. However, we were able to correctly estimate effects on separate samples of low- and high-status students using a different dependent variable but the same independent variable. These analyses provide some assurance that the results at the classroom level are not the product of some strange fluke of the data.

Middle School Data: 1991–92

Observations of middle school teachers reveal low levels of assignment of competence, similar to rates observed among elementary school teachers. The average rate of assigning competence per 10 minutes for middle school teachers was .27 in comparison to .25 for elementary school teachers in 1984–85. However, unlike data on assigning competence among elementary school teachers, there was more variation within observations on a given teacher than between observations on different teachers. Teachers who had more than one class of complex instruction a day appeared to treat different classes differently. Middle school teachers made much more frequent use of the multiple-ability treatment (.94 per 10 minutes) than did the elementary school teachers (.29). In comparison to assigning competence, the multiple-ability treatment showed less variation between middle school classes. We combined all status treatments into one index for purposes of analysis.

Effects on Status Problems of the Classroom. Teachers' rate of status treatment varied significantly according to the status structure of the classroom. As shown in Table 6.4, the correlation between the rate of status treatment and the congruence of the classroom status structure was $r = .431, p < .05$. In other words, in those classrooms where peer and academic status were positively correlated, the teachers made more frequent use of status treatments. In highly status congruent classrooms, there were more low-status students ($r = .59, p < .01$). Perhaps the teachers perceived many more students in need of treatment in these congruent classrooms.

There was no association between the rate of status treatment and the index of status problems. Having documented in Chapter 5 the effects of

Table 6.4: Intercorrelations for Classroom Level Variables: Middle School ($n = 19$)

	1	2	3	4
1 Status Problems	1.00	.08	.02	-.24
2 % Status Treatments		1.00	.43*	.30
3 Congruence			1.00	.59**
4 % Low Status				1.00

$*p<.05; **p<.01$

classroom status structure on the index of status problems, it is essential to control classroom characteristics. In a series of regressions of the index of status problems on the teachers' rate of status treatment, we controlled one classroom characteristic at a time. With a sample of 19 classrooms, there were major limitations on the number of predictors we could enter into a regression. The rate of status treatment was not a significant predictor of status problems in *any of these regressions*. Moreover, once the rate of status treatments was entered into the regression, the classroom characteristics such as congruence and percentage of low-status students also failed to predict the severity of status problems.

Effects of Individual Participation. At the individual level, with a sample of 58 students, we used simultaneous controls for a number of features of the status order. Table 6.5 shows again that the teachers' rate of status treatments appears to have no effect on the rate of task-related talk for low-status students. This lack of effect is in contrast to the impact of congruence and mainstreaming, which continue to have marked negative effects on the participation of low-status students. As in the analysis in Chapter 5, the percentage of low-status students continues to have a significant positive effect.

Discussion of Middle School Data. Variation in the observed rate of status treatments among teachers and classrooms appeared to be unrelated to participation of low-status students or to the index of status problems. Two major interpretations are possible: (1) The complexity of the status struc-

Table 6.5: Regression of Rate of Task-Related Talk for Low-Status Students on Teachers' Rate of Status Treatments: Controlling for Middle School Classroom Characteristics ($n = 58$)

Predictor	B	Beta	t	p (one-tailed)
Constant	6.06	.00	2.67	.010
		(2.28)[a]		
Status Treatments	-.06	-.01	-.08	.468
		(.96)		
Congruence	-5.46	-.36	-1.97	.027
% Low Status	.20	.47	2.91	.003
		(.07)		
Mainstream	-4.39	-.37	-2.63	.006
		(1.67)		

[a]Standard Error in parentheses
$R^2 = .149$

ture at the middle school prevents the research design from tracking the effects of status treatment; or (2) the status treatments, for some theoretically inexplicable reason, do not work as well at the middle school as they do at the elementary school.

Starting with the problems of design, it is impossible in this more complex social structure to disentangle what may have been differences in degree of status problems in the fall from effects of teachers' treatments during the academic year. Status incongruent classrooms had significantly fewer status problems. It is possible that the independent operation of peer status acts as a natural status treatment (see Chapter 5). If this were the case, status problems might have been much less frequent from the beginning of the class, making the teacher's rate of status treatment a poor predictor of status problems. In contrast, the mainstreamed classrooms may have had very severe problems from the beginning. The major efforts at treating these problems made by the two teacher trainers in these classrooms may have resulted in moderating these problems from very severe to moderately serious. However, the high rate of status treatments in the mainstreamed classrooms would not show up as effective in the regressions unless we had a measure of what the problems were in the fall. In other words, given the variability between classrooms arising from differences in initial status structure, we need a pre–post design.

The design assumed that the only factors restricting teachers' rate of status treatments were lack of skill and of comfort with the technique. The design also assumed that the teachers would have no difficulty in identifying as candidates for assignment of competence, the same low-status students whom we selected as target students. However, something about the variation in classroom status structure was associated with variation in the rate of status treatment. Table 6.6 presents the results of regressing the teacher's rate of status treatment in a given classroom on a number of predictive factors. As we suspected, teachers in status congruent classrooms treated status more frequently than teachers in incongruent classrooms. This is not surprising given that status problems were more severe in such classrooms. Also, the greater the percentage of African-American students in the classroom, the higher the rate of treatment, suggesting that teachers worked much harder on status problems with Black students. In some cases, the teachers may have incorrectly attributed low status to African-American students, who, as a group, were no more likely to have low costatus scores than Whites or Asians (see Chapter 5). They may have assigned competence to students whom the sociometric measures did not identify as low status. Finally, the two teachers who were in their second year of work with complex instruction and who were trainers, had higher rates of treatment.

Table 6.6: Regression of % of Status Treatments in Teacher Talk on Classroom Congruence, Teacher Status as a CI Trainer, and % of African-American Students in the Class ($n = 19$)

Predictor	B	Beta	t	p (two-tailed)
Constant	-.097	.000	-.028	.786
		(.349)[a]		
Congruence	1.235	.437	2.548	.022
		(.485)		
Teacher Trainer	.900	.553	3.378	.004
		(.267)		
% African-American	.013	.345	2.053	.058
		(.006)		

[a]Standard error in parentheses
$R^2 = .539$

In review, the research design is not sufficiently powerful for the complicated status structure of the middle school classroom. We need to know the level of status problems in a given classroom *prior* to the teacher's treatment. We also need to be sure that the teacher is treating the students we define as low status. This design left it up to the teacher to figure out who was a low-status student to whom they would assign competence. Teachers may have treated different students from those we selected as target students. Middle school teachers have much more limited exposure to their students and the students' social relationships. Particularly when peer status is independent of academic status, it may be very difficult to tell which students have relatively low status.

These design problems call for a classroom experiment rather than observation of natural variation. In future research, we propose to randomly assign low-status students to a treatment of assignment of competence. By taking measures of status problems before and after treatment, and by comparing treated and untreated low-status students, we will be able to make a more powerful evaluation of the effectiveness of treatments at the middle school level. We also may have to use a design that controls some of these pre-existing status structure variables such as congruence, mainstreaming, and the percentage of low-status students.

We must also consider the possibility that we are not facing a design flaw but a genuine failure of the treatment. Many teachers reported to us that students were reluctant to be singled out for favorable evaluations. However, other teachers reported very good response to their attempts to assign competence, and a noticeable improvement in the behavior of the low-status students they tried to help. In those classrooms where peer and academic status are negatively related, students may feel that an increase in their academic status will cause a loss in their peer standing.

Assigning competence depends on the students' viewing the teacher as a high-status source of evaluations. Theoretically, it is possible that some of these teachers were not a high-status source of evaluations (perhaps some middle school classes do not trust the evaluations of their teachers). In general, the peer orientation of the middle school students is remarkably strong. Perhaps status treatments from peers would be more effective than status treatments from teachers. Table 5.2 in the preceding chapter showed the significant effects on status problems of having a low-status student play the role of facilitator. The effect was much stronger in the middle school than in the elementary school. We plan to experiment with a peer assignment of competence in future research on middle school students.

PRACTICAL IMPLICATIONS

From an educator's perspective, the practical implications of status treatments lie in the indirect effect of status on learning. We have shown repeatedly that interaction is a precursor of learning in the context of complex instruction. The impact of status on interaction therefore results in high-status students learning more and low-status students learning less (Cohen, 1984). In other words, the effect of status on learning is mediated by the interaction. Theoretically, when teachers are successful in raising expectations for competence on the part of low-status students, these students will increase effort on school tasks.

These strategies of treating status are practical and workable. Teachers in many parts of the United States, Canada, Israel, the Netherlands, Sweden, and Jamaica are using status treatments. Teachers are particularly pleased with the change in behavior and accomplishment of low-status students. They are delighted to discover the abilities of students they previously had seen as undistinguished.

As one of the teachers of complex instruction reports, a single successful treatment may be sufficient to change a student's standing with the class.

> One day I had a student named Juan. He was extremely quiet and hardly ever spoke. He was not particularly academically successful and didn't have a good school record. He had just been in the country for two or three years and spoke just enough English to be a LEP student. I didn't notice that he had many friends, but not many enemies either. Not that much attention was paid to him.

We were doing an activity that involved decimal points and I was going around and noticed he was the only one out of his group that had all the right answers. I was able to say, "Juan! You have figured out all of this worksheet correctly. You understand how decimals work. You really understand that kind of notation. Can you explain it to your group? I'll be back in a minute to see how you did." And I left. I couldn't believe it: he was actually explaining it to all the others. I didn't have faith it was going to work, but in fact he explained it so well that all of the others understood it and were applying it to their worksheets. They were excited about it. So then I made it public among the whole class, and from then on they began calling him "the smart one." This spread to the area where he lived, and even today kids from there will come tell me about the smart one, Juan. I thought, "All of this started with a little intervention!" (Graves, & Graves, 1991, p. 14)

CHAPTER 7

The Effect of Gender on Interaction, Friendship, and Leadership in Elementary School Classrooms

Anita Leal-Idrogo

Barrie Thorne (1993) characterizes gender separation among elementary school students as a "variable and complicated process, an intricate choreography aptly summarized by Erving Goffman's phrase 'with-then-apart'" (p. 36). Although extensive earlier research emphasized voluntary gender segregation among young children, Thorne's more recent work brings out how the organization of the classroom can and does bring boys and girls together. However, it is still the case that girls and boys are seldom encouraged to utilize each other as social and academic resources in the classroom. This inhibition of interaction aggravates and reinforces the tendency to separate on the basis of gender. It also reinforces gender stereotypes, allowing children to carry these stereotypes into puberty.

GENDER INEQUITIES

In this chapter, I present the results of an investigation that explored how gender operates in CI classrooms in comparison to gender inequities typical of traditional co-educational classrooms. The research focused on three gender inequities: (1) the operation of gender as a status characteristic, (2) voluntary gender segregation, and (3) leadership as a male realm.

Gender as a Status Characteristic in the Classroom

Status effects are observable in a variety of settings, including the classroom. Since 1968, expectation states theory (Berger, Cohen, & Zelditch, 1972) has been the basis for extensive laboratory and applied research on status characteristics and their effect on group interaction. This theory is discussed in detail in Chapter 5.

Research consistently shows that gender operates as a diffuse status characteristic in mixed-sex groups of adults (Berger et al., 1972; Lockheed & Hall, 1976; Ridgeway & Diekema, 1992). There is some evidence that it operates among young children in the classroom, although the results are less clear. In Zander & Van Egmond's (1958) study, boys dominated in the areas of talking and influencing in second- and fifth-grade classrooms, which supported the notion that gender can operate as a diffuse status characteristic among children in classrooms. Webb (1982) reported supportive findings from an observational study where seventh- and eighth-grade boys were perceived to be more competent and where both girls and boys sought assistance from boys more than from girls. Lockheed, Harris, and Nemceff (1983) provided the strongest and most rigorously controlled test of whether gender operates as a status characteristic among young children. In their study of 168 White fourth- and fifth-grade students, there were no gender differences in observed activity or influence. Girls initiated and received as many verbal acts as did boys. In a pilot version of CI, Cohen (1982) also found what appeared to be equal-status relationships between girls and boys in elementary school: Girls and boys had similar rates of participation while working at learning centers. However, in that study, children had not been clearly assigned to mixed-sex groups at the learning centers and no data were available about the gender of the child with whom the target child interacted.

Voluntary Gender Separation

The long-standing tradition of formally separating the genders in schools has shifted over time, in part because of federal legislation. Yet, among school-age children, voluntary separation on the basis of gender, that is, greater frequency of interaction between the students of the same gender rather than between the genders, continues both in encounter and in friendship (Grant, 1983; Lockheed et al., 1983; Thorne, 1993). In ethnographic studies in elementary schools, Thorne (1993) described "same-sex clusters" and separate territories on the playground.

In a study of 51 elementary school classes, friendship cliques were single-sex (Hallinan, 1977). Subsequently, in a study of fourth, fifth, and sixth graders in 18 classrooms, Hallinan and Tuma (1978) found that same-gender, best-friend choice was the dominant pattern (77%) on a sociometric instrument. Other studies showed similar patterns (DeVries & Edwards, 1977; Foot, Chapman, & Smith, 1980). Voluntary gender separation is a strikingly tenacious phenomenon among children.

However, studies also revealed that task structure mitigated the typical separation in interaction between girls and boys in classrooms. For example,

Hallinan and Tuma (1978) documented that the way teachers grouped students for instruction affected children's friendships. Comparisons of cross-gender interaction in nontraditional elementary and middle school classroom settings (i.e., small groups or teams) with traditional settings (i.e., large groups or individuals) revealed an average of 45% cross-gender interaction for the former, and 33% for the latter (DeVries & Edwards, 1977).

Leadership as a Male Realm

Studies of children's leadership experiences and attitudes are rare. This may be because leadership generally is perceived as a psychological dimension or trait experienced exclusively by adults (Lockheed, 1983).

Children, like adults, possess gender stereotypes, and children's attitudes become more stereotyped as their awareness of gender stereotypes increases (Stein & Smithells, 1969). Children also have stereotypical attitudes about leadership ability; both boys and girls view leadership ability as a male characteristic (Nash, 1975). The association of leadership with masculinity may arise because males tend to hold more positions of leadership in the larger society compared with females.

Research on leadership experiences of children revealed a gender bias, both in actual leadership role experiences of girls and boys as well as in stated preferences for leaders of one gender. In one of the few studies of leadership among children, Lockheed (1981) found that among fourth and fifth graders, boys reported holding more leadership positions than girls. Further, boys were perceived as leaders more often than girls even though girls and boys were involved in the same "leader-like" behavior. In Lockheed's 1983 study, even though videotaped observations of children's mixed-sex task groups revealed no gender differences in contributions made toward the task, when members of the four-person, mixed-sex task groups were asked to identify the leader, boys were chosen more frequently, receiving 94% of the children's votes.

RESEARCH QUESTIONS

The specific research questions derive from what I would expect to find in CI classrooms if each of the three types of inequity existed and what I would expect to find if these classrooms were free of each type of inequity. First, if gender were indeed operating as a status characteristic, I would expect to find, according to the theory (Berger et al., 1972), that boys were more likely than girls to initiate interaction in the mixed-sex context. If, on the other hand, gender were not activated as a status characteristic in this situation, the percentage of mixed-sex interactions initiated by boys should equal the percentage of mixed-sex interactions initiated by girls. In this study, gender was the primary status characteristic considered. I used costatus to control for other status characteristics that are known to operate in the classroom, such as academic ability and social attractiveness (see Chapter 5).

The second research question asked about the extent of voluntary gender separation. I selected verbal interaction and friendship choice as indicators for observation and analysis. Specifically, I compared the observed probabilities of cross-gender and same-gender verbal interaction and friendship choices with the probabilities generated by a simple chance model called the Social Integration Model (described below). To what extent did cross-gender interaction match or exceed the proportion expected under the Social Integration Model?

Assuming that interaction is a source of friendship (Hallinan & Tuma, 1978), I also used the Social Integration Model to compare the probability of cross-sex/same-sex friendship choice to the probabilities generated by the model. I expected an increasing tendency for cross-sex friendship choice to develop over time as a result of increased interaction opportunities.

The third research question examined whether complex instruction modified the typical sex bias in the leadership perceptions of girls and boys. Was there a higher probability of girls or boys being chosen as leader than in a comparable study conducted by Lockheed (1981) in which 94% of the boys were chosen as leader by both girls and boys? Given that girls acted as facilitators, a legitimated leadership role in complex instruction, I expected that a greater proportion of females would be chosen as leader compared with Lockheed's 1981 mixed-sex group study.

The Social Integration Model

As part of this study, I constructed the Social Integration Model as a standard for comparison of theoretical to observed rates at which girls and boys talked to each other, and probabilities of choosing each other as friends. According to this model, social integration occurs when gender is irrelevant to observed verbal interaction and reported friendship choice between girls and boys. The model provides a rate of expected verbal interaction and expected friendship choice based on the ratio of girls to boys in a classroom. I then compared this standard with observed interaction and reported friendship choice in the classroom. This model rests on the strong assumption of a student's independence of choice in talking and/or choosing a friend. The model assumes that the only factor affecting the probability of a girl or boy talking to either sex or choosing a friend is the number of females or males available for choice.

PARTICIPANTS

Subjects for this study were elementary school students in the second through fourth grades whose classrooms were participating in CI, 45 minutes per day, 5 days per week for the 1982–83 school year. Children were primarily of Latino descent, with a small proportion of African-Americans, Asians, and Whites. Parental social status was working class and lower white collar.

The teachers in 10 classrooms selected a total of 100 children, mostly 8 and 9 years of age, for purposes of systematic observation of verbal interaction. While these students did not constitute a random sample, they did represent a sample that was heterogeneous with respect to gender, achievement, and language.

The sample for the sociometric friendship data was larger than the verbal interaction sample. A sociometric questionnaire was administered to a total of 343 children in 13 classrooms (inclusive of the 10 classrooms from which verbal interaction subjects were selected) comprising all students in all complex instruction classrooms. Of the 343 students who filled out the sociometric questionnaire, 290 responded to the leadership question and cast 290 votes.

INSTRUMENTS

Observers used the Target Student Instrument, detailed in Chapter 5, to score task-related interaction. Observers also noted the gender of the target of the talk. They scored target children on a weekly basis during 3-minute-per-child observations as students talked and worked together in small groups at the learning centers in each of the 10 classrooms. Interrater reliability was measured both prior to initiation of observation in the classrooms as well as midway through the school year. The average percentage of agreement between observers and the supervisor was .90.

The sociometric instrument was administered early (October 1982) and late (April 1983) to all children, including the target children, in all classrooms. It consisted of eight questions in the fall and 11 questions in the spring. To measure friendship choice, I analyzed girls' and boys' responses to the following statement appearing in both the fall and spring questionnaire: "Circle the name of your best friends." This directive preceded a list of all classmates' names. The subjects were instructed to circle as many names as they wanted, including their own.

To measure leadership choice, only the late sociometric questionnaire included the following statement: "Circle the name of the student who was the best leader in the group." This statement preceded a list of all classmates' names. Again, subjects were instructed to circle as many names as they wanted, including their own.

RESULTS

In this section, I report the results of the data analyses as they relate to the three research questions.

Evidence for Gender as a Status Characteristic

Was there evidence to indicate that gender operated as a diffuse status characteristic in complex instruction classrooms? Was gender a predictor of cross-sex talk? Were there higher rates of initiation of verbal activity for males than for females, given mixed-status interaction? Table 7.1 allows us to compare the overall rates of initiation of verbal interaction of 99 girls and boys, without respect to the gender of the target of the talk.

The mean rate of verbal acts initiated varied from class to class and ranging from 9.8 to 23.10 for girls, and 11.60 to 25.90 for boys. The Wilcoxon matched-pairs, signed-ranks test showed that across the 10 classrooms, the

Table 7.1: Mean Rate of Acts Initiated for Ten Observations of Three Minutes Each by Class, Grade, and Gender

Class ID	Grade	Mean Rate of Total Acts Initiated By Girls	Mean Rate of Total Acts Initiated By Boys	Difference
01	3	13.7 $(n = 4)$	25.9 $(n = 5)$	-12.2
04	3	16.4 $(n = 7)$	16.8 $(n = 4)$	+0.4
05	3	17.2 $(n = 4)$	11.6 $(n = 5)$	+5.6
06	3	14.4 $(n = 6)$	22.3 $(n = 6)$	-7.9
08	3	9.8 $(n = 4)$	12.5 $(n = 5)$	-2.7
09	2	12.5 $(n = 4)$	21.0 $(n = 6)$	-8.5
11	3	18.0 $(n = 6)$	15.0 $(n = 5)$	+3.0
12	2	17.5 $(n = 4)$	24.0 $(n = 6)$	-6.5
13	2	17.7 $(n = 4)$	23.6 $(n = 4)$	-5.9
14	4	23.1 $(n = 6)$	15.8 $(n = 4)$	+7.3
		Grand Mean = 16.03	Grand Mean = 18.85	Mean Difference = -2.82

differences between the mean verbal acts of boys and girls were not statistically significant. Furthermore, the average rate of acts initiated for boys in
each classroom was uncorrelated with the average acts for girls (r_s = – .06,
n.s.).

Regression Equation. With the individual child as the unit of analysis, I used a multiple regression to assess the relationship between the
dependent variable—the average rate of cross-sex interaction—and a set of
predictor variables that included the following: gender of the subject, available number of target students that were cross-sex, costatus score for the
subject, and total number of complex instruction curricular units completed.
I expected that the more target students of the opposite sex that were available, the greater would be the probability of cross-sex interaction.

I selected the dependent variable of cross-sex talk to restrict observations to the mixed-sex group and to ensure that the genders were not being
observed as they separated within the small group. Because of the varying
ratio of girls to boys in a class, I also entered the raw number of target students of the opposite sex available to the subject as a predictor variable in
the regression. The number of curriculum units completed was an additional
predictor variable because it affected the amount of treatment and opportunities for cross-sex interaction.

Table 7.2 shows that gender, as a predictor of rate of cross-sex verbal
acts initiated, was not statistically significant. However, the predictor
variables as a set had a significant effect on the rate of cross-sex verbal

Table 7.2: Regression of Rate of Cross-Sex Talk on Gender, Status, Number of
Target Students of Opposite Sex Available, Total Talk, and Curriculum Units
Completed (n=99)

Independent Variable	B	Beta	Standard Error	t	Probability
Gender	-.235	-.134	.145	-1.61	.108
Status	-.008	-.126	.008	-1.68	.096
Target Students of the Opposite Sex	-.007	-.162	.003	-1.99	.049
Total Talk	.430	.716	.048	8.82	.0001
Curriculun Units Completed	-.020	-.099	.018	-1.23	.219

Adj. R^2= .453 F = 17.59
Total Talk is girls' and boys' talk to same-sex and cross-sex targets.

acts initiated. Forty-five percent of the variance of the dependent variable was explained by the model. Further, two independent variables were statistically significant as predictors of rate of cross-sex verbal acts of initiation.

First, the number of target students of the opposite sex in the class had a statistically significant effect (Beta = 0.162, $p < .05$). However, there was an inverse relationship between the number of these target students in the class and the probability of cross-sex talk being initiated. That is, as the number of opposite-sex students in a class became greater, the probability of cross-sex talk being initiated became smaller. Evidently, when the boys or the girls were distinctly in the minority, that group withdrew from cross-sex interaction. Second, the results show that the total talk of both girls and boys to each other was a statistically significant factor (Beta = 0.716, $p = .000$). The higher the general rate of interaction in the classroom, the higher the probability of cross-sex talk.

Evidence of Voluntary Gender Separation

I determined social gender integration by the extent to which cross-sex talk and cross-sex/same-sex friendship choice matched or exceeded the proportion expected under the Social Integration Model described earlier. Specifically, I calculated the deviation of the observed proportion of same-sex and cross-sex talk and reported friendship choice from what would be expected in the Social Integration Model. The expected proportion or ratio of cross-sex talk was calculated by dividing the number of girls *or* boys in the class by the total number of students minus the initiator of the verbal act. This was necessary because self-talk was not recorded. For example, if there is a ratio of 60% girls to 40% boys in the class, the model expects 60% of the interaction of a particular girl to be directed toward girls. The observed proportions of cross-sex verbal interactions were calculated from the task-related talk item on the Target Student Instrument and compared with expected proportions of cross-sex and same-sex interaction to determine the extent to which cross-sex talk matched the proportion expected under the model.

The expected proportion of same-sex/cross-sex friendship choice was calculated in the same manner as described above, except that the choosers were not subtracted because they could choose themselves. Further, for each classroom, I compared the proportion of all same-sex friendship choices in the early and late administrations of the sociometric instrument. I also compared cross-sex talk and same-sex friendship choice with previously cited studies to provide additional information about interaction between girls and boys in both traditional and nontraditional classroom settings.

Cross-Sex Verbal Interaction. According to the Social Integration Model, if there were equal numbers of girls and boys in a class, 50% of both girls' and boys' interaction should be cross-sex. The calculation of expected proportions of cross-sex talk depended on the average number of girls and boys in a classroom. I used the average number because the number of children in each class changed from fall to spring.

The total number of interactions for girls was 1,603, for boys, 1,885—a very high rate of talk. Overall, both girls and boys had observed proportions of cross-sex talk that were close to the proportions predicted by the Social Integration Model. For example, the percentage of girls' talk that was addressed to boys was 45.35. The expected percentage according to the Social Integration Model was 54.18. Similarly, the observed percentage of boys' talk that was addressed to girls was 41.63, while the expected percentage was 49.40. Both girls' and boys' proportions of cross-sex talk fell short of the expected proportions, yet were higher than those in previously cited studies. The mean of the proportion of observed cross-sex talk was higher for girls than for boys.

The difference between the expected and observed proportions of cross-sex talk for girls or boys was not significant as measured by the Wilcoxon matched-pairs, signed-ranks test. To see if there were classroom effects on proportions of cross-sex talk, I calculated the Spearman rank order correlation. It was not statistically significant ($r = .08$).

Same-Sex/Cross-Sex Friendship Choice. Was there gender integration in friendship choice in CI classrooms in contrast with the characteristic pattern of sex segregation in previous research? As in the discussion above, the terms "sex integration" and "sex segregation" or "gender separation" are used, the first being the inverse of the other two, but in contrast to the presentation of results for children's verbal interaction, here the emphasis is on same-sex friendship choices.

The results show that, for both the early and late test administrations, girls and boys were more likely to choose friends of the same sex than was predicted by the Social Integration Model.

Using the Wilcoxon matched-pairs, signed-ranks test, the difference between the expected and reported proportions of same-sex choice was significant at the .001 level. In all classrooms, the proportions of reported early same-sex friendship choice were above 70%, while the expected proportions were 48.18% for the girls and 51.82% for the boys.

An examination of the probabilities of observed same-sex choices shows a slight decrease over time for girls, and a statistically significant increase for boys ($p < .01$). For both sexes, there was a statistically significant correlation ($r = .779$; p < .01 for girls, and $r = .848$; p < .01 for boys) between early and late choices, by classroom.

The boys were significantly more likely than the girls to choose friends of the same sex in the spring sociometric instrument (82.28 for the boys compared with 78.78 for the girls). When I combined same-sex choices of boys and girls, I found that the percentage was 80.43 in the fall and 81.30 in the spring.

Evidence of Leadership as a Male Realm

By analyzing girls' and boys' responses to the sociometric leadership question administered in the spring, I investigated the question of whether children who had experienced CI would exhibit bias in leadership perceptions typically held by elementary schoolchildren in favor of males. Two hundred ninety leader votes were cast in 11 classrooms, that is, one vote per child. A total of 158 or 54% of the total votes were cast for boys. This result is substantially different from Lockheed's (1983) study in which 94% of the leader votes were cast for boys. One hundred thirty-two votes or 46% were cast for girls. There was a marked tendency for boys to choose boys as leaders (72%) and for girls to choose girls (63%). This means that girls made more cross-sex leadership choices than boys.

DISCUSSION

The results of this study point to several changes from the usual inequities based on gender reported in elementary school classrooms. First, there was no evidence of gender operating as a status characteristic. As a matter of fact, not only did girls talk just as much as boys, but the rates of cross-sex talk were also the same. If gender were operating as a status characteristic, one would expect the high state of the status characteristic (i.e., male) to be a significant predictor of rate of cross-sex talk. However, this was not the case.

Second, two contrasting pictures emerged on voluntary gender separation in CI classrooms. On the one hand, the theoretical Social Integration Model was very close to the observed cross-sex verbal interaction for both girls and boys. On the other hand, there was a sharp contrast in friendship choices, where there was a significant departure from the Social Integration Model. Consistent with the findings of other studies, where interdependent task structures have been shown to encourage both cross-sex and cross-race interaction, friendship choice remained highly segregated. Further, the significant correlation between girls' early and late friendship choices and between boys' early and late friendship choices indicated stability over time.

The results of the analysis of the leadership portion of the sociometric data revealed that leadership did not appear to be a male characteristic or realm, as reported in previous research. Compared with other studies, there was a substantial difference in the perception of girls as leaders. The girls in this study were much more likely than the girls in past studies to select other girls as leaders.

The results of past studies suggest that some selected features of the task structure may account for gender-equitable behavior such as I observed in complex instruction classrooms. Specific features of CI that may account for such behavior are mixed-sex small groups at learning centers, training in cooperative group behaviors, rotating roles such as the facilitator (i.e., leaderlike roles), and the multiple-ability status treatment designed to show children that they each had an important contribution to make to the completion of the group task.

Like Lockheed, Harris, and Nemceff (1983), I did not find gender operating as a status characteristic in elementary classrooms. Was this result a function of students' experiences in CI or a function of the youngsters' age? My design cannot distinguish between these alternatives.

Results of the study also illustrate the tenacity of gender separation in friendship choice at this age. Teachers might assume that girls and boys spontaneously separate from each other and that it may even be part of the "normal" developmental process and so there is no necessity for intervention. However, gender separation among children does not have to be accepted as a normal state of affairs.

The findings of this study suggest that it is possible to design classroom task structures for children where they can have verbal interaction with members of the opposite sex, enabling both sexes to benefit from the interdependency that is formed. Having boys and girls act as social and academic resources for one another can do much to modify stereotypes based on gender.

PART IV

Changing the Curriculum

CHAPTER 8

Principles of a Principled Curriculum

Rachel A. Lotan

The goal of complex instruction is to foster and enhance conceptual learning of students in heterogeneous classrooms. As explained and illustrated in the various chapters of this book, to accomplish this goal, complex instruction, as a pedagogical intervention, relies on changing *the social structure of the classroom* when students work in small groups. These changes, consisting of establishing new roles for teachers and students, increasing peer interaction, and equalizing rates of participation of different-status students during groupwork, are contingent upon the structure of the task, that is, the learning activities in which students engage when in small groups. For example, in Chapter 3, we document the positive relationship between peer interaction and learning gains, *given uncertain, open-ended tasks*. In Chapter 6, we explain how teachers use status treatments *when group tasks incorporate multiple intellectual abilities*.

In small groups, dimensions of the collective task affect the nature of the interaction among participants and their rate of success in completing and contributing to the task. This proposition is the foundation for the design of learning tasks for complex instruction, where group tasks are crafted deliberately to support the pedagogical practices associated with positive student outcomes.

While group activities are its core, groupwork is not the exclusive mode of teaching and learning in CI. Rather, group activities are incorporated into the curriculum when the goal is conceptual learning, the development of higher-order thinking, and deep understanding of content. Teachers who have made CI part of their repertoire of teaching strategies continue to share factual information through short lectures, have students work in pairs to practice spelling or computation, assign individual work such as reading silently or writing in journals, and allot time for extensive research projects.

At times, teachers use CI activities as the culminating point of a unit; at other times, these activities serve as springboards for further work that may develop into lengthy individual or group projects. Some teachers schedule groupwork rotations in the middle of a unit to vary instructional strategies and keep their students' interest. Many social studies teachers found that when students returned to the textbooks after the rotations, their comprehension and retention of the material were greatly enhanced.

In this chapter, I describe the elements of a groupwork activity and the structure of a curricular unit used in CI. Then, I present four principles that have guided the construction of these group activities. Since 1989, staff members of the Program for Complex Instruction at Stanford, who are also subject matter experts in mathematics, science, social studies, and language arts, have designed curricular prototypes and have piloted and evaluated their implementation. The examples used to illustrate the principles of curriculum development are taken from these prototype units.

FORMAT OF GROUP ACTIVITIES AND UNITS

A learning activity that supports complex instruction consists of *an activity card*, *resource cards* that include necessary background information or primary sources, and *resource materials* such as audio- and/or videotapes, visuals, cartoons, manipulatives, science laboratory equipment, or props. An activity also includes *individual reports* to be completed by each member of the group during groupwork or as homework. Six to eight activities, organized around a big idea or a central concept, constitute a CI unit. Many teachers have extended this definition of a unit to include the readings, discussions, lab activities, or vocabulary lessons that precede the group activities, as well as the individual assignments and assessments that follow them.

The activity card contains the instructions for the group's task, the questions to be discussed by the group as they refer to the resource materials, as well as the stipulations for a final group product. The activity card is a symbol of the teacher's delegation of authority, one of the key concepts of the classroom management in complex instruction. As they pick up the materials to start their work in groups, students understand that they are to assume full responsibility for completing the assignment and for creating the group product that attests to their concerted efforts.

The individual reports are one of the main vehicles for ensuring and enforcing individual accountability through a written assignment. As explained later in the chapter, individual accountability is an important feature of the learning task and of the group processes in CI.

DESIGN FEATURES OF CI CURRICULUM

Group activities for CI are different from frequently used curricular materials. More often than not, when they work with traditional materials, students engage in individual seatwork: they read, answer questions, calculate or apply formulas, or follow detailed instructions to conduct lab experiments, if equipment is available. When assigned to work in pairs or in small groups, tasks remain essentially unchanged; individual seatwork becomes collaborative seatwork, and not necessarily a sound group task.

The principles that underlie the design of true group tasks in CI make for a tighter connection between the content to be learned and its delivery, between the learning task and the recommended instructional practices. The development of these principles began when the program spread beyond the use of the *Finding Out/Descubrimiento* (De Avila & Duncan, 1982b) curricular package. As the developers at Stanford as well as teachers and educators in the field sought to expand the strategies of complex instruction to additional subject matters, to different grade levels, and to countries other than the United States, the lack of open-ended, multiple-ability group tasks became a severe stumbling block to the reach of the program and its survival over time.

Four generic principles underlie the group activities in CI, across subject matters and across grade levels.

1. Constructing tasks that are open-ended.
2. Incorporating multiple intellectual abilities.
3. Bolstering group interdependence and enforcing individual accountability.
4. Connecting activities through central concepts and big ideas of the disciplines.

Open-Ended Learning Tasks

The significant positive relationships between the proportion of students talking and working together and learning gains at the classroom level, and the rate of participation and learning at the individual level are among the most robust findings of the research on CI. As detailed in Chapter 3, these propositions hold only under the condition of uncertain, open-ended tasks.

Many teachers describe as "open-ended" the kinds of learning activities that sociologists and psychologists call "uncertain, ill-structured tasks" (see Cohen, 1994a; Qin, Johnson, & Johnson, 1995). I define open-ended tasks as those problem-solving learning activities for which a shorthand, standard answer or solution is: "It depends." To avoid sounding facetious, I have chosen to illustrate this definition with an open-ended mathematics problem, mainly because many still doubt that "It depends" could be a legitimate answer to any problem in mathematics.

The following is an activity from a seventh-grade unit on "Area and Perimeter," developed at Stanford:

We have three, rather large tables with the following dimensions (in meters): 2.5L × 1.2W × 0.75H. How many guests can we invite to a festive dinner?

"It depends," is clearly the quickest and shortest answer to this question. More seriously, before they can figure out the number of guests that can be accommodated comfortably, the groups have to make some decisions. Do the hosts prefer a sit-down or a buffet-style dinner? Will they place the tables in one straight line, in a T- or in a U-shape? How much elbow room (specified in centimeters) will they allow for each guest? Will youngsters need less room than adults or possibly more?

Only after clarifying, deliberating, drawing, or building models while carefully considering the dimensions of the tables, are students ready to proceed and calculate the answer to the problem as posed on the activity card. Although each group presents one correct answer, *the* answer varies from group to group, since each group has specified different preconditions. Furthermore, the process of problem solving continues as groups listen to each other's reported solutions and discuss the advantages and disadvantages of prior decisions.

Potentially, through this problem-solving task, students see applications of mathematics in a real-life context, rather than as futile classroom exercises. This problem illustrates the tight connection between perimeter, a mathematical concept, and a real-world application. It also illustrates why and how students working on such problems learn to state explicitly assumptions and conditions, how calculating and arriving at a numerical answer is but one aspect of "doing mathematics," and also how one makes decisions as a member of a group.

Educators tend to accept open-ended tasks in language arts or social studies more readily than they do in mathematics or science, because notions of interpretation, point of view, or multiple perspectives are inherent in the humanities, but seemingly antithetical to the "hard" sciences. For example, when students work on a unit called "Discovering Poetry" (Program for Complex Instruction, Stanford University, n.d.), they read "A Dream Deferred" by Langston Hughes. As they struggle to define the word *deferred*, group members offer different ideas about what kind of dream the poet might allude to and how dreams could possibly explode like dried raisins. After group members deliberate literary questions for which a single answer is too restrictive and for which multiple explanations and responses are legitimate, they discuss with great fervor how to construct a mobile to best represent their personal as well as collective interpretations of the poem's message and, possibly, the poet's intent.

Open-ended group activities in science are radically different from traditional lab activities. While lab activities are usually crowded with details and include minute directions to be followed carefully to avoid potential mistakes (i.e., they are tightly controlled), group tasks in science designed for CI pose problems in a different way. For example, in an activity entitled "Plasmids and Protein Production," (Stanford University Middle Grades Life Science Curriculum Project, Field Test Version, 1994), students design a model to show how bacteria are genetically engineered to produce insulin. Consulting a diagram of the process included on the resource card, students discuss and decide how to extract a plasmid from a bacterium or how to insert a new plasmid into a bacterium. Rather than following step-by-step, recipe-like instructions, students use the diagram, the materials at their table, and perhaps additional resources to devise a procedure and to decide as a group how to go about completing the task.

As they discuss where to draw the line in producing and using genetically altered organisms or the pros and cons of using bacteria in the genetic engineering of food, groups decide on different answers and present different arguments. After reaching consensus, groups reflect on their decision-making process—an important step in learning how to collaborate.

In completing the activities of this unit, students explore not only what genes do and how they work, how bacteria, plants, and animals are genetically altered, but, in a culminating activity, they also plan, design, and present a genetic engineering project. In this project, students are mindful of the ethical implications and consequences of the technological advances: Should genetic engineering technology be used to cure genetic diseases? Should money and effort be spent on developing a "human youth hormone" to keep people looking and feeling young? Should a gene for being thin or tall be inserted into some people's genetic makeup? In combining aspects of science and technology with societal considerations, students come to realize that science is not an abstract subject detached from everyday life. As educated consumers of science, they understand how scientists work and the ramifications of scientific research.

An open-ended task means that the teacher expects no single outcome and that there is no prescribed way to approach a question or a problem. Given the intellectual heterogeneity of the group and the students' rich and varied repertoires of problem-solving strategies, group members can draw upon each other's abilities and expertise. When working with open-ended group tasks, students have opportunities to use each other as resources, to explore alternative solutions, to communicate their thoughts effectively, to justify their arguments, and to examine issues from different perspectives. These are some of the processes that contribute to the development of higher-order thinking.

By assigning tasks that are open-ended in their process and in their outcome, teachers effectively delegate *intellectual* authority to the students. Because no "answer keys" are possible for truly open-ended tasks, some teachers worry that they will be put on the spot as students might (and often do) come up with unexpected, and sometimes quite uncomfortable, answers or solutions. As they struggle to minimize direct supervision and unnecessary interventions in the groups, many teachers try to maintain control by "hovering" through the tasks: overspecifying the instructions or preteaching the assignment to remove much of the uncertainty.

Like the teachers, many students handle the task's uncertainty with varying degrees of comfort and success. Some groups and individuals proceed cautiously at first, as if checking whether schoolwork has indeed changed so dramatically: Are they to think for themselves, ask for and value their classmates' opinions, submit and defend their own? Many students (paradoxically, older students more so than younger ones) find the existence of more than one legitimate outcome and more than one path to a solution first surprising, then disturbing, and sometimes infuriating. Realistically, a delicate balance between open-endedness and adequate guidance makes for productive, rather than frustrating, uncertainty: Too much uncertainty is unmanageable, but too many details short-circuit the problem-solving interchanges, and thus the learning process.

With practice and with frequent and consistent exposure to open-ended tasks, teachers and students grow increasingly comfortable dealing with uncertainty. As they recognize the potential benefits of these activities and the intellectual richness for which they set the stage, open-ended activities provide a necessary and much needed balance to traditional classroom tasks.

Multiple Intellectual Abilities

The notion of multiple abilities is central to complex instruction and crucial for successful status treatments. It sets the stage for changing the teacher's and the students' expectations for competence and their view of what it is to be "smart" in a complex instruction classroom. Multiple-ability tasks are in stark contrast to most traditional classroom tasks for which students use a narrow range of intellectual abilities such as listening to lectures, reading textbooks, highlighting key passages and sentences, memorizing information, or filling in blanks.

Activities of a CI unit are multidimensional in that students use different intellectual abilities and various problem-solving strategies, and can push toward and arrive at different levels of depth in the assigned task. For example, in the Genetics unit described earlier, students use different intellectual abilities as they rotate through the tasks. In addition to reading and writing (the traditional academic abilities), students learn how to use and create models, how to locate and interpret information from different sources, and how to use different media to convey their own messages persuasively. Just like scientists, students learn to summarize their data and findings in diagrams, graphs, charts, and tables.

In one of the activities of a unit on the "Visual System" (Stanford University Middle Grades Life Science Curriculum Project, Field Test Version, 1994), sixth- and seventh-grade students prepare a presentation for younger children to explain the uses of lenses in correcting people's vision. Students examine different converging and diverging lenses and experiment with distance from a light source. They talk about near- and far-sightedness. They refer to their text as questions arise about how light rays, lenses, the eye, and the other parts of the visual system interact. They summarize what they have learned, prepare an interesting, multimedia presentation, and discuss effective strategies for teaching others about lenses. As many teachers know from their own experience, successful teaching calls for a gamut of intellectual abilities and problem-solving strategies.

In the integrated social studies/language arts unit for middle grades developed by the staff of the Program for Complex Instruction at Stanford, and called "How Do Historians Know About the Crusades?" (Program for Complex Instruction, Stanford University, n.d.), students rotate through different tasks to learn how historians examine texts, artifacts, and the music and art of the period to make sense of historical events. In the first type of task, students examine visual representations of historical artifacts: photos and a floor plan of the ruins of Crac des Chevaliers, a Crusaders' castle built in Syria during the eleventh century. Students analyze the pictures, hypothesize about the architectural strengths and weaknesses of the castle, and consider why the Crusaders chose that particular location. They speculate about the lives of women and children in this setting, and set out to find further information about questions raised in the course of their discussions. Next, the students design and build a three-dimensional model of a fortress that will protect their group from enemy invaders. Designing this model requires careful planning, mechanical ingenuity, and translating a two-dimensional sketch into a three-dimensional model—each a highly valued intellectual ability.

In the second type of task, students listen to medieval ballads, identify musical instruments, and describe the mood and the message of the songs. Because of their fascination with and attraction to music, youngsters understand and empathize deeply with the troubadour's pain over the inevitable separation from his beloved, or his yearning for the promised salvation if only he would join the march of King Louis to the Holy Land. As they create their own song that conveys a political or personal message, students deal more consciously with the emotional power of music and with the various elements of musical expression. Among the many intellectual abilities students use in these tasks are identifying or creating melodies and rhythmic patterns, appreciating musical expressions, and understanding how a song's melody and its lyrics play off or compliment one another. Such musical activities have great appeal for students. Teachers are often pleasantly surprised by how thoroughly students enjoy these musical activities and by how much they learn from the activities even without formal musical education.

The third type of task relies on understanding textual sources such as excerpts from Pope Urban II's speech calling the masses to join the Crusades, or Muslim and Christian eyewitness accounts of the siege of Jerusalem. After thorough analysis of the text, students translate the verbal messages into different media: They create a mural depicting the siege of Jerusalem and dramatize the events from the perspective of the Muslims, who were overpowered by the invading Crusaders. In addition to decoding, these activities require a host of intellectual abilities: understanding sophisticated texts, detecting sources of bias, being emphatic, relating a single textual passage to the larger scheme of events, and translating the message of the text into nonverbal forms.

Such use of multiple abilities might be less obvious in mathematics. However, after careful analysis of mathematical tasks developed for CI, one enthusiastic and expert CI teacher listed them in alphabetical order and posted them in his classroom: from analyzing, through generalizing, justifying, modeling, and recognizing patterns, to zipping through calculations. Frequently he points to these multiple abilities as evidence of his students' mathematical power.

By expanding the range of intelligences (Gardner, 1983) necessary to accomplish the tasks, more students have access to the tasks since they can understand what needs to be done not only through written instructions, but also through resources and representations other than text. Manipulatives, visuals, costumes and props, audio- or videotapes pique the students' curiosity and are often more enticing to them than plain text. Many students, turned off by reading as a classroom activity (mainly because they have been unsuccessful at it before) are lured into group tasks by multimedia resources.

As more students who have poor academic skills gain access to the tasks and participate more, they read, write, and compute in the context of the group activities. They use basic skills in meaningful, relevant contexts; they use language to communicate and to problem solve. Indeed, reading comprehension increases along with gains in conceptual understanding.

Multiple abilities, including reading and writing, are apparent in the resource materials, which are an integral part of the task and tightly connected to the assignment posed on the activity card. Using multiple-ability resources, students learn how to analyze and extract meaning from visuals, musical compositions, or paintings, to understand their messages thoroughly and deeply. In effect, these resources are multiple representations to be "deconstructed" as if they were text.

While students use these multiple representations and have multiple opportunities to access the task, as well as multiple ways of contributing intellectually to the group's effort, both teachers and students need to resist the urge to pigeonhole certain members of the group and declare them "the artist," "the musician," "the reader," or, for that matter, "the thinker." Just as all members of the group are expected to think, so are they all expected to participate actively and make important intellectual contributions. For example, if a student likes to draw and is particularly good at it, he or she can propose to the group how to go about designing a poster. However, all members have input into the choice of colors, the elements to be included, or the content of the poster. When all members of the group participate in creating the group products and make relevant intellectual contributions, the teacher can find more opportunities to observe and document the students' intellectual competence and thus more opportunities for successfully addressing status problems.

Group Interdependence and Individual Accountability

Many teachers worry that often in groupwork academically strong students quickly complete the task by themselves, and others drift along either copying the answers or doing nothing at all. Many teachers also worry that they have no way of holding students individually accountable for their contributions to the work of the group or for their mastery of the content of the learning activity. The third principle of the design of group tasks addresses both these concerns.

Group Interdependence. Johnson and Johnson (1994) define interdependence as the essence of collaboration. Thompson (1967) views interdependence as an essential feature of group technology. Building uncertainty into the task, providing opportunities for voicing multiple perspectives, and making activities multiple-ability foster interdependence. The responsibility for the group, as a collective, to interpret a challenging text, and to fashion a single product or presentation—the group product—further increases interdependence among group members. When students collect individual data to pool into a group data sheet (e.g., measuring changes in one's heart rate after various physical activities) and the report is dependent on finding more and more data points, interdependence is increased.

When a task is rich, intricate, and multifaceted, it becomes impossible for a single student to complete it successfully in the limited time of a classroom period. When teachers can successfully instill in their students a sense of urgency to complete the task in the allotted time while incorporating everybody's input, interdependence increases. For example, all group members have speaking parts in a skit that dramatizes an imaginary encounter between Martin Luther and Pope Urban II in a social studies unit called "Challenging the Authority of Institutions" (Program for Complex Instruction, Stanford University, n.d.). In a foreign language activity for high school students developed at Stanford, group members fan out to survey their classmates on favorite pastimes. Members of the group collect the data and figure out ways to summarize them in a poster to report to the class. In a unit on the societal consequences of the Industrial Revolution, the group's assignment is not only to devise a useful invention, but also to identify a potential market and design an advertising campaign to penetrate that market. For such elaborate tasks to be completed in a reasonable time, the contributions and the work of all members are crucial.

Often, while working on the group products, which is the last phase of groupwork and before the final wrap-up, students apply the big idea or the central concept of the unit to their own experiences or explore their own thoughts and feelings about certain events or ideas. This application not only deepens their understanding but also makes schoolwork more relevant to them.

Individual Accountability. Like interdependence, individual accountability is a critical feature of groupwork. That is why individual reports to be completed after the group's discussion and presentation are an indispensable part of the group activities. In these written reports, students respond in their own words to some of the key discussion questions posed on the activity cards and summarize what they have learned. In answering questions in the individual reports, students learn to express their opinions clearly and explicitly and to construct a written argument. As they present their personal reactions, students might elaborate on how their thinking is similar to or different from that of other members of the group.

The quality of the students' writing on these individually completed worksheets in *FO/D* was found to be significantly related to learning (Stevenson, 1982). We have found a positive relationship between the index that includes the requirement for completing individual reports and learning at the middle school level (see Chapter 10, this volume).

As they complete the individual reports, students have excellent opportunities to develop, practice, and improve their writing skills. These reports are also a vehicle for teachers to assess the conceptual understanding and progress of individual students.

Big Ideas and Central Concepts

Activities of a complex instruction unit cluster around a central concept, a "big idea," or a key epistemological question of a discipline. As they rotate through the activities, students encounter this central concept or idea in different contexts and in different situations. Students have multiple opportunities to grapple with the content and to explore related questions, to examine different representations, and to consider different applications.

Big ideas and central concepts are different from themes or topics, which are other common organizing devices for curricular materials. When deciding on the conceptual content of a unit, we draw upon the fundamental principles, concepts, and methods of a discipline, or build activities around real-life issues, problems, or dilemmas.

The relationship between human activity and its impact on the environment is the organizing idea of the group tasks in the Ecology unit (Stanford University Middle Grades Life Science Curriculum Project, Field Test Version, 1994). By examining the causes and consequences of air and water pollution or the greenhouse effect, by learning about the components of a landfill or how to clean up after an oil spill, students understand how they and their community (families, friends, and neighbors) affect land, water, air, and other species. Rather than ringing alarm bells, this unit sets the stage for students to plan their individual and collective actions and, based on scientific information and analysis, devise ways to benefit rather than harm the environment. In another unit, students learn about the physiological and psychological effects of drug use on the various systems of the human body. They also learn about the historical origins of medicinal and recreational drugs as well as the sociopolitical pressures associated with their use.

Social stratification is the central concept of the social studies unit entitled "Taking Your Proper Station: Life in Tokugawa Japan" (Program for Complex Instruction, Stanford University, n.d.). In the context of feudal Japan, students learn to recognize the various manifestations of societal barriers in the layout of a castle town, where the highest-ranking samurai lived in greatest proximity to the shogun's castle, and where the outcasts lived across the river, apart from all others. Students compare the clothing worn by nobles, merchants, and peasants; they read and discuss a story in which two young people, like Romeo and Juliet, sacrifice their lives—for love is impossible across the deep social divide.

In "Voices in Japanese Poetry," a language arts unit that accompanies the above social studies unit, students investigate the differences in form, tone, imagery, and point of view in the poetry of merchants, ladies of the court, and women who toil in the fields, as well as in the classic haiku of the social elite. Closely aligned with the central concept of the social studies unit, the central principle of the language arts unit is the relationship between a poet's voice and his or her social position. Although the context is feudal Japan, students and their teacher often proceed to explore the concept of social stratification and its consequences as it relates to contemporary American society.

When group activities of a unit are organized around a central concept or a big idea and as students rotate through the activities, building on each other's experiences, they can understand concepts at a deeper level, make connections to other units or to other events, and explore different perspectives. These rotations contribute to increased learning gains (see Chapter 10 of this volume).

CONCLUSION

Using the curricular prototypes, teachers first practice the implementation of the instructional strategies of CI. Few teachers resist the temptation of creating new units. However, in addition to much time and effort, the development of new curricula requires extensive feedback from experts in CI and in the various subject matters, sustained collegial interaction among teachers, and piloting of the activities in the classroom.

Teachers who have had the opportunity to participate in these activities report that the quality of their implementation of CI has deepened: They put greater emphasis on the big idea and the central concepts of the unit during wrap-ups, they make more connections among the different activities of the unit, and they are better able to hold students accountable for the subject matter content of the activities. Furthermore, teachers report that through the work on curriculum, they have extended their understanding of CI, its theoretical principles, and their relevance to the classroom. In short, developing their own curricular materials constitutes advanced professional development in CI for many teachers. How to support them in this process and how to demonstrate the effectiveness of these professional development activities is the next challenge to be addressed by the Program for Complex Instruction.

CHAPTER 9

Effects of the Multiple-Ability Curriculum in Secondary Social Studies Classrooms

Bert Bower

Tracking in the secondary school poses a fundamental dilemma for social studies teachers. Although a crucial goal of social studies education is to prepare students for effective participation in our pluralistic society, strategies that separate students from one another according to academic ability also tend to separate them from one another on such key measures as social class, race, and language. Academic segregation of social studies classes sends students at every level a clear message: Equal participation and cooperation by diverse groups in society is possible in theory only—a theory they will learn in academically segregated classrooms.

Many social studies educators have responded to the call for increased equity by doing away with ability grouping and tracking. They have embraced a variety of cooperative learning techniques—dividing their students into small, cooperating groups and encouraging students to help one another learn—as a primary tool for making learning more equitable. But even with these methods, teachers face a host of technical challenges. How can students with a wide range of perceived academic abilities learn together at the same pace? How can students from a variety of social and academic backgrounds work together effectively in small groups? What types of academic tasks are appropriate in the heterogeneous classroom?

Cohen and Lotan have found that cooperative learning can be more effective at fostering positive student interaction and learning in heterogeneous elementary classrooms if expectations for competence are treated (see Chapter 6). Researchers have found that students' perception of academic ability among peers is one of the most powerful status characteristics leading to unequal student interaction (see Chapter 5). They have also shown that competency expectations can be altered by using multiple-ability groupwork tasks that engage a wider range of intellectual skills than traditional groupwork tasks and make it possible for different students to be seen as competent during groupwork activities.

RESEARCH DESIGN AND HYPOTHESES

The objective of this study was to test whether cooperative learning strategies combined with a multiple-ability treatment diminish effects of status on interaction and lead to higher achievement gain scores than cooperative learning strategies without a multiple-ability treatment. Rather than design the study with control and treatment groups, two treatment groups were studied (see Figure 9.1).

Students in the Primary Source treatment were trained in cooperative norms and roles and interacted on a series of collective tasks requiring only conventional academic abilities such as reading, writing, and discussion. Students in the Multiple-Ability treatment were also trained in cooperative norms and roles. But these students were told that a wide range of abilities —not just reading, writing, and discussion—would be crucial to the completion of a groupwork task and that every student would have at least one of the key abilities to contribute, while no one student would have all the relevant abilities. Then they interacted on a series of collective, multiple-

Figure 9.1: Primary Source and Multiple-Ability Treatments Within Cooperative Social Studies Classrooms

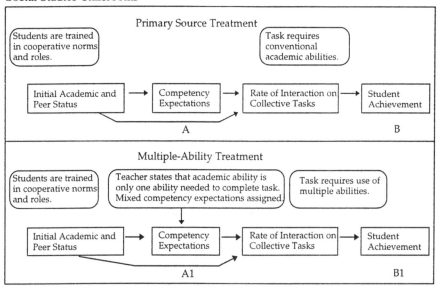

Hypothesis 1: A1 is weaker than A.
Hypothesis 2: B1 is greater than B.

ability tasks utilizing such abilities as visual interpretation, kinesthetic skills, artistic talents, intuitive thinking, and graphic capabilities.

Since training in cooperative norms and roles constituted a treatment in both cases, no untreated control group was studied. Using two treatment groups allowed me to answer the study's fundamental question: Which of these two types of cooperative groupwork more effectively treats unequal-status interaction and leads to higher achievement gains?

To carry out the study, five U.S. history teachers from the San Francisco Bay Area learned cooperative groupwork strategies. A unique feature of the study's design was that those five teachers were involved in a curriculum development project that created the two curricular treatments. Another unique feature of the study was that each of the five teachers agreed to teach both treatments to two different classes. This enabled me to hold constant the effects of particular teachers on students in the two treatment groups.

By recording student-interaction rates and comparing student-achievement results on a criterion-referenced test between the Primary Source and Multiple-Ability treatments, I tested the following two hypotheses:

1. In cooperative classrooms where students are told that many abilities will be needed to solve a series of collective social studies tasks and are given tasks that specifically require them to use these multiple abilities, there is a weaker relationship between academic status and task-related interaction than in cooperative classrooms where students are told nothing about the abilities they need to solve tasks and are given conventional academic tasks requiring only linguistic abilities.
2. Low-status students in cooperative classrooms who are told that many abilities will be needed to solve a series of collective social studies tasks and are given tasks that specifically require them to use these multiple abilities, will have higher gain scores than low-status students in cooperative classrooms who are told nothing about the abilities they need to solve tasks and are given conventional academic tasks requiring only linguistic abilities.

RESEARCH SETTING AND SAMPLE

As noted, this study involved five teachers, with each teacher agreeing to teach both the Primary Source and Multiple-Ability curricula to two different eleventh grade U.S. history classes in 1989–90. Thus, there was a total of 10 classrooms in the study. The Primary Source treatment group had 137 students in 5 classrooms. The Multiple-Ability treatment group had 140 students in 5 classrooms.

The teachers in this study were self-selected. They responded to a flyer sent to social studies departments in the San Francisco Bay Area. The two requirements for participation as volunteers for the study were (1) that they teach at least two periods of U.S. history, and (2) that each classroom be composed of mixed-ability levels. The motivation for the teachers to participate was a collegial enterprise in which they could help to discover which of two approaches was more effective for heterogeneous cooperative groups. As a result of their participation, they received professional development in cooperative learning and very attractive curriculum materials.

To measure the academic- and peer-status ranking for each student, I had all students complete a questionnaire before beginning the treatment. Data from the questionnaire were used to create a costatus variable: a composite index of perceived ability in social studies and perceived popularity. Information about the costatus variable was based on two questions in the sociometric questionnaire: One asked students to circle the names of their fellow students whom they thought to be best in social studies, and the other asked them to select peers whom they considered to be the most popular in the class. The distribution of choices in each classroom for perceived ability was divided into quintiles, and each student was assigned a score ranging from 1 to 5. The distribution of choices for popularity was also divided into quintiles, and each student was assigned a costatus score from 1 to 5 (using the same method reported in Chapter 5). Observational and achievement data were collected on target students in each classroom who fell into both the top quintile (high-status) and the bottom quintile (low-status). Ten target students were selected from each class for observation, giving a total of 100 target students.

The teachers were instructed to use their professional judgment to place students into academically heterogeneous small groups. This meant that all observations of low-status students took place in a group with at least some higher-status students, and that observations of high-status students took place in a group with at least some lower-status students. The teachers also knew that they could change the composition of the small groups during the course of the study without affecting the study's outcome, since only individual target students, and not the groups, were observed.

DESCRIPTION OF TREATMENTS AND TRAINING PROCEDURES

Both the Primary Source and the Multiple-Ability curricula were designed to use groupwork activities to supplement a chapter in *History of the American People* (Risjord, 1986). Since they rely on the content choices and reading activities in a leading U.S. history textbook, the two curriculum units (1) could easily fit into the teachers' year-long curriculum, (2) modeled a process of curriculum development teachers could replicate with their own textbooks in the future, and (3) represented an option that might be attractive to commercial publishers as a possibility for further development and dissemination. In both curricula, students were assigned groupwork tasks. Unlike in CI, however, these tasks were similar for each group. For example, all groups might create multimedia presentations, although each group would have a different subject to present.

The curriculum for both treatments focused on "The Roaring Twenties, 1919–1929." The unit consisted of three major lessons, each of which had an introduction, a series of behavioral objectives, a list of necessary materials, and a description of procedures for the teacher to follow. Before each lesson, students read a selection from their textbooks on the topic of that lesson.

For the Primary Source treatment classes, Lesson 1: "Postwar Tensions" began with a lecture about national tensions following World War I. Then students focused on the Nicola Sacco and Bartolomeo Vanzetti case as an example of postwar tensions. In small groups, they read and interpreted primary source documents about the case. Lesson 2: "Republicans in Command" included a lecture about the presidencies of Warren G. Harding and Calvin Coolidge, and the election of Herbert Hoover, as well as a groupwork task highlighting the differences between primary and secondary sources about the Republican Era. Lesson 3: "Social Tension and Transformation in the Golden Years" featured a lecture on the widespread social changes that swept the nation in the 1920s, in conjunction with a groupwork task that asked students to interpret six primary source documents related to those changes.

For the Multiple-Ability treatment classes, Lesson 1: "Postwar Tensions" introduced students to social tensions in the United States following World War I. Teachers asked students several questions about a series of eight slides depicting the main themes of postwar tensions. Then, in small groups, students prepared some type of presentation—a skit, dialogue, pantomime, or narrative—that dramatized the Sacco and Vanzetti case. Lesson 2: "Republicans in Command" covered the presidencies of Harding and Coolidge, and the election of Hoover in a slide lecture. Then students were given 10 political cartoons to interpret as a groupwork task. Lesson 3: "Social Tension and Transformation in the Golden Years" included a slide lecture on the widespread social changes that swept the nation in the 1920s and a groupwork activity in which students combined written resources, slides, and music to create a multimedia presentation about one aspect of social change in the 1920s.

To successfully complete each of the three multiple-ability groupwork activities, students were required to use a wide range of intellectual competencies. For example, in Lesson 3: "Social Tension and Transformation in the Golden Years," students were asked to create a multimedia presentation on one of six key areas of change in 1920s society: the role of women, changing ideas about alcohol, the advent of the movies, new forms of transportation, the sports mania, and changing consumer habits. Each group was given specific background information on the subject, five slides, overhead transparency pens, and blank overhead transparencies. The students were told they could seek additional resources, such as library books, musical selections, simple costumes, and the textbook. Students were told that different abilities—organizational skills, speaking ability, visual thinking, musical appreciation, teaching ability, reading comprehension, interpretation, writing skills—would be needed for the successful completion of this task. They were encouraged to use all their abilities and resources to create memorable presentations that combined several media. For example, they might act out, in front of a slide image of the era, a short vignette depicting the changing role of women in society. They might follow this up by playing a bit of period music and revealing a slogan about the role of women that they had created on an overhead transparency.

Comparison of Treatments

The two curricula were carefully developed to incorporate the comparative design features of this study. Since this study was designed to disentangle the effects of cooperative training from the effects of a multiple-ability status treatment, both curricula included the use of small groups. In this way the curricula were similar. Both treatments had three cooperative, small groupwork tasks in which students were given roles (usually, facilitator, checker, recorder, presenter, and harmonizer). Since both treatments included cooperative training and cooperative tasks, I was able to hold constant this variable, thus enabling me to vary only the competency expectations treatment and the types of abilities students used to complete the cooperative tasks.

A crucial similarity between the two curricula was content. Since the pre- and posttest was the same for both treatments, the content covered in the two curricula had to be similar, if not identical. Toward this end, students in the Primary Source and the Multiple-Ability treatments

1. Read the same section in their textbook before each lesson
2. Heard the same lecture, although the Multiple-Ability treatment included slides

3. Focused on the same guiding questions
4. Worked with the same concepts in small groups (although if students in the Primary Source treatment read a primary source about Prohibition, students in the Multiple-Ability treatment talked about a picture showing Prohibition)
5. Engaged in class discussions on similar if not identical historical events and concepts

Every effort was made to make the content objectives of both units parallel so that this variable, like cooperative training, could be held constant.

The two treatments differed most significantly in two ways. First, no treatment for competency expectations was given during the Primary Source curriculum unit. Before groupwork, teachers simply told their students: "Historians recreate the past by studying primary source documents. When you interpret primary sources, you are playing the role of an historian." This directive to students had no relevance to competency expectations, but was included in the curricular procedures so as not to raise teachers' suspicions about which treatment was hypothesized to be more effective. In the Multiple-Ability curriculum unit, however, the teachers were instructed to give a true competency expectations treatment in which they told students before each groupwork task: "No one is going to be good at all these abilities. Everyone is going to be good on at least one." Students were told, and received in writing, a specific list of the abilities they would need in order to successfully complete each project.

The second major difference between the two treatments was in the abilities students needed to complete the groupwork tasks. In the Primary Source unit the students used conventional academic abilities such as reading, writing, and discussion as they discussed each primary (written) source in their small groups. In the Multiple-Ability unit, however, students used a whole host of abilities in addition to conventional academic ones.

The design of the units with these similarities and differences enabled me to compare the rates of student interaction in small groups, as well as the differences in pre- and posttest scores, between the Primary Source and the Multiple-Ability treatments and to account for any differences I found as a function of the two intervening variables: (1) competency expectations treatment, and (2) multiple-ability groupwork tasks.

Teacher Training Procedures

The five teachers who volunteered for this study attended three training sessions, helped develop the two curriculum units, and agreed to teach the 2-week units to two separate classes. In the first training session I covered characteristics of the heterogeneous classroom, the dilemma tracking poses for the social studies, the applicability of cooperative groupwork to the high school social studies classroom, how cooperative groupwork supports the goals of the *History-Social Science Framework for California Public Schools* (California State Department of Education, 1988), the advantages and disadvantages of groupwork, and a discussion of types of groupwork tasks applicable to the U. S. history classroom. Then the teachers participated in a model Primary Source groupwork task and a model Multiple-Ability groupwork task.

In the second workshop, I showed teachers how to train their students in cooperative norms and roles. Teachers listened to a definition of cooperative groupwork. They then discussed the advantages of groupwork and participated in a demonstration of two cooperative skill builders. Next, they heard a detailed explanation of how best to form heterogeneous small groups, assign group responsibilities, assign individual roles, and deal with groups that finish before others. Then teachers participated in an extensive discussion on how to train students for both Primary Source and Multiple-Ability groupwork. Finally, the teachers collaborated with the researcher to brainstorm ideas for the curriculum development effort. They decided they wanted the experimental curriculum units to deal with U.S. history in the 1920s and gave the researcher a textbook and a series of topics to include.

In the third workshop, I introduced the two newly created curriculum units on "The Roaring Twenties, 1919–1929"—one designed for Multiple-Abilities groupwork and the other for primary source groupwork. As I reviewed each of the lessons, teachers made suggestions for changes and asked for clarification of procedures.

MEASUREMENT OF STUDENT INTERACTION AND ACHIEVEMENT

The two dependent variables for this study were student interaction and achievement. Student interaction was defined as verbal and nonverbal exchanges between students during groupwork tasks. This talk and behavior were recorded on the Target Student Observation Instrument, which was designed and used like the one described in Chapter 5 (see Appendix C). The key differences were that my instrument included two nonverbal behaviors, "on-task kinesthetic/bodily," such as acting out a part or making a movement that expresses an historical idea, and "on-task visual/spatial," such as pointing to a visual or drawing a diagram.

In this study, on-task nonverbal behavior was indicated by the average frequency with which a student was observed using nonverbal behaviors with other group members in a task-related manner during the cooperative groupwork task. Before calculating these average rates of task-related interaction for each individual, an analysis of variance was carried out on both frequency of on-task talk and frequency of on-task student behavior, in order to be sure there was sufficient stability in the measures taken of each student. The *F* values for all the variables except *requests assistance* and *offers or gives assistance* were statistically significant. Except for these two variables, there was more difference between observations taken on different students than within the set of observations taken on the same student.

Achievement was defined as a student's mastery of the social studies knowledge objectives included in the units. In this study I looked at achievement gains on a criterion-referenced test that measured the students' mastery of knowledge about the period of U.S. history between 1919 and 1930. The pretest was a criterion-referenced test including 40 multiple-choice questions, 30 of which were factual-recall questions reflecting the content objectives of the two curricular units. The other 10 questions depended on the critical-thinking skill of recognizing analogies. Students were asked to relate historical concepts from the 1920s to similar concepts in contemporary society. One question, for example, asked: "The federal government's efforts to enforce Prohibition in the 1920s was like today's efforts to: *a*. stop the spread of AIDS via illegal drug use, *b*. open drug rehabilitation centers, *c*. give addicts prescribed drugs, or *d*. stop drug trafficking." These 10 questions were designed to test students' deeper understanding of the concepts they were studying.

The posttest was administered at the end of the curriculum unit. It was identical to the pretest except that it included a 10-point essay question. This provided an additional measure, besides the 10 critical-thinking questions, to analyze how well the students achieved the conceptual objectives of the unit.

Teachers scored these essays blind, based on a list of criteria supplied by the researcher. That is, essays from both treatments were combined into one batch, and students' names were removed. To assess interscorer agreement, I read and scored six essays in each of the 10 classrooms of this study. The six essays included two written by low-status students, two written by midstatus students, and two written by high-status students. A scorer was considered reliable when he or she attained at least 90% interscorer agreement with me. All scorers reached reliability. The average interscorer reliability was 93%.

IMPLEMENTATION OF TREATMENTS

During the 2–3 weeks teachers taught the Primary Source curriculum and the Multiple-Ability curriculum, several measures helped determine whether the two curricula were implemented according to the research design criteria. All observers were carefully apprised of the research design and were asked to note both the similarities and differences of the curricular implementation in each teacher's pair of classes.

Classroom Observations

Three observers and I carried out all classroom observations. The observers reported several similarities among the teachers. All teachers trained their students in cooperative norms and behaviors prior to beginning the content of the two curricular units, using a variety of cooperative skill builders (see Cohen, 1986). The teachers clearly assigned students roles for each groupwork task. They rotated these roles for each of the three groupwork tasks. The teachers had been carefully trained not to hover over small groups and not to intervene during the groupwork process. The observers reported that teachers rarely intervened directly during the groupwork process, although one teacher regularly hovered over the whole class and talked about cooperation for about 5 minutes during each day of groupwork while the students were busily engaged in the cooperative tasks. Most of the teachers reinforced cooperative norms during whole class discussions by noting the cooperative behaviors they observed and by discussing the group process. Many teachers were observed managing conflict among students in particular groups by asking the group to discuss other ways they might handle a problem. Teachers rarely intervened to solve major intellectual and interpersonal problems that a group was having. All teachers gave the same textbook reading assignments to both groups and discussed the same guiding questions about the 1920s with each group.

We also observed the differences between the two curricular treatments. The teachers were given a bright blue binder with the materials for the Primary Source curriculum and a bright red binder with the materials for the Multiple-Ability curriculum. They were instructed to keep these binders in different places and to have only the appropriate one out during Primary Source or Multiple-Ability teaching. This helped them successfully implement those parts of the curricula that were different. In the Primary Source classrooms, the teachers were observed discussing carefully with the students the process historians use to analyze primary sources. They discussed why historians, using divergent source material, often arrive at differing conclusions. We observed the teachers telling students: "Historians recreate the past by studying primary source documents. When you interpret primary sources, you are playing the role of an historian." Then the teachers distributed the primary source accounts and moved about the room to check to see if students were using their reading as a basis for interpreting the past.

During the wrap-up sessions, teachers held a class discussion about the differences between fact and opinion and the students' interpretation of several key documents. During the class discussion, the presenters in each group described how their group interpreted each document. The teachers reported no difficulty teaching this unit, although they did universally note that students became tired and bored with some of the documents.

In the Multiple-Ability classrooms, the teachers were observed describing what multiple-ability groupwork activities would be like. They discussed with students several of the abilities the upcoming tasks would require. They also pointed out how these abilities would be useful in adult problem-solving situations. The three observers listened carefully for teachers to say the following: "No one is going to be good at all these abilities. Everyone is going to be good on at least one." The observers noted when teachers said this. The notes reveal that each teacher gave the multiple-ability introduction at least three times (at the beginning of each groupwork task) during the course of the Multiple-Ability treatment. During the groupwork tasks, the teachers moved about the room to make sure the groups were working independently and productively. During the wrap-up session the teachers discussed the multiple abilities students used and allowed the students to use these abilities while making group presentations. The presentations ranged from slide shows about social conditions in the 1920s to elaborately staged minidramas about the Sacco and Vanzetti case. The only difficulty teachers expressed about teaching this treatment was that the first groupwork task (to present a minidrama about Sacco and Vanzetti) took a bit longer than they had expected.

Cooperative Behaviors Observed

To confirm the use of cooperative behaviors among students in both treatments, I included several measures of cooperation on the Target Student Observation Instrument. In the "talk" category I included "requests assistance" and "offers or gives assistance" and in the "behavior" category I included "helping behavior." Students had been trained specifically for these types of cooperative interactions. I found ample evidence to support my claim that students worked together cooperatively, but on every measure of cooperation I found that the students in the Multiple-Ability treatment had higher rates of cooperative talk and behavior than those in the Primary Source treatment. To arrive at the mean rates of cooperative talk and behavior, I first averaged the rates of talk and behavior collected during five observations for each target student. I then calculated a grand mean for each treatment. The largest difference in cooperative interaction between the two treatments was for "helping behavior." Students in the Primary Source classrooms had an average rate of .16 per 3 minutes, while the Multiple-Ability students had a rate over three times as great (.49 per 3 minutes). This was the only difference in cooperative behavior that was statistically significant ($p < .001$).

Assignment to Small Groups

To find out if teachers assigned students to heterogeneously mixed small groups, I collected overhead transparencies of each teacher's classroom seating arrangement for each small group activity. These classroom maps showed the names of the students in each group and the roles they were assigned. I used these maps as a measure of the assignment of students to heterogeneously mixed small groups. I looked to see if the groups were mixed by sex and costatus scores. My analysis confirmed that the teachers did assign students to heterogeneously mixed groups.

To find out if teachers assigned students roles to play in their small groups, I used three measures. First, I collected the handouts on which students had recorded their role assignments. Second, I noted that each teacher used the overhead transparencies provided entitled "Group Roles" for class discussion of roles. Third, I used the classroom maps to see if each student was assigned a role to play. On all three measures, I found that roles were clearly assigned and discussed.

To find out if teachers rotated the roles among small groups, I looked at three classroom maps per class (there were three small group activities in each classroom). I found that not only were the roles rotated among students, but the group composition changed as well. In no class did the teacher keep the same students in the same group for all three activities. In only a few classes were groups the same for two activities. Most of the teachers changed students' assignments after each activity, keeping close track of who played what role so that roles would not be repeated.

Use of Multiple Abilities

One of the purposes of the Target Student Observation Instrument was to measure and compare the types of abilities students used in the Primary Source and Multiple-Ability treatments. The Target Student Observation Instrument included two types of nonverbal behaviors that are measures of the implementation of the Multiple-Ability curriculum: (1) on-task behavior that is kinesthetic/bodily and (2) on-task behavior that is visual/spatial. The observed rates of behavior on these two measures were higher among students in the Multiple-Ability treatment than in the Primary Source treatment. The average rate for kinesthetic/bodily behavior was .07 in the Primary Source treatment as compared with .31 in the Multiple-Ability treatment, and the average rate for visual/spatial behavior was .80 in the Primary Source treatment as compared with 2.56 in the Multiple-Ability treatment. However, I found that students in the Primary Source treatment had an average rate of task-related reading/writing behavior of 6.56 as compared with 4.00 in the Multiple-Ability treatment.

Students in the Multiple-Ability treatment had a mean rate of kinesthetic/bodily behavior over 4 times greater than their counterparts in the Primary Source treatment. Examples of kinesthetic/bodily behavior that I observed in the Primary Source treatment included students pointing to text passages and students using body language to communicate simple ideas, such as a shrug to show confusion. I observed a greater variety of kinesthetic/bodily behavior in the Multiple-Ability treatment, including students recreating the actions of historical figures, students standing in front of photographic slides to recreate the events depicted in the slide, students expressing concepts such as "oppression" and "tension" through complex body language, and students arranging props for historical minidramas.

Students in the Multiple-Ability treatment had a mean rate of visual/spatial behavior over 3 times greater than their counterparts in the Primary Source treatment. Examples of visual/spatial behavior that I observed in the Primary Source treatment included students pointing to a picture in their textbook and students drawing a simple diagram. I observed a far greater variety of spatial/visual behavior in the Multiple-Ability treatment, including students drawing complex diagrams for drama sets, students pointing out the complex visual images found in photographic slides, students drawing political cartoons, students watching their classmates re-enact historical dramas, and students drawing metaphors.

Students in the Primary Source treatment had a mean rate of reading/writing behavior 1.5 times greater than those in the Multiple-Ability treatment. I observed these students silently reading historical documents and recording answers on worksheets after discussing them with the group. I observed students in the Multiple-Ability treatment reading directions, writing their own dramatic scripts, and reading quotes from historians. However, because these students were more active using nonlinguistic abilities, they had a lower mean rate of reading/writing behavior.

Thus, the Target Student Observation Instrument revealed that the two curricula differed widely on the types of behavior and, presumably, the underlying skills or abilities students exhibited during small group interaction. These differences in mean rates of behavior for kinesthetic/bodily, visual/spatial, and reading/writing activities between the Primary Source and Multiple-Ability treatments demonstrated that students used mostly linguistic ability in the Primary Source treatment, whereas in the Multiple-Ability treatment students used multiple abilities to a far greater extent.

RESULTS

Although task-related interaction increased in the Multiple-Ability treatment as compared with the Primary Source treatment (see Figure 9.2), there was not a significantly weaker relationship between academic status and task-related interaction in the Multiple-Ability treatment. When I regressed the correlation of status and talk on the treatment variable and controlled for prior achievement, I discovered that the treatment was not a significant predictor of the correlations observed between status and interaction in the classroom.

On closer examination of the data, I discovered that several classrooms had extremely severe status problems that were created by the composition of students in those classrooms. Significant status problems occurred in classes that had high numbers of low-achieving students. Because the classrooms in this study differed so widely in the severity of the status problems prior to treatment, it was very difficult to disentangle the effect of treatment from initial variability in the severity of the status problem to be treated. Although the treatment did not have a statistically significant effect on the correlation of status and interaction in the classrooms in this study, four out of five Multiple-Ability classrooms did have weaker correlations between status and talk than their Primary Source counterparts. That is, the Multiple-Ability treatment worked in the predicted direction to mitigate the negative effects of status on interaction, although this effect did not reach statistical significance. I suspect that the reason for this is that there were more-severe status problems in the Multiple-Ability classrooms. The severity of the status problem

Figure 9.2 Mean Rate of Talk for Low- and High-status Students in Primary Source and Multiple-Ability Treatments

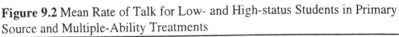

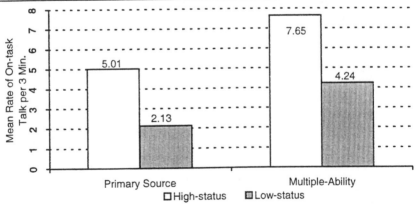

in each classroom was identified by creating an index of status problems that is the correlation coefficient (Pearson r) of target students' costatus scores and the observed average rate of on-task talk for each student. The value of this index ranged from .259 to .865 in the Primary Source classrooms, and from .342 to .918 in the Multiple-Ability classrooms.

Results of the data analysis supported the achievement hypothesis. Students in the Multiple-Ability treatment began with a lower mean pretest score, and ended with a higher mean posttest score, which caused their mean gain score to be significantly higher than the mean gain score of students in the Primary Source treatment. Furthermore, low-status students in the Multiple-Ability treatment had a significantly higher mean gain score than low-status students in the Primary Source treatment. The high-status students in the Multiple-Ability treatment also had a higher mean gain score, although this difference was not significant, probably due to the mismatch of high-status students on the pretest measure.

I was also interested in measuring the achievement gap between low- and high-status students in each treatment. I found that in the Primary Source treatment, low-status students began with a lower mean pretest score than their high-status classmates and ended the study with a mean posttest score that was significantly lower than that of the high-status students (see Table 9.1). That is, the Primary Source treatment actually worked to widen the achievement gap between low- and high-status students. While low-status students in the Multiple-Ability treatment also began with a lower mean pretest score than their high-status peers, they did not end the study with a significantly lower mean posttest score. The Primary Source treatment resulted in a statistically significant posttest achievement gap, whereas the posttest achievement gap in the Multiple-Ability treatment was not statistically significant.

IMPLICATIONS FOR SCHOOL CHANGE

The results of this research show that techniques of treating status are practical and workable in nonexperimental, heterogeneously grouped classrooms. Although the five teachers who taught the two treatment curricula in the research project were not apprised of the hypotheses of the study, during the debriefing session they clearly recognized the problem of dominance of high-status students during groupwork tasks and wanted to know what they could do to further ameliorate its effects. They also wanted to find ways of reaching the low-status students in their classes and of ensuring their equal participation during groupwork tasks.

This study resulted in several practical ideas for infusing cooperative, multiple-ability groupwork tasks into the secondary social studies curricu-

Table 9.1: Comparison of Mean Scores on Criterion-referenced Test, Gain Score, and Essay for High- and Low- Status Students Within Each Treatment

Treatment		Pretest			Posttest			Gain Score	Essay
		Multiple Choice	Critical Thinking	Total	Multiple Choice	Critical Thinking	Total		
Primary Source									
Low status	X	11.78	4.48	16.26	16.96	5.09	22.44	6.22	7.13
(*n* = 23)	SD	2.86	1.65	3.78	4.43	1.83	5.51	4.06	1.60
High status	X	12.84	5.72	18.56	20.20	7.08	26.88	8.32	8.48
(*n* = 25)	SD	4.72	1.90	6.09	5.25	2.77	5.97	4.81	1.23
Achievement Gap[a]		1.06	1.24	2.30	3.24	1.99	4.46	2.10	1.35
t-statistic		.93	2.41*	1.55	2.30*	2.92**	2.67**	1.63	3.29**
Multiple-Ability									
Low status	X	11.17	4.09	14.83	19.35	5.87	25.22	9.83	7.48
(*n* = 23)	SD	3.04	1.65	4.32	3.92	1.84	5.45	4.99	1.95
High status	X	11.84	4.12	15.96	20.32	6.08	26.40	10.36	7.84
(*n* = 25)	SD	3.53	1.79	4.47	4.34	1.55	5.42	4.42	2.15
Achievement Gap[a]		.67	.03	1.13	.97	.21	1.18	.53	.36
t-statistic		.70	.07	.89	.81	.43	.75	.39	.61

*$p < .05$; **$p < .01$
[a]Calculated by subtracting the mean score of low-status students from the mean score of high-status students in the same treatment group.

132

lum. Each teaching unit in a semester- or year-long course might include one or two multiple-ability groupwork activities. Plenty of time should be allotted to these experiences, and the curriculum manual should give clear instructions on how to debrief each activity.

Interviews with the teachers in this study revealed that they were genuinely pleased with the groupwork tasks. Both the Primary Source and Multiple-Ability treatments included three groupwork tasks over a 2–3-week teaching unit, but the teachers felt that this was too much groupwork at too fast a pace. While the Multiple-Ability groupwork tasks developed for this research project utilized five-member groups, there are a host of other ways to divide the classroom that also rely on cooperation and use of multiple abilities. The use of several types of student grouping—whole class, half class, groups of four, pairs—while at the same time creating cooperative, multiple-ability opportunities for students to interact, will ensure that students do not become saturated with "always doing groupwork." Such curriculum development will also give teachers several different types of activities to choose from. Thus, they will not simply be augmenting conventional, linguistic teaching with an occasional cooperative, multiple-ability groupwork activity, but will be integrating the principles of cooperation and multiple abilities into their daily teaching repertoire.

CONCLUSION

Social studies educators who believe that equal participation and cooperation by diverse groups in society is a critical goal of citizenship education, can teach this value if they accept the challenge of teaching heterogeneously grouped classes. But they need help. This research has shown that multiple-ability curricula, by successfully challenging students to use a far greater array of human abilities, can lead to an increase in student interaction and achievement. These positive outcomes should inspire researchers, publishers, and curriculum developers to work collaboratively with teachers to create effective cooperative, multiple-ability curricula and teacher training sessions. If supported in this manner, social studies teachers facing the daily challenge of diversity can convey to all their students a clear message: Equal participation and cooperation by diverse groups in society is possible in practice, as well as in theory.

PART V

Effects of Complex Instruction on Academic Achievement, Linguistic Proficiency, and Cognitive Development

CHAPTER 10

What Did Students Learn?: 1982–1994

Elizabeth G. Cohen, Julie A. Bianchini, Ruth Cossey, Nicole C. Holthuis, Christopher C. Morphew, and Jennifer A. Whitcomb

From the beginning of the program, educators considering adoption of complex instruction, funding agencies, researchers in cooperative learning, and even sociologists have wanted to know the bottom line: What did students learn? Were the learning/achievement gains statistically significant? Did students in complex instruction learn more than comparable students in conventional classrooms? To answer these questions, the authors of this chapter describe achievement data collected by the program with a variety of tests, both standardized and content-referenced.

The first part of the chapter summarizes and interprets the results of repeated evaluations of the effects of complex instruction, using the *Finding Out/Descubrimiento* (De Avila & Duncan, 1982b) curriculum in Grades 2–5. At the elementary level, evaluators used the California Test of Basic Skills (1982), and an *FO/D* content-referenced test.

The next section of the chapter reviews and interprets achievement results for the middle school. The middle school data include results of content-referenced tests for social studies, mathematics, and Human Biology. Table 10.1 contains summary information on tests, grades, and numbers of students and classrooms that will assist the reader in following the discussion.

Certain patterns emerge from a review of results of these evaluations. In the concluding section of the chapter, we synthesize what we have learned from these results. Some of these generalizations are substantive and have to do with the conditions under which the most impressive gains in achievement occur. Others foreshadow the methodological discussion of Chapter 11, which offers a critique of achievement testing. Finally, we discuss important products of CI, such as intellectual and social skills, that these achievement tests have not measured.

Table 10.1: Summary of Test Data

Year	Test Type	Subscale or Subject Matter	Grade	Number of Classrooms	Number of Students	Tables/ Figures
Achievement Tests for Elementary School						
1982–83	CTBS	Math Concepts, Math Applications, Computation	2, 3, 4	12 *FO/D* 3 comparison	102	Tab.10.2 Fig.10.2
1983–84	CTBS	Science Math C & A Computation	2, 3, 4, 5	17	334 230 252	Tab. 10.2
1987–88	CTBS	Total Math	3, 4	4	65	Fig.10.1
1989–90	Content-Referenced Multiple Choice	Science	2, 3, 4	10	202	Fig.10.3
Achievement Tests for Middle School						
1991–92	Content-Referenced Multiple Choice	Social Studies	7, 8	26 CI 9 comparison	84–382	Tab.10.3 Tab. 10.4
1992–93	Content-Referenced Multiple Choice	Social Studies	7, 8	25 CI 2 comparison	669	Tab. 10.5
1992–93	Items from QCAI Rubric-scored	Mathematics	7, 8	14	272	Figs.10.4 & 10.5
1992–93	Content-Referenced Rubric-Scored	Human Biology	8	10	260	Tab.10.6
1993–94	Content-Referenced Rubric-Scored	Human Biology	6	3	80	Tab.10.6

ACHIEVEMENT RESULTS IN ELEMENTARY SCHOOLS

We review three sets of data from standardized tests: 1982–83, 1983–84, and 1987–88. The data set for 1982–83 included three comparison classrooms where *FO/D* was not used. For the *FO/D* content-referenced test, there is one set of data from 1989–90 (see Table 10.1).

Nature of Schools and Classrooms

Audiences hearing about CI often assume that the program works in university laboratory schools or at least in the wealthy suburbs near Stanford University. Actually, the elementary schools represented in this chapter were from the San Jose Unified School District, from working-class suburbs of the Bay Area, and from a rural district near Fresno. Classrooms varied from largely segregated Latino or Southeast Asian to heterogeneous classrooms with a mix of middle-class Anglos and working-class Latinos. Many of the participating students were from non-English-speaking backgrounds and were experiencing difficulties in basic skills. Educators implemented *FO/D* in an attempt to improve basic skills while at the same time addressing the need for development in conceptual aspects of science and mathematics.

Standardized Tests

Three subscales of the CTBS math tests are relevant to the curriculum activities of *FO/D*: Math Concepts, Math Application, and Computation. In addition, in 1983–84, the school district chose to administer the science portion of the CTBS test to all elementary classrooms, including those where *FO/D* had been implemented. Results for *FO/D* students were examined, even though the test did not include physics and chemistry, the major scientific content of the *FO/D* materials.

Pre-Post Test Gains: NCE Analysis. Using data from the CTBS standardized achievement test, we first present a comparison of student performance in the fall of the school year with performance in the spring. De Avila, in an unpublished proposal, examined the gains statistically by testing for significance of the difference between average fall and spring scores for the 1982–83 and 1983–84 school years. This analysis employs Normal Curve Equivalents (NCEs). At the time of this statistical analysis, NCEs were the preferred statistic for evaluation of programs such as Title I. NCEs are normalized standard scores with a mean of 50 and a standard deviation of 21.06 (Linn, 1979). These statistics permit standardization across a variety of forms of the normed test administered at different grade levels and in different years. Improvement in NCEs between fall and spring means that students gained more than the nationally normed population. If they gained the same amount as the normed population, their score would stay the same. Thus, any increase in average NCE means that students are gaining more than is to be expected.

Table 10.2 presents pre- and posttest scores for the math computation, concepts, and application subscales, total math scores, and science scores, where available. The average NCE for the 1983–84 sample starts off considerably higher than that for the 1982–83 sample. The higher pretest scores for 1983–84 were probably due to the inclusion of one magnet school with a significant number of middle-class students. Also included was one school with gifted bilingual classes.

Students made statistically significant gains from fall to spring in mathematics in both years and in science in 1983–84, when the science test was

Table 10.2: Pre–Post Math and Science CTBS Test Scores: Normal Curve Equivalents for 1982–83 and 1983–84, Grades 2–5, for Classrooms Using FO/D

Test	1982–83		1983–84	
	Pretest	Posttest	Pretest	Posttest
Computation				
Mean	24.92	35.5	44.88	54.6
SD	(9.86)	(7.04)	(16.71)	(24.71)
t	13.47*	($n = 102$)	11.16*	($n = 252$)
Math Concepts				
Mean	29.93	36.64	47.47	52.61
SD	(7.74)	(6.13)	(16.98)	(15.87)
t	8.53*	($n = 102$)	6.11*	($n = 241$)
Math Applications[a]				
Mean			46.52	51.78
SD			(18.74)	(15.97)
t			5.33*	($n = 230$)
Total Math				
Mean	37.08	57.04	43.47	53.47
SD	(18.56)	(20.87)	(15.11)	(15.28)
t	8.36*	($n = 102$)	15.24*	($n = 329$)
Science[b]				
Mean			44.67	51.32
SD			(18.82)	(17.79)
t			8.17*	($n = 334$)

* $p < .001$
[a] Concepts and Applications Subscales combined for 1982–83
[b] Data not available for 1982–83

administered. The gains in all subscales and in the math total battery were markedly higher than would have been expected according to national norms. The gains in Math Computation were even greater than the gains in Concepts and Application. Gifted bilingual students and the students from the magnet school showed excellent gains, along with those whose pretest scores were lower.

Gains in 1987–88: A Shift in the Distribution. These data come from a suburb of Fresno, California, where Professor Teresa Perez of Fresno State University had worked with several schools in implementing CI. A sample of students on whom there were spring scores in 1987 were tested once more, in Spring 1988, after a year of *FO/D*. Data are available on 89 students in 2 second- and 2 third-grade classrooms from two schools in 1987. Of these youngsters, 65 experienced *FO/D* in third and fourth grades during the following school year.

For this set of data, the analysis compared the percentage of students falling into each quartile of the percentile distribution on the CTBS. Figure 10.1 shows these percentages for the students before and after experience with CI for the total math score. There were similar results on the CTBS reading scales. Examination of the bar chart shows the dramatic increase in the percentage of students in the top quartile (from 24% to 37%) after the year of experience with CI. In the previous spring, this sample was much more likely to be in the second quartile than anywhere else in the distribution. It was also the case that there were 5% more students in the lowest quartile in Spring 1988 than in the previous spring.

Use of "untreated" comparison groups. De Avila (Cohen & De Avila, 1983), using standardized achievement test data from 1982–83, compared

Figure 10.1: Percentage of Students per Quartile, Pre vs. Post *FO/D* for Math, 1987–88

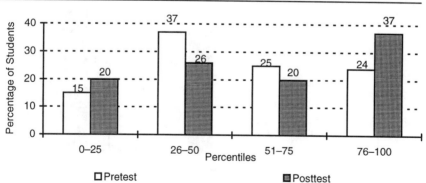

the 12 classrooms that experienced *FO/D* with students from three classrooms (*n* = 41) that did not. All these classrooms were members of the Bilingual Consortium of San Jose, a federally funded project that offered extensive staff development to teachers of all member classrooms. The teachers in the *FO/D* classrooms received staff development from program staff members in addition to the regular offerings of the Consortium. Figure 10.2 presents the average percentiles for pre- and posttests for *FO/D* students and for the comparison students (Cohen & De Avila, 1983).

The percentiles are more directly interpretable than the normal curve equivalents in Table 10.2. For Total Math and Computation, the *FO/D* students moved from a very low standing in terms of the nationally normed population (around twenty-fifth percentile) to grade level, or fiftieth percentile. Clearly, the comparison students also gained relative to the nationally normed population. De Avila used *t*-tests to assess the difference in gain scores between the *FO/D* and comparison students. The *FO/D* students showed significantly greater gains in Math Computation (*t* = −1.7, *p* < .05) and in the Total Math scores (*t* = −2.55, *p* < .01) than the comparison students. Although the *FO/D* students also gained more on average than the comparison students on the Concepts and Application subscales, the difference in gain scores was not statistically significant. Cohen and De Avila (1983) pointed out that it was difficult to show significance with only 41 comparison students.

In Figure 10.2, one can easily see the differences between pre- and posttest scores for the two groups on each of the subscales and on total test

Figure 10.2: *FO/D* vs. Non-*FO/D*, Pre–Post Test Scores in CTBS Math, 1982–83: Grades 2–4 (*N* = 104)

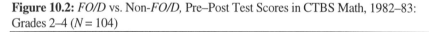

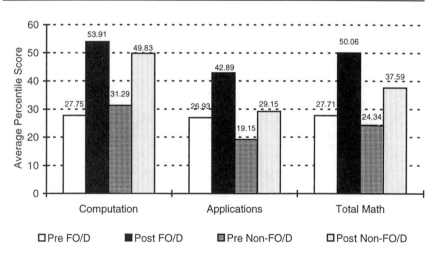

scores. The difference in the height of the pretest bar and the posttest bar displays graphically the larger gains of the *FO/D* students. One can also see how both groups moved upward in comparison to the national norms from fall to spring (Cohen & De Avila, 1983).

A Content-Referenced Test for *FO/D*

The *FO/D* content-referenced test contains items that reflect the vocabulary, concepts, and applications of the *FO/D* curriculum. The first version of this test was created and administered in the pilot year 1979–80. Ten years later, in 1989–90, the test was revised with the help of classroom teachers and administered once more as a pre- and a posttest during the school year.

The revised test consists of 100 items, 65 items covering science and 35 on mathematics. As a result of the revision, there were items for all 17 units of the *FO/D* curriculum, although teachers were not able to cover all these units in one academic year.

There were three types of items: concepts and vocabulary, simple applications, and complex applications. The term *concepts and vocabulary* refers to science and mathematics vocabulary, including concrete items such as candle or washer, and abstract concepts such as circumference or fulcrum. *Simple applications* refer to the recognition of a concept embedded in its context, either in a question or in a fill-in-the-blank item. For example:

Which of the following is a liquid?
_____Dough _____ Milk _____ Salt ____ Measuring cup
Liters are useful for measuring _____.
____Bugs _____ Milk ____ Your height ____ Your weight

Complex applications refer to concepts that involve abstractions that are outside the students' everyday life experience or that use more than one kind of abstraction. For example:

Rachel put some white powder into a cup. Then she added vinegar. She noticed bubbles in the cup. What did Rachel observe?
Acid _____ Base _____ Solution _____ Reaction

The test sample was 202 students in 10 classrooms from Grades 1–4 in Redwood City and Milpitas, California. The sample included classrooms where only a handful of students were reading at grade level. Eleven non-English-proficient students and 87 limited-English-proficient students took the test. Teachers administered the test orally in English and in Spanish. The students could choose whether to take the test in English or in Spanish. The students circled responses, often choosing between pictures. The test did not require that students be able to read or write at grade level. In the case of other language minority students, the teacher used the English version, but an instructional aide who spoke the student's native language often helped. In the lower grades, most teachers took several days to administer the pretest. The posttests were administered during May 1989.

Students gained an average of 11 points out of the 100 points on the test. The average pretest score was 50.3. On the posttest, over 80% of the students answered more than half the items correctly. Figure 10.3 illustrates student growth on the test by dividing the percentage of correct items into quartiles. The percentage of students who fell into each of the quartiles in the pre- and posttest can be directly compared. Only a few students fell into the lowest quartile on the pretest and none did on the posttest. On the pretest, 45.54% of the students fell into the second quartile, while in the posttest, only 19.80% were in this category. Half of the sample scored in the third quartile at the time of the pretest, but this category increased to 65.84% on the posttest. Most impressive, however, was the increase in the proportion of students in the top category from 1.49% to 14.36%.

With respect to the different subscales, the highest gain, 6.4 items out of 50, or 12.8%, was achieved on the Concepts and Vocabulary subscale. The lowest gains were in the Complex Applications subscale, which is, by definition, the most challenging. Out of 15 items on this subscale, the average gain was only 1.3 items. There were about equal gains on the items drawn from science and mathematics.

According to the final report on this evaluation (Cohen & Lotan, 1990), when data were analyzed according to groups divided on the basis of English

Figure 10.3: Percentage of Students per Quartile Pre vs. Post *FO/D* Content-Referenced Test, Grades 2–4, 1989–90

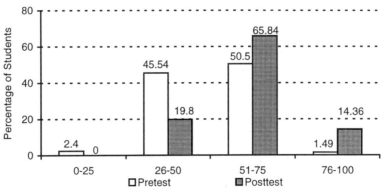

language proficiency (non-English proficient; limited English proficient; and fully English proficient), all groups made considerable gains, but the limited-English-proficient group showed the highest gains. With respect to gender, although girls scored somewhat lower than boys on the pretest, the gains of the former were somewhat higher than those of the latter. As a result, there was no difference between boys and girls on the posttest.

Interpretation of Elementary Achievement Results

Initially, De Avila viewed the two CTBS subscales of Math Concepts and Application as the most theoretically relevant to the curriculum (Cohen & De Avila, 1983). The children repeatedly solved word problems on the FO/D worksheets. Unlike the decontextualized problems in the typical arithmetic lesson, these problems were a natural adjunct to their group activities: How many liters do you think this will hold? How many liters did it hold? How far off were you? The children were not only gaining experience with word problems, but were using computation to answer questions about their own activities.

De Avila and Cohen were initially surprised by the strength of the results in computation. They viewed computation as relatively routine learning in comparison to the problems included in the Math Concepts and Application subscales. Since FO/D stressed the development of thinking skills, they did not expect it to have a dramatic effect on computation items. However, there were strong results in computation in the earliest evaluation (1979–80), and the gains in computation were even more dramatic in the analyses of 1982–83 and 1983–84. In retrospect, De Avila and Cohen realized that there were multiple opportunities to practice computation in connection with the worksheets. Even more important, students in the second and third grades could understand the underlying concepts of arithmetic in ways that the ordinary classroom drills did not provide. Instead of the drills of arithmetic lessons, students carried out arithmetic operations to solve real problems in which they manipulated materials, discussed solutions, and made estimates. Conversations with classroom teachers revealed that they did not ordinarily teach arithmetic with emphasis on concepts. It was probably the combination of the drills in the regular classwork and the more conceptual approach to arithmetic built into the worksheets, that regularly produced dramatic gains in the Computation subscale.

The significant gains on the science test in 1983–84 were also surprising. The science content of FO/D was physics and chemistry and was not directly related to the science content of the tests. Nonetheless, the general emphasis on scientific reasoning, analysis, and construction of hypotheses may have assisted the students in taking this test.

The overall results of achievement testing at the elementary school showed strong gains according to the standardized tests and the content-referenced test. From an absolute perspective, over 80% of the students answered more than half the items on the content-referenced test correctly. This is an impressive accomplishment by any criterion. It means that a considerable proportion of the students, many of whom belong to linguistic minorities, improved their general knowledge of mathematics and science. The gains among the students with limited English proficiency were also remarkable. Observers often noted these students making full use of activity cards in English and Spanish. Having individual reports and the content-referenced test, as well as the activity cards, in both languages represented a great advantage for the limited-English students with a Spanish-speaking background.

Differences by Grade Levels. From the earliest studies, the youngest children made the most impressive gains. This was always surprising to the teachers of the second graders, who felt that the program was too difficult and was stretching the children to their utmost. Both in 1982–83 and in 1983–84, the analysis of normal curve equivalent scores on the CTBS shows a consistent pattern of the highest gains for the second grade. The lowest gains were for Grade 5, which was included in the 1983–84 sample. For example, in the total math battery, the average gain for second graders was 20.86 points in 1982–83 and 13.20 in the following year. In contrast, the gains for Grade 4 were 12.95 in the first year and 12.24 in the second year. Fifth graders in the second year gained only 7.29 points.

A similar pattern was found in the *FO/D* content-referenced test. Whereas the first and second graders showed an average gain of 13.6 and 13.0 points, respectively, the fifth graders gained only 6.9 points. The comparison of gain scores according to grade showed a systematic decrease with each grade.

These grade differences are probably a joint function of characteristics of the curriculum and of the achievement measures. With respect to the curriculum, *FO/D* was designed for the early elementary years. Program staff advised fifth-grade teachers to use supplementary materials and to demand more writing of the students because the curriculum was developmentally appropriate for younger children. Because so many of the fifth-grade students were functioning far below grade level, some teachers felt that the curriculum was just right for their students. However, without enrichment, *FO/D* did not present as many opportunities for growth to fifth graders as to second graders. The curriculum was enormously stimulating for second graders, and they had so much more to learn. With respect to measurement, the content-referenced test contained simple vocabulary like the word *candle* that was no challenge for fifth graders, and as a consequence they received relatively high pretest scores.

In the case of the standardized achievement tests, CTBS Computation scales were directly relevant to the regular mathematics curriculum in the second and third grades and to the kinds of computations required by the worksheets. In contrast, fifth-grade CTBS tests in mathematics did not center on simple computation and included mathematics that was not represented in the worksheets. Thus, the measurement was a much better match to the curriculum in the early elementary grades.

ACHIEVEMENT RESULTS IN MIDDLE SCHOOLS

In this section of the chapter we present the achievement results for social studies, mathematics, and science in the middle school. There are two data sets for social studies from 1991–92 and from 1992–93, each including results from comparison classrooms that did not work with multiple-ability curricula. For mathematics, we report on results for 1992–93, and for science for 1992–93 and 1993–94.

Social Studies

We have 2 years of social studies test results in classrooms that used curricula especially developed for CI and designed to fit within the California curriculum framework (California State Department of Education, 1988). Researchers constructed content-referenced tests designed to reflect material that students were supposed to cover, according to the California curriculum framework. Teachers administered these tests before and after the multiple-ability curricular units in 1991–92 and 1992–93. In both years there were comparison classrooms in which teachers who did not use CI also administered the pre- and posttests.

Test Construction and Administration. The multiple-choice tests for the seventh and eighth grades in social studies had two major sections: factual information and higher-order thinking. The pre- and posttests were identical. The seventh-grade test had 50 items, 33 factual and 17 higher-order thinking items.[1] It covered topics on Feudal Japan, the Crusades, the Mayan culture, and the Reformation. The higher-order thinking items were analogies, using simple language but requiring very abstract thinking. A sample item follows:

> The way the Muslims felt after the Crusaders captured Jerusalem was like the way you would feel after

    a. winning the lottery.
    b. not getting invited to a party.
    c. catching a cold.
    d. having your home robbed of all its valuables.

The eighth-grade test had 40 items, 30 factual and 10 higher-order thinking items.[2] It covered materials on the following topics: Manifest Destiny, the Civil War, and the Rise of the Industrial Era. These topics/eras are all covered in the textbook used in the classrooms and in the materials from the Teachers' Curriculum Institute program[3] that the teachers utilized with multiple-ability groupwork tasks.

For each of the higher-order thinking items in the 1991–92 administration, some students were asked to explain why they chose the answer they did. Analysis of student responses led to modifications of the test for 1992–93. In an attempt to reduce the impact of reading skill on test outcome, teachers read test items out loud in the second year.

In the first year, students took the pretest before any units had been implemented and the posttest after all units for the year had been completed. Conditions of administration were changed in the second year so that teachers were instructed to administer a pre- and a posttest directly before and after the relevant unit. This strategy was designed to avoid the poor motivation of some students to do well on a test administered in June that had no connection with their grades in social studies. All but one teacher in a CI classroom and one teacher in a comparison classroom complied with this directive.

Results for 1991–92. Pre- and posttests were administered in 26 seventh- and eighth-grade social studies classrooms from 5 schools and in 9 comparison classrooms, all from the same school. In an attempt to control on school effects, comparison classrooms were selected from a school where CI was also being implemented. Teachers of comparison classrooms received no preparation in CI. There were 5 comparison classrooms at the seventh-grade level taught by two teachers, and 4 comparison classrooms at the eighth-grade level taught by two teachers.

Not all the teachers taught all the units for which there were test items. Therefore, the size of the sample varies by unit. In analysis of the data, test items were divided into subtests according to the unit to which they referred. Only subtests on units that were covered were scored for a given class. The total number of students taking each subtest varied from 84 students who studied the Crusades, to 382 students who studied the Civil War.

Table 10.3 presents the average pretest scores and posttest scores for CI classrooms and for comparison classrooms. The table is divided according to

Table 10.3: Average Pretest and Posttest Scores for Middle School Social Studies by Unit: For Seventh- and Eighth-Grade Complex Instruction vs. Comparison Classrooms, 1991–92

| | | Average Scores | | | | | |
| | | Pretest | | Posttest | | *n* | |
Grade	Unit	CI	Comp.	CI	Comp.	CI	Comp.
7	Feudal Japan	3.39	3.85	4.99	4.9	118	99
7	Crusades	4.94	—	7.33	—	84	—
7	Maya	4.59	—	6.89	—	298	—
7	Reformation	4.73	—	7.31	—	300	—
8	Manifest Destiny	5.51	5.82	6.8	6.13	305	38
8	Civil War	8.69	8.87	10.62	10.99	306	76

the unit and the grade to which the specific test items apply. There is only one unit on which comparisons could be made at the seventh-grade level and two at the eighth-grade level. The average pretest scores for CI classrooms are a little lower than those in comparison classrooms, while the posttest scores are somewhat higher in CI classrooms than in comparison classrooms in two of the units. This is also the case for the size of the gain scores.

Statistical analysis of these data showed a consistent effect on posttest scores of the individual's sixth-grade reading score, for each of the units, even when the pretest score was controlled. Thus, there is a clear effect of lack of reading skills on the scores on this test.

On the items requiring analogies between central concepts and other settings, the average gain scores of the CI seventh- and eighth-grade classrooms are significantly higher than those in the comparison classrooms ($t = 2.366$, $p < .05$). The lower gains in the comparison classrooms were not due to a ceiling effect, because their pretest scores allowed ample room for improvement. Table 10.4 examines the effects of being in a CI classroom on posttest scores on items requiring higher-order thinking. The regression analysis controls for the effects of differing pretest scores and differences in reading scores. The table shows significant favorable effects of being in a CI

Table 10.4: Regression of Social Studies Posttest Score on Pretest Score, Complex Instruction vs. Comparison Classrooms, and Reading Score: For Higher-Order Thinking Items in 1991–92, Seventh and Eighth Grade

Predictors	B	Beta	p
Seventh Grade (n = 356)			
Constant	.214	.000	.000
Pretest Score	.271	.265	.000
CI vs. Comparison	.087	.201	.000
Reading Score	.002	.300	.000
$R^2 = .226$			
Eighth Grade (n = 344)			
Constant	.121	.000	.000
Pretest Score	.201	.200	.000
CI vs. Comparison	.081	.147	.001
Reading Score	.004	.449	.000
$R^2 = .324$			

classroom for both seventh and eighth graders. There were no effects of being in a CI classroom for items requiring factual recall.

Results for 1992–93. Achievement data were collected for 11 seventh-grade and 14 eighth-grade classrooms. Among the seventh-grade classes were a number from one school where a combination of factors made implementation very difficult. These included a minimum of support from the school administration, teachers who had severe disciplinary problems, and a school with a long history of low expectations for student performance and problems with deviant student behavior. There were only two comparison classrooms; they were both seventh grade and came from the problematic school site.

Different teachers taught different numbers of units. In order to standardize for this variation in number of items, Table 10.5 presents "batting averages," or the average percentage of correct items for pre- and posttests on higher-order thinking and factual items for seventh and eighth graders separately. The results for the two comparison classrooms appear separately under the seventh grade heading in the table. The seventh graders showed statistically significant gains on higher-order thinking skills, moving from an average of 37 to 49% correct ($t = 3.31$, $p < .05$). The gains for the eighth graders were larger, moving from 40 to 55% ($t = 9.78$, $p < .001$). On factual items, the seventh graders showed only a 5.6% gain, while the eighth graders gained 19.6%.

Table 10.5: Average Percentage Correct Answers for Seventh and Eighth Grade Social Studies Tests on Higher-Order Thinking and Factual Items: Complex Instruction Classrooms and Two Seventh Grade Comparison Classrooms, 1992–93

		Higher-Order Thinking Items		Factual Items	
		Average % Correct	n	Average % Correct	n
Seventh Grade					
Complex Instruction	Pretest	37.1	265	38.6	266
	Posttest	48.8	237	44.2	237
Comparison Classroom A	Pretest	36.9	25	31.4	26
	Posttest	47.5	22	38.5	22
Comparison Classroom B	Pretest	32.9	28	38.87	29
	Posttest	91.4	18	75.7	18
Eighth Grade					
Complex Instruction	Pretest	40.3	344	38.4	348
	Posttest	55.4	304	58.0	304

Of the two comparison classrooms, Classroom A did a little less well than CI seventh graders on higher-order thinking skills, and a little better on factual items. Classroom B had scores higher than anything ever seen with these tests: a batting average of 91.4% on the posttest items that required higher-order thinking skills and 75.7% on the factual items. The pretest scores were similar to those of the CI seventh graders, if not a little weaker, so the improvement scores were very large.

Multivariate analysis revealed two additional factors that affected individual achievement. One was the percentage of students with below grade level skills in reading in the classroom. The more of these students there were, the lower were the batting averages as well as the gains. The second factor was the number of units the teacher had taught and tested. The more units students had experienced, the better they tested.

Interpretation of Social Studies Results. The results for 1991–92 show the strong effects of CI on the ability of the students to answer the items requiring analogies, clearly an example of higher-order thinking. Being in a CI classroom had a significantly favorable effect on these items but no effect on factual items. Many of the activities in the social studies units created for CI required students to draw analogies between historical events and current events. For example, when students studied political cartoons of the

Reformation period, they drew analogous political cartoons for current events illustrating the theme of challenging of authority of institutions. They composed a song on current events analogous to a Crusader song they heard and analyzed. It is very encouraging that a set of lively activities can help students to think abstractly—students for whom this kind of test question is frequently difficult.

The purpose of the CI activities is to develop concepts rather than to increase factual knowledge. The latter goal does not require such elaborate curricula, although it is significant that teaching in this way does not impair students' gains in factual knowledge.

In the second year, the results for the seventh graders, although statistically significant, were puzzling. The absolute gains were very small in comparison to those of the eighth graders. In addition, one of the comparison classrooms did better than any of the CI classes. How can one account for these results? Questionnaire data from these seventh-grade teachers revealed the fact that for most units, students experienced only one multiple-ability activity per unit. They rarely had the chance to grasp the central concepts through experiencing multiple activities. These seventh-grade teachers spent far less time per unit than teachers in the previous year or the eighth-grade teachers of the second year. They did not take time to prepare the students for the historical period with readings, direct instruction, or lecture/discussion before they moved into the group activities. In contrast, the eighth grade teachers had a wealth of supporting materials from the Teachers' Curriculum Institute and spent much more time per unit both with supporting activities and with CI. Moreover, the eighth-grade teachers' topics were more familiar; teachers had a better background for teaching the Civil War than a seventh-grade unit such as Feudal Japan.

In order to assess the effects of these implementation problems on achievement in social studies, we regressed posttest scores in social studies on pretest scores and two measures of implementation. The Rigor Index was the first of these measures. It contained a measure of the frequency with which teachers took the time to rotate groups of students among activities; a measure of the frequency with which students finished their individual reports; whether these reports were completed during class time; and the proportion of reports on which the teacher provided feedback to the students. This information came from a teacher questionnaire administered at the end of the first year of implementation. In addition to the Rigor Index, we used the average percentage of students who were disengaged according to staff observation with the Whole Class Instrument. Both the Rigor Index and the percentage disengaged had powerful effects on posttest scores, holding constant pretest scores. Thus, the lack of time and management problems were clearly major barriers to achievement in 1992–93.

The results for the second comparison classroom were very strange. Careful examination of the figures shows that as many as 10 students who took the pretest were missing on the posttest. This dropoff is not characteristic of any other classroom in the sample. Inquiries revealed that this teacher was a newcomer to the school, had transferred from a high-achieving school, and was disappointed to be teaching in such a problematic school. This teacher had a reputation for drilling students. Moreover, he was one of the teachers who gave all the unit posttests together at the end of the school year. We have no way of knowing what happened in this classroom, but in any case this comparison classroom raised as many questions as it answered.

Mathematics

Ruth Cossey developed the mathematics curricula for CI and designed the evaluation. In the 1992–93 school year, she conducted an evaluation of what students learned in mathematics classrooms using CI. This chapter reports results with one of the assessment instruments she used. (For information on other instruments, see Cossey, 1997).

Because there was variation in the particular units used in different classrooms, Cossey sought an assessment instrument that would capitalize on the commonalities of the math programs. All teachers agreed to provide a mathematics program that emphasized problem solving, reasoning, and communication. All teachers taught a statistics unit that was either developed by CI staff or enhanced in consultation with CI staff, and all teachers treated geometric concepts such as area and perimeter in their curricula.

QUASAR Cognitive Assessment Instrument. Cossey selected the assessment tool Quantitative Understanding: Amplifying Student Achievement and Reasoning (QUASAR). QUASAR (Silver & Lane, 1995) is a national middle school mathematics program, launched in 1989 to demonstrate the feasibility of implementing mathematics programs that promote thinking and reasoning skills in schools located in economically disadvantaged communities. To help monitor the adequacy of the new program, the project developed the Quasar Cognitive Assessment Instrument (QCAI) (Lane, Liu, Stone, & Ankenmann, 1993). QCAI seemed to match the general programmatic goals of the teachers, even though it did not match the specific content of any teacher's curriculum.[4]

From this 36-item instrument, Cossey selected 18 open-ended tasks for CI classrooms. There were two different forms of the test, each using a different set of nine items. The tasks were "open" either in the solution paths possible, the answers, or both. In these tasks students are asked to construct rather than select correct responses. In some of the items students are asked to show their work; some ask them to explain their answers. The emphasis on divergent thinking and mathematics communication was consistent with principles of CI curricula in mathematics. The items assessed such abilities as estimating the area of an irregular shape or recognizing the underlying mathematical structure of a number pattern. Relevant to the work on statistics was a task assessing students' understanding of the concept of average in which they are required to interpret information presented in a bar graph.

Use of an instrument designed for another mathematics program to evaluate CI had particular strengths and weaknesses. Among the instrument's strong points were meticulous attention to making the test items friendly and accessible to inner-city youth through extensive field testing and external equity panel reviews. Another strength was its alignment with the general instructional goals of the National Council of Teachers of Mathematics. Still a third strength was its attempt to uncover divergent thinking.

Finally, QUASAR agreed to provide focused holistic scoring of the responses on each task by an ethnically diverse, highly trained cadre of scorers with an interrater reliability of at least 90%. QUASAR developed a general rubric incorporating three components: communication, strategic knowledge, and mathematical conceptual and procedural knowledge. Criteria representing the three overlapping components were identified for each of five score levels (0 to 4). For example, under the heading "mathematical knowledge," a score level of 4 requires an understanding of the problem's mathematical concepts and principles, the use of appropriate terminology and notations, and algorithms that are executed completely and correctly. A score of 4 under the heading "strategic knowledge" requires identification of all the important elements of the problem and an appropriate and systematic strategy for solving the problem as well as clear evidence of a solution process that is complete and systematic. To obtain a score of 4, the student must also communicate clearly and unambiguously and use supporting arguments that are sound and complete. The other levels of scoring specify less satisfactory levels of performance on these components. Using criteria specified at each level of the general rubric, QUASAR staff developed specific rubrics for each task. External reviewers examined the specific rubrics along with sample student work scored at each of the five levels (Lane & Parke, 1992).

There were also certain weaknesses in the choice of this instrument as an evaluation tool for CI. As mentioned earlier, QCAI does not represent a tight curricular match for any of the CI classrooms. Moreover, given that only one of the teachers had a strong mathematical background, the 5-month span between pre- and posttest administrations of the measure may not have allowed teachers sufficient time to demonstrate an increased ability to provide a program with a radically new emphasis on mathematical thinking and communication. Still another weakness is that QCAI does not provide a direct measure of students' sustained mathematical performance. Students had less than 5 minutes to respond to each task. (The time was equivalent to that allowed students in the QUASAR project to complete the same instrument.) The requirement of quick responses may have prevented some students from showing the full range of their mathematical problem-solving and communication ability.

Administration. The QCAI was administered in a 45 minute time period in 14 classrooms of eight middle grade mathematics teachers in the fall and spring of the 1992–93 school year. As described above, there were two forms of the test; for each form, there were two different versions of the booklet, with the same items arranged in different order. As an aid to Spanish-speaking students, each task was presented in both Spanish and English on facing pages. The distribution of the two test forms was in random order in the fall in each class. In the spring, each student present in class was given a booklet with preprinted name, teacher, and class identification to ensure that each would receive a different form in the spring. Cossey employed this strategy to avoid practice effects of taking the same test twice. There were 272 students who took both fall and spring assessments; 113 students from Cohort 1 took Form 1 in the fall and Form 2 in the spring; 159 students from Cohort 2 took Form 2 in the fall and Form 1 in the spring.

Scoring. Under QUASAR's supervision, personnel at the Learning Resource Development Center at the University of Pittsburgh scored the tests holistically. Raters used the specific rubrics developed on a large sample of student responses. Initially, two raters read each student's response. If the two initial raters disagreed by one point, the final score was the average of the two ratings. If the two initial raters disagreed by more than one point, the response of the senior adjudicating rater became the final score. Additionally, as part of an interrater reliability check, a senior rater scored every tenth response. Cossey examined the incidence of disagreement for a subsample of students and found that raters disagreed by more than one point on fewer than 5% of the responses.

Results. A student could not earn a score of 2.5 or better on a question without a reasonable level of mathematical communication. Initial examination of the percentage of items with scores equal to or greater than 2.5 showed that the two forms of the test were not equivalent. Cohort 1 had 31.09% items with score of 2.5 or better on the pretest, whereas Cohort 2 had 40.04% of the items with these scores. The nonequivalence of the two forms made it impossible to talk about gains. Adjusting for differences in the forms did not clarify the data analysis.

The most conservative solution to this problem of analysis was to consider the assessment as one of the program in general, rather than an assessment of individuals. (This is similar to QUASAR's treatment of data from this instrument.) Thus, the analysis is of test forms separately, recognizing that the people who had posttest scores were not the same people who had pretest scores on a given form.

Cossey and Holthuis examined the shift in the sample from low scores to medium or high scores on the posttest. For this purpose, an average score was calculated for each student. These averages were then classified on the pre- and the posttest according to three categories: low (0–1.5); medium (1.52–2.5); and high (2.52–4.0). Students in the low category were those who were not able to communicate their strategies, a dimension required for higher scores. Figures 10.4 and 10.5 show the distribution of scores on the pretest and posttest by test form. These two bar charts indicate that a greater percentage of students were able to achieve a high average score on the posttest than on the pretest, regardless of form. Conversely, fewer students scored low on the posttest than on the pretest. On form 1, 39.9% of the students fell in the medium category on the posttest as compared with 31.9% on the pretest. The equivalent figures for form 2 were 42.1% on the posttest and 39.6% on the pretest. On this form, the easier of the two, the sharpest rise in percentage of students was in the high category (from 22.6% to 35.1%). While these results are encouraging, the grand mean of average scores on both posttests falls within the medium range.

There were no effects of grade on individual pretest or posttest scores either for the percentage of points earned on the whole test or for the percentage of items with scores over 2.5. There was, however, a positive correlation between CTBS reading score and the percentage of questions scored

Figure 10.4: Comparison of Distribution of Total Scores on Pretest and Posttest, QCAL: Test Form 1, Mathematics, Grades 7 & 8, 1992–93 (*N* = 159)

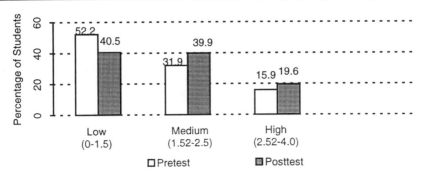

Figure 10.5: Comparison of Distribution of Total Scores on Pretest and Posttest: Test Form 2, Mathematics, Grades 7 & 8, 1992–93 ($N = 159$)

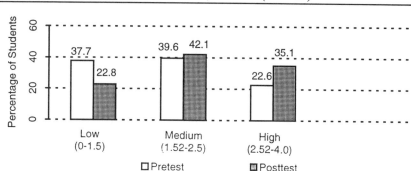

high on the pretest ($r = .554$, $p < .001$) and on the posttest ($r = .516$, $p < .001$). There were no gender differences on the pre- and posttest scores.

Interpretation of Results in Mathematics. The analysis documented a modest shift among these students in the direction of improved mathematical communication. Even if the test forms had been equivalent, it was more desirable to examine shifts in overall categories than the average size of individual gain scores. Individuals can show changes in scores from pre- to posttest that represent a change from no understanding to a very weak understanding of what was required. Although the absolute size of the gain score may look impressive, this person is not reaching the level of performance desired. This person's gain is indistinguishable from that of a student who gained the same number of points, but actually moved from an average to an excellent understanding and ability to communicate. The shift to higher categories is especially important because scores in these categories were only given to students who showed some skill in mathematical communication.

Of all the multiple-ability curricula, the program in mathematics was the most challenging from the teachers' perspective. Because it was developed in line with the most recent reforms in mathematics, teachers were quite unfamiliar with the goals and objectives, such as improved mathematical communication. Moreover, there was no supporting textbook for the units, nor were there specially developed supporting materials. Thus, beyond the group activities and what staff developers offered, teachers had to draw on their own understanding of the mathematics involved. When students arrived at novel solutions to the open-ended problems, it was up to the teacher to provide feedback as to whether they had gone astray entirely or had a solution that reflected the central concepts, such as proportionality. Few teachers had the mathematical background to do this. Thus, modest results for many of the classrooms are not too surprising.

Science

Julie Bianchini conducted an extensive evaluation of CI classrooms using the Human Biology Middle Grades Life Science Curriculum (Hum Bio) (Stanford University Middle Grades Life Science Curriculum Project, Field Test Version, 1994). The goal of this curriculum is to challenge students to learn key science concepts, to apply scientific information to real-world situations, and to practice decision-making skills. The text, laboratory activities, and multiple-ability group activities integrate the natural and social sciences (Heller & Kiely, 1997). As a result of a collaboration between the Program for CI and the Human Biology Project, Bianchini and Nicole Holthuis created multiple-ability activities suitable for CI to accompany selected units of the curriculum. They designed these activities to accompany textbook modules and laboratory activities that were in the process of development.

Bianchini and her team conducted an evaluation study of 13 middle school science classrooms over the course of 2 years. During the 1992–93 school year, approximately 260 sixth- and eighth-grade students in 10 classrooms participated, as did 80 sixth-grade students in three classrooms during 1993–94.

Nature of the Tests. Bianchini constructed content- referenced tests for four of the six Hum Bio units: Circulation, Respiration, Digestion, and Systems. The purpose of the tests was to assess students' factual knowledge, conceptual understanding, and ability to apply and synthesize scientific information. In constructing tests for particular units, Bianchini tried to reflect the multiple-ability nature of CI group tasks within the constraints of a paper-and-pencil format. Many of the questions contained diagrams or illustrations in an attempt to make the test less reading-dependent and easier to understand. For example, in one question regarding the concept of systems, students were given a drawing of an ecological system, including a forest, stream, factory, and polluted factory waste water. They were asked to identify the system's components, to offer three consequences of the system, and to predict the effects of changing one component. Other questions asked students to represent their knowledge with pictures instead of words. Many of the questions were open-ended, requiring students to construct their own short answers.

Administration and Scoring. Teachers administered tests on a unit-by-unit basis: They gave a pretest prior to implementation and a posttest upon unit completion. During the 1992–93 school year, sixth- and eighth-grade students completed one to three CI unit tests: Systems, Circulation 1, and/or Digestion. The following school year, sixth-grade students completed two CI unit tests: Circulation 2 (a revised Circulation 1 test) and Respiration.

Researchers scored these unit tests in 2–3 hour blocks over the course of a year. The rubrics included both criterion- and norm-referenced guidelines. For example, for the Systems unit test, the researchers established a point scale and a set of general criteria for each of the six questions. Then they used a sample of students' pre- and posttests to construct more specific guidelines for those questions requiring open-ended responses. They made adjustments to the range of acceptable answers and/or the point scale to better fit the kind and quality of student work.

There were one to seven rounds of reliability completed for each open-ended question. The researchers began by selecting a set of six to ten pre-tests and posttests. After each researcher had given initial scores to the set, the group discussed answers and reached consensus on final scores. Then reliability for each researcher was calculated by dividing the number of initial scores that matched final scores by the total number of scores. If the reliability score or calculation was low, researchers pulled a different set of tests and completed another round. The group did not move to scoring until after they felt very comfortable with the question. For several questions, researchers were unable to achieve individual reliability. For these items, the questions were scored in pairs or as an entire group. The average percentage agreement among the scorers was 80%. On average, researchers spent 75 hours per 100 tests.

Results of Science Tests. The five tests were not of equal value (a total of 56 points was possible on Systems, 43 on Respiration, 51 on Digestion, 93 on Circulation 1, and 83 on Circulation 2). To make the tests comparable, percentage totals were calculated for the pretest, posttest, and gain scores by dividing the test scores by the total number of points possible. Table 10.6 provides a summary of the percentage pretest, posttest, and gain scores for each test.

T-tests indicated that the posttest scores were significantly higher than the pretest scores for each of the five tests ($p < .001$ for each). The average scores on the Systems pretest (36.0%) and posttest (60.9%) were the highest of the five tests. Learning gains were greatest for Systems (24.9%) and lowest for Digestion (7.3%).

Because a major objective of CI is the development of higher-order concepts and processes, it is important to analyze higher-order questions separately. Bianchini, Holthuis, and Nielsen (1995) categorized higher-order questions as those that asked students to apply, analyze, and/or synthesize

Table 10.6: Percentage Correct for Pretests, Posttests, and Percentage Gain
Scores: Science Testing with Five Tests, Grades 6 and 8, 1992–93 and 1993–94

Test	n	% Pretest	%Posttest	% Gain
Systems	206	36.0	60.9	24.9
		$(16.2)^a$	(18.9)	(17.4)
Respiration	65	27.4	42.2	14.8
		(13.3)	(19.1)	(11.8)
Digestion	172	35.4	42.7	7.3
		(16.2)	(16.8)	(10.8)
Circulation 1	135	21.6	35.6	14.0
		(10.2)	(14.4)	(10.5)
Circulation 2	69	17.3	36.1	18.8
		(8.2)	(18.1)	(12.8)

[a] *SD* in parentheses

scientific knowledge. When these researchers analyzed the percentage of
pretest, posttest, and gain scores on the base of the total number of higher-
order questions per test, they found similar trends to those for the overall
scores. The posttest scores on the higher-order questions were significantly
higher than the pretest scores for each of the five tests, as determined by
t-tests. Gains on higher-order thinking items were largest on Systems (students scored 21.8% better on the posttest) and smallest on Digestion (5.6%).

The inclusion of diagrams and pictures in many of the test questions
and the requirement for drawings and diagrams in answers were strategies
intended to make the tests more accessible. However, students did not consistently score higher on the pictorial questions. A qualitative analysis
(Bianchini et al., 1995) suggested that in some instances pictorial questions
constrained or confused student responses. In other instances, students clearly
benefited from the acceptance of drawings as answers; they were better able
to convey what they knew through an illustration than through words. Despite
these and other attempts to make tests more accessible to all students, reading scores were significantly correlated with pre- and posttest scores on each
of the five unit tests. Moreover, reading scores were significantly correlated
with percentage gain scores on Respiration, Circulation 1, and Circulation 2.

Given the widely discussed gender gap in science achievement, it was
particularly important to compare the scores of boys and girls. Because some
tests were given to eighth graders, it was possible to see whether there was

evidence of a gender gap beginning among the older students. Among the sixth graders, although gain scores for boys and girls did not differ significantly, girls scored significantly higher than boys on some of the pre- and postests (Circulation 1 and Digestion). The evidence from the eighth grade is mixed. Girls did significantly better than boys on the Systems pretest, but boys made significantly greater gains than girls on that test. On the digestion test, girls once again had significantly higher pretest scores, but there was no difference between the boys and girls in the percentage gain.

Interpretation of Science Results. The evaluation documented significant gains on all of these assessment instruments. Of course, without standard for comparison, it is impossible to know if the students gained more than they would have without the use of CI. Even from the perspective of absolute scores, it is difficult to assess whether the scores signal a reasonable level of understanding of the topics covered. The only a priori criterion of what students were supposed to gain was a better understanding of the central concept of each unit of multiple-ability activities. There were no a priori criteria of what additional skills, factual knowledge, and concepts students were supposed to learn about circulation, digestion, and respiration.

Most of these students had little background in science. Although teachers had the draft of the new textbook for the Middle Grades Life Science Curriculum as well as laboratory exercises suitable for many of the topics (Stanford University Middle Grades Life Science Curriculum Project, Field Test Version, 1994), they varied as to how much use they made of these materials. Thus, some teachers relied heavily on multiple-ability group activities to do the bulk of the teaching, something the activities were not designed to do. This was not helpful to students with a minimal background in science, who therefore came to the group activities with a minimum of understanding and orientation. In addition, some students lacked skills required by the test, such as the ability to draw a well-labeled diagram.

Some of these units, like Circulation, were much larger than others, such as Systems. Circulation had more than 15 multiple-ability activities available to the teacher. Not all of these activities were used, nor was all the other available material from the unit presented. As a result, it was probably the case that some students were tested on material they had never studied or experienced.

The use of open-ended assessment requiring scoring with rubrics proved to be an expensive and time-consuming strategy. Nevertheless, the answers provided by students were a rich source of information about the strategies and limitations of the curriculum, their understanding of science, and particularly their misconceptions and gaps in background.

SUMMARY AND IMPLICATIONS

In this chapter we have chronicled years of achievement testing with standardized tests and with content-referenced tests for elementary students and for middle school students. Sometimes we have examined the absolute gains from pretest to posttest, and sometimes we have made comparisons between CI classrooms and other classrooms that did not use these strategies but covered similar curricular materials. Overall, students in CI classrooms showed significant gains from pre- to posttests and in comparison to students in other classrooms. The learning gains are both in the areas of factual knowledge and in higher-order thinking skills. The younger children show impressive gains on standardized achievement tests in math computation and in math concepts and application. They also significantly increased their understanding of science concepts and vocabulary and their ability to apply these ideas. At the middle school level, we have demonstrated gains in knowledge of science, social studies, and mathematics. Only in social studies do we have reasonable data from comparison classrooms, permitting the conclusion that CI resulted in greater improvement in higher-order thinking skills than alternative educational treatments.

We have been frank about the limitations of any one of these evaluations. Many lack comparison groups. Others used tests that were less than ideal. Still others revealed problems in test administration. Yet, across all these studies, there is real strength in the consistency of significant learning gains for CI students across varying content, grade levels, individual achievement levels, levels of English language proficiency, and different schools. One could select only the most successful of these evaluations for presentation, but we believe that it is the *array* of findings over a long time under varying conditions that is truly impressive.

Lessons Learned

These results illustrate some important underlying lessons to be learned from a study of achievement data. The first lesson is that the strength of the gains in test scores appears to depend on the match of the test to the curriculum. For example, the gains in middle school mathematics were not very great, but the test was by no means an exact match to the curriculum. Similarly, if we examine the outstanding gains on the Systems unit in the science curriculum, we can see that this success was partly a product of a brief, self-contained unit where the test items faithfully reflected the nature of the group activities and the central concept of the unit. This was less true of the other units where items referred to a wider body of knowledge and did not always reflect group activities. In middle school social studies, where the test questions reflected the analogies students had to construct in the course of activities, there was a clear superiority in higher-order thinking for students who had experienced these activities in comparison to students who had not.

The second lesson was a sad but important generalization: There will not be impressive learning gains if CI is not implemented properly and/or if there are severe problems of classroom management (see Chapter 3). The second year of testing in social studies revealed weak gains for the seventh-grade classrooms, gains that were smaller than those of the eighth grade classrooms. Analysis showed that the smaller achievement gains were a product of failure to rotate students between activities, failure to give adequate time to the curriculum, and high rates of student disengagement in some of the classrooms. It is significant that these failures took place in a school that did not give teachers adequate support. It would appear that CI requires a modicum of organizational and classroom "health" for successful learning outcomes.

In addition, teachers need considerable support from staff developers and from department chairs if they are to spend more time on particular curricular themes or topics. If teachers feel pressured to cover curriculum by their departments or by their own desire to get through the textbook, they are likely to sacrifice rotation in CI. This means that each student participates in only one activity exemplifying the central concept, a serious dilution of the organizing principle of the curriculum. This particular problem was characteristic of middle schools and was not present at the elementary school level.

A third lesson to be learned from the results is the importance, beginning at the level of middle school, of supporting materials to prepare students before they begin the group activities. Learning outcomes for the middle school typically require more than small group activities. The understanding and knowledge that is tested cannot all be achieved in a group activity.

In the case of the new mathematics curriculum, there was no textbook and a lack of supporting material. Some of the modest learning gains probably should be attributed to these problems. In the case of some of the larger science units, such as Circulation, the teachers varied in their use of textual material and often omitted laboratory activities. Qualitative analysis showed that students had many misconceptions and lacked a basic understanding of the scientific method. They needed something more than the group activities in order to do well on the test.

An excellent example of the need for basic instruction in addition to CI was observable in the responses of students when asked why they answered some items the way they did on the seventh-grade Crusader unit. The responses made it painfully clear that they didn't know what was meant by the term *Muslim*. Teachers (and curriculum developers) had assumed this word was understood; thus, they never included necessary direct instruction and explanation. This lacuna caused students considerable difficulty on the test.

It is necessary for the teacher to combine CI with other teaching activities. Materials from the Teachers' Curriculum Institute include excellent slides for slide lectures and discussions, and exercises in other social studies skills designed for pairs of students. All of these activities are intended to accompany textbooks. The results in achievement for the eighth graders using these materials are markedly superior to the results for the seventh graders who did not have the rich, supporting materials and activities.

The final lesson has to do with the relationship of reading skills to the test scores. Despite efforts to revise the tests to make them less dependent on reading skills, there was a continuing relationship between an individual's reading score and gains on these tests. We have frequently found these relationships between gain scores and reading scores, even when the test items are read out loud in English and Spanish. Such a correlation does not tell us whether the problem lies in an inability to read and comprehend the test, or with a failure to learn in response to instruction and interaction.

In some analyses, holding the individual's reading score constant, there were additional effects of the percentage of students in the class with low reading scores. Teachers in such classes may be less demanding of their students, or there may be a lack of resources within many of the small groups to interpret the activity cards and the individual reports. For optimal results with CI, it is necessary to seek out truly heterogeneous classrooms where there are some students in each group who represent grade level reading skills.

Unmeasured Results

We would like to close this chapter with the issue of what we are and are not measuring with the instruments described. CI always involves multiple-ability curricula as well as particular instructional strategies. It is not possible to generalize about what students have learned as a result of CI without dealing with the particular content of these curricula. Given the range of conventional achievement measures we have used, we have only measured learning objectives that relate to the content of the curricula.

There are other intellectual and social skills that are not measured by these tests. Students in CI learn to deal with uncertain problems and to use resources among fellow students rather than to depend on adult authority; they also learn how to plan and carry out projects as a cooperative group. These are the kinds of learning outcomes that we have not measured and do not even know how to measure. Yet, in some sense, these are among the important learning outcomes that teachers and students discuss when they talk about CI.

We have confined ourselves in this chapter to paper-and-pencil instruments administered at the individual level. Yet students in this approach do their learning in groups; and their learning is of a particularly active variety. Clearly, performance assessments of individuals and groups have a better chance of reflecting the outcome of a classroom experience that features active group learning. Performance assessments might have the additional advantage of overcoming the persistent relationship we have documented between reading scores and measures of what students have learned.

The task of assessing what students have learned, although not a standard sociological problem, has raised many new questions relevant to the work of sociologists of education. Sociologists use data from achievement tests as a dependent variable, but they do not often reflect on the nature of these instruments. Chapter 11 considers limitations and potential of paper-and-pencil assessment instruments from a sociological perspective.

NOTES

1. Jennifer Whitcomb and Elizabeth Cohen took primary responsibility for constructing the seventh-grade test. Many of the factual items were adapted from published tests of the textbook *Across the Centuries* (Armento, Nash, Salter, & Wixson, 1991a).

2. Bert Bower and Elizabeth Cohen took primary responsibility for constructing the eighth-grade test. All content was available in the text, *A More Perfect Union* Armento, Nash, Salter, & Wixson, 1991b). Seven teachers reviewed a prototype of this test. Based on their comments, Bower and Cohen made changes.

3. The Teachers' Curriculum Institute, under the leadership of Bert Bower, produces commercially available social studies materials that contain slide lectures, activities for pairs, and multiple-ability activities for four- and five-person groups.

4. QUASAR uses different but overlapping versions for seventh and eighth graders. Cossey used the same form for both grades. Technical information about reliability and validity studies of QCAI is provided in Lane, Stone, Ankenmann, and Liu (1994); Lane, Liu, Stone, and Ankenmann (1993); and Stone, Ankenmann, Lane, and Liu (1993).

CHAPTER 11

Sociologists in the Land of Testing

Elizabeth G. Cohen

Achievement measures are traditionally the province of psychometricians and educational evaluators. It was partly accidental that a group of sociologists of education working with CI became deeply involved in developing and analyzing achievement tests for such a long time. Funding agents required achievement data, but they provided no special funds for the major work of test construction, administration, or analysis.

Researchers in the Program for Complex Instruction were perpetually dissatisfied with their attempts to assess achievement gains in the short term. Although everyone agreed that achievement was an important outcome for CI, they never saw the assessment of achievement as a major objective. They were more concerned with issues of equity and change in the social structure of the classroom than in achievement gains. Nonetheless, unless the staff could offer evidence in the form of achievement data to schools, school districts, and foundations, these groups would have been uninterested in supporting the goals of equity. Despite their sociological view of achievement gains as a social construct, the staff were convinced that educators and funders thought of "achievement gains" as real and concrete. Ignoring this reality would put all the work at risk. Therefore, the program staff have continued their efforts to assess achievement for over 15 years. From all the struggles and puzzles of this work and from a persistently and peculiarly sociological and theoretical point of view came a new perspective on the problem of assessment.

SOCIOLOGICAL WORK WITH ACHIEVEMENT TESTS

Work with achievement tests is not unique to sociologists in the Program for Complex Instruction. To the contrary, sociologists of education make routine use of achievement tests as a dependent variable in their investigations of the effects of schooling. They use an achievement measure as an indicator of the educational system's productivity, whether at the district, school, or classroom level. They typically use tests constructed by nonsociologists for measurement of achievement. Most common in the literature are the tests created for large national longitudinal studies such as High School and Beyond and the National Educational Longitudinal Study (NELS). The Educational Testing Service created the tests for these studies, using teachers to construct and review items.

Sociologists also use achievement as an outcome measure of social processes in schools, such as tracking and restructuring. Since so many other variables, such as family background and measures of ability, also affect achievement scores, this tradition uses multivariate analysis. The designs hold some individual background factors constant while examining the effects of schooling experience on achievement.

Sociologists have been generally uncritical of the achievement tests they use, partly because they have little choice in achievement measures in working with national databases and partly because test construction is outside their expertise. Nonetheless, there are some important questions about the suitability of these tests as measures of the consequences of student experience within the organization of the schools. For example, it is not uncommon to find tests of reading administered early and late in the high school career as a way to measure high school achievement (Peng, Fetters, & Kolstad, 1981), but reading (with the possible exception of remedial reading) is not directly taught in high school. Thus, there is some doubt about which experiences account for observed changes in reading scores over time. Perhaps those who read at grade level in their first year of high school continue to read on their own time, thus increasing their skills.

A similar problem results when sociologists use subject matter achievement tests (e.g., in mathematics) to reflect the effects of different tracks or ability group placements. Students in lower tracks or ability groups may never have covered the subject matter in the test. The researcher cannot disentangle the alternative explanation of differential curriculum coverage from social psychological explanations such as being in a low-status group or having a different peer group. To make this important distinction, it is necessary to find out what students are being taught in various tracks and groups. Differences in material coverage are a simple but powerful alternative explanation to some of the preferred explanations for the effects of tracking (Gamoran, 1989).

Achievement Testing in CI

In addition to the need to legitimize the innovation with achievement gains, we also valued achievement data as a measure that would reflect the character of the program's implementation. A wide variety of tests, both standardized and content-referenced, described in Chapter 10, have proven sensitive to features of implementation such as the percentage of students talking and working together or the amount of time teachers allow for students to work in groups. Implementation at the classroom level affects scores on standardized achievement tests and on content-referenced tests in social studies, mathematics, and science (see Chapter 3).

Results of a valid achievement test can and should vary according to the quality of implementation in a classroom. This variation makes it possible to test hypotheses about which features of the program produce learning outcomes. For example, we have repeatedly found that under conditions of uncertain group tasks, there are better achievement results in classrooms with more interaction. We conclude that interaction is a key feature of the program. Such knowledge is invaluable in preparing teachers and for disseminating the innovation; it supports our insistence that teachers must not sacrifice student interaction as they make adaptations.

The achievement tests have also allowed program researchers to develop what we call "quality control" indicators. One of these indicators is a measure of interaction among the students. By examining the relationship between the percentage of students talking and working together and achievement outcomes, we were able to determine the minimum amount of student interaction that is sufficient to produce achievement gains at the classroom level. The quality control indicators provide a way to check the character of implementation in the United States and abroad.

When variations in classroom implementation show consistent relationships to achievement tests, it is, to some extent, a measure of the construct validity of those tests. By holding measures of implementation constant in multivariate analyses, we avoid some of the problems encountered by sociologists who use tests as a measure of schooling without direct information about classroom experience.

A CRITIQUE OF ACHIEVEMENT TESTING

Chapter 10 described the wide array of achievement tests used by the program in elementary and middle schools and for different subject matters. Despite the documentation of many statistically significant achievement gains, there were continuing concerns with the limitations of our assessment. Ideally, one would want the assessment to reflect the changes in students that have come about as a result of instruction, as well as the curricular materials and activities within the groups. Sometimes, however, the assessment reflected other variables such as the student's reading level or the weak match of the assessment to the curriculum. We also struggled with the problem of a reasonable comparison classroom for evaluation designs.

As a result of these and related concerns, I offer a sociological critique of the use of achievement testing as a way to evaluate the educational results of a classroom experience. The criticisms apply not only to our own work but also to work done by other educational evaluators. Following this discussion of problems, the chapter closes with an alternative plan for future assessment that meets many of the objections concerning current practice.

The Case of the Uncontrollable Control Group

There is a tradition within educational evaluation of comparing innovative classroom treatments with a set of classrooms using more "conventional" approaches. If the experimental classrooms have higher test score gains than the comparison classrooms, the evaluator concludes that the treatment is effective.

The use of comparison classrooms presents two major problems. First, this comparison group is often referred to as a control group, although there is nothing controlled except the withholding of the special classroom treatment. Actually, the term *control* is a misnomer because the evaluator often has very little idea of what happened in the comparison classrooms. The teachers could be using a strong alternative approach to the experimental intervention; they could be participating in another innovative program; or they could have such terrible management problems that little in the way of formal teaching activities takes place. The comparison classrooms could even have teachers who are determined to prove that the experimental innovation is ineffective and unnecessary, and thus work harder than at any time in the past to produce good results on the achievement test.

The second problem is that random assignment to an experimental or a control group has often proved impractical in actual work with schools. Typically there is very little control over the selection of treated versus untreated classrooms. In our experience, there is a distinct bias in the teachers and classrooms that participate in CI. Knowing that the intervention is designed to work with problems of inequity, the teachers who volunteer and the classrooms that principals select for participation tend to have a higher percentage of poor readers and students with limited English proficiency than any comparison classrooms we can locate in the same school and grade level. Thus, the selection of classrooms for treatment stacked the deck against us in most comparisons we made.

Absolute Gains in Test Scores

An alternative to the use of comparison classrooms is examination of absolute gains from pre- to posttests, administered before and after the intervention. For the examination of gains in test scores, standardized achievement tests (such as the CTBS) have the advantage of a nationally normed comparison population. As we were able to show while evaluating CI in the elementary school, students gained markedly more than would have been expected in the national norm group. An additional advantage of standardized achievement tests is that they still have the greatest legitimacy in the eyes of most constituencies.

However, there are two major disadvantages to the use of standardized tests. The first drawback is that the test items may have only a marginal relationship to the curricular content of the intervention. In the case of *FO/D* (De Avila & Duncan, 1982b), at least part of the curriculum, the mathematics portion, related to the content of the second-, third-, and, to a lesser extent, fourth-grade CTBS achievement test. However, the CTBS math subscales for the fifth grade were largely irrelevant to the curriculum. Moreover, the CTBS Science Test for the early elementary years did not reflect the physics and chemistry of the curriculum at all.

The second disadvantage arises from the fact that school districts often control the administration of standardized tests; this was the case in California. When state school funds declined precipitously, hard-pressed districts eliminated fall testing. Instead, they relied on comparisons based on a single annual spring testing. Given the lack of a unique identification number for each child in school records, staff had to laboriously collate scores from the previous year's records. Since the students were frequently transient, there was a large percentage of students for whom no pretest was available. Eventually, we gave up the attempt to use data from annual testing.

We have also examined absolute gains on content-referenced tests constructed by staff members. Content-referenced tests have one advantage over standardized tests: They are more likely to reflect the intended curriculum (although they still may not reflect the implemented curriculum). In almost all the comparisons of absolute gains on content-referenced tests that we examined, there were statistically significant gains from pre- to posttest.

However, statistical significance says nothing about the educational significance of those gains. In order to estimate the significance of gains, it is helpful to have an a priori set of standards concerning what students are supposed to learn from the curricular materials. For example, in a unit on statistics, an absolute standard might be: The student is able to transform data from tabular form into bar charts. Without such a standard, the evaluator runs the risk of seeing as favorable a shift from total ignorance to a weak and confused grasp of curriculum materials. To follow the example, if a student improves from no understanding of this transformation of data to a confused and incorrect bar chart, the improvement may not be educationally significant. From an educational perspective, it is important to find out something about the absolute grasp of skills and concepts. We did not set such absolute standards in the development and analysis of our content-referenced tests.

The setting of standards itself raises additional questions: Who is to set such a priori standards for particular curricular materials? Should curriculum developers prepare the standards and communicate them to teachers? Dictating to teachers exactly what students are supposed to gain from a particular set of educational experiences not only is undesirable from a professional perspective but does not work very well. Unless the teacher also understands and believes that these standards represent worthwhile goals of instruction, instruction will vary widely as teachers pick and choose what they think is important.

Control over Conditions of Testing

A third criticism of assessment stems from lack of control over the conditions of testing. For the most part, we had relatively poor control over conditions of testing; we were certainly not allowed to administer standardized achievement tests. Many teachers also did not want us to come in and administer content-referenced tests. Even when they were willing, there were too few staff members for the task.

When observers were present at the time of testing, the variability in student motivation made a strong impression on them. There were often no consequences for the student; testing was almost never linked to grading. Many students appeared to regard the assessment as an unimportant evaluation and therefore put out less effort.

By and large, teachers seemed uninterested in the outcome of the tests. They frequently told us that they distrusted standardized achievement tests; school officials often failed to provide teachers with the results for their classrooms. Some of the teachers were uninterested in the results of the content-referenced tests; this was probably a product of our failure to involve them sufficiently in the development of the tests.

Teachers rarely used results of even content-referenced tests as formative evaluation for the following year. The teachers' failure to use the test results was partly our fault because scoring and analyzing the tests was a very time-consuming process. We were very slow in returning information to them on their own classes. Even when they were interested, they were sometimes put off by the format of the results and seemed unprepared to deal with numbers and what they represented. If teachers are to use external assessments constructively, it will be necessary to work with them in developing the requisite skills to interpret the results.

Match of Tests and Curriculum

Perhaps the most serious criticism of achievement tests is that they often are a poor match to the curriculum. There are two kinds of mismatches: The test may not reflect what students were supposed to do and learn in the curriculum as envisioned by the curriculum developer, or the test may reflect the intended curriculum, but the teacher may have departed from that curriculum sufficiently in topics or emphasis so that the test does not match student experiences in the classroom.

The match of the test to the intended curriculum is particularly problematic when the goal of the curriculum is the development of higher-order thinking skills. Because CI curricula have always emphasized goals of higher-order thinking, the ability to solve uncertain problems as a group, and the grasp of abstract concepts, we were in deep trouble using paper-and-pencil, multiple-choice instruments administered to individuals as the principal measure of achievement. The very form of the test did not complement the form of the goals of instruction. According to Glaser and Silver (1994), multiple-choice formats are severely limited in their relationship to goals such as the development of complex reasoning. Testing experts readily admit that standardized achievement tests do not measure these kinds of objectives at all well. For example, Shepard (1989) describes needed reforms in mathematics assessment.

> Twenty years ago, standardized tests served as reasonable indicators of student learning. In today's political climate, tests are inadequate and misleading as measures of achievement. Assessment tasks should be redesigned—indeed, are being redesigned—to more closely resemble real learning tasks. Tests should require more complex and challenging mental processes from students. They should acknowledge more than one approach or one right answer and should place more emphasis on uncoached explanations and real student products. (pp. 6–7)

Assessment specialists, in response to this challenge of measuring more than factual knowledge, are now working with portfolios and performance assessment. Portfolio techniques, although promising, have problems of unreliability as well as lack of legitimacy in the eyes of the outside world. Moreover, the current work is experimental, while the most common practices in current assessment of achievement have changed little in the past 50 years (Glaser & Silver, 1994).

Within the confines of a written instrument, we have tried in a number of different ways to capture higher-order thinking. In the earliest evaluation of *FO/D*, for example, De Avila (De Avila, Cohen, & Intili, 1981) used the

Cartoon Conservation Scale (De Avila & Pulos, 1978), a measure of conceptual development. The test is made up of pictures, and the child selects the correct picture answer. In the middle schools, the analogy items in the social studies tests used simple vocabulary but required very abstract thinking. In the middle school science tests, students had to demonstrate their understanding of concepts when they answered open-ended questions. Finally, in the mathematics test, students had to provide a rationale for their answers. Evaluation of student responses included criteria such as strategic thinking as well as communication.

As soon as there are comparison classrooms included in the design, an additional problem arises. If the comparison classrooms do not receive the same curricular treatment, one can only assess that part of the knowledge or skills that one can assume was covered in all classrooms. In the case of curricula created for seventh-grade social studies, this dilemma forced us to emphasize on the tests factual knowledge that was in the state-adopted textbook. Many of the concepts central to the multiple-ability curricula were not represented in the test. Only the use of analogies allowed us to include some abstract concepts presented by the textbook and represented in our curricula. Precisely these items showed the unique effects of CI.

The life sciences and mathematics curricula for the middle school had no counterpart in other classrooms, so comparisons were impossible. However, mismatches between the content of the test and instruction remained. The use of the QUASAR cognitive assessment instrument in mathematics (Lane, Liu, Stone, & Ankenmann, 1993) had the limitation of representing only an approximation of the formal curriculum. As explained in Chapter 10, the assessment instrument for mathematics was developed independently of the curriculum. Bianchini's content-referenced tests in the Middle Grades Life Science Curriculum (see Chapter 10) were a better match. Because teachers often taught only selected activities and textual materials from the larger units, sometimes the students were tested on materials they had never experienced. Where the match of test to the implemented curriculum was good, as in the small Systems unit, the results were excellent.

Students' Awareness of Criteria for Evaluation

If the matching problem just described could have been solved, we believe that the achievement results would have looked even more favorable. However, there is still something critically wrong with the evaluation process: The students have no chance to learn the criteria for evaluation. This is particularly the case when the researcher fashions an assessment and asks the teacher to administer it. If it were a teacher-made test, the teacher would warn the students that they had better pay attention to particular skills because they would be on the test.

Sociological theory provides a strong basis for giving students explicit criteria. According to the theory of evaluation and authority in organizations, setting the criteria is a critical feature of the evaluation cycle (Dornbusch & Scott, 1975). "Criteria setting refers to the process of determining which properties will be taken into account in evaluating task performance" (Natriello & Dornbusch, 1984, p. 44). Unless criteria are clear, the person being evaluated is unlikely to perceive the evaluations made as soundly based. In the classroom, not only must the students know what the criteria are, but they must receive evaluations that are sufficiently frequent and challenging to direct their efforts (Natriello & Dornbusch, 1984). According to the theory, lack of clear criteria and infrequent evaluations, even if they relate to the criteria, will undermine student effort. From a pedagogical perspective, preparation for a test based on a unit of groupwork is inadequate if students work their way through the group tasks with no clear idea of what aspects of those tasks will be evaluated and with few opportunities to receive information on how well they are doing according to those criteria.

Cultural Capital × Measurement Interaction

There is one remaining criticism of the use of achievement tests as a measure of learning outcomes of a particular set of educational experiences. Even if there is an excellent match between the test and the intended and implemented curriculum, even if there is some strong basis of comparison, and even if students are well aware of the criteria used in the evaluation, the researcher must still contend with what the student brings to the experience of taking a test. Ideally, an assessment should be able to find out what students have learned independent of the limitations they may have in taking tests. For example, students reading well below grade level typically have difficulty reading a test. Questions that are open-ended do not solve this problem, because the answers require writing skills.

Thus, it is difficult to separate students' understanding of concepts from their ability to read and comprehend the test and their ability to write clearly. We have consistently found correlations between reading scores and pretest and posttest scores as well as gain scores. We have observed these relationships even when other variables affecting posttest scores were controlled. Students who lacked English proficiency were at a distinct disadvantage in test taking. (The exception was Spanish-speaking students who took the Spanish language version of some of our tests.)

Beyond these obvious factors, a form of cultural capital is relevant to test taking. Teachers report that many lower-class children do not see the importance of making an effort on tests. Particularly in the case of very young students from parents with little formal education, it is necessary to explain to them why it is important to try hard on a test. According to the observers, some teachers of elementary schools students did this when administering the content-referenced test as a measure of *FO/D*. However, other teachers did not take the time to motivate students, and the children made little effort to perform well.

Another form of cultural capital affects test taking. The test items sometimes assume knowledge that has not been explicitly taught by the teacher or the textbooks. Without the cultural resources from outside of school, students may simply not have the requisite knowledge to perform well on these items. The best example of this problem was our discovery that many seventh graders did not understand who the Muslims were or that there was a Muslim religion. Teachers had assumed this as general cultural knowledge. This lack of information on the part of some students undermined their ability to understand the test items in connection with the unit on the Crusades.

In the psychological literature, there is much discussion of interaction between the student's ability and the treatment offered by the teacher. In this case, I am positing an interaction effect between the student's cultural and linguistic background and the assessment instrument itself. We have made numerous attempts to get around this problem, including reading the test items out loud, using pictorial items, and simplifying the language but not the concepts on the test. None of these devices has completely removed the effects of reading on test scores.

ALTERNATIVE ASSESSMENT

One overall conclusion of this critique is the fundamental limitation of an assessment created by outsiders. Unless the teacher has a strong role in assessment, there will always be gaps between what the students experience and the nature of the assessment. Of course, one might imagine loss of autonomy of the teacher and a standardized form of instruction that would guarantee a match between instruction and assessment. However, such a solution is antithetical to the CI model.

The analysis of student knowledge of the criteria of evaluation leads to a second conclusion: Assessment should be part of instruction. To tie assessment more closely to instruction means that the process of assessment must be in the hands of the teacher. Moreover, students should actively participate in the process of assessment, and not just be objects of evaluation.

The sociological theory of authority and evaluation (adapted from Dornbusch & Scott, 1975) that program staff use in providing feedback to teachers (see Chapters 2 and 14) can help in constructing a model for student participation in assessment. To apply these principles to students in order to produce maximum effort to improve, several features of the evaluation system must be in place.

1. Criteria for evaluation must be absolutely clear.
2. Students must perceive criteria as fair and valid.
3. There must be an adequate sampling of work.
4. Students must receive specific feedback on how well they are meeting these criteria.

If all these conditions are in place, students will perceive feedback as soundly based. To the extent that they do, they will put out more effort.

The general implications of this theoretical work are clear. Teachers must develop specific criteria for evaluation. They have to present these criteria in such a way that students will see them as fair and valid. Furthermore, evaluation must be an ongoing process in which students have multiple opportunities to meet these criteria and receive feedback on how well they are doing.

These recommendations for teachers imply the elimination of the sharp distinction between assessment and instruction. Assessment becomes part and parcel of the way teachers think about what they are trying to teach and the way they provide feedback to individuals and groups. Moreover, if an alternative assessment requires that teachers make students aware of the criteria for evaluation and that they give students practice in using those criteria, then teachers must change not only assessment but the way they teach. These changes in teaching constitute an advanced form of professional development.

My emphasis on students having access to criteria for evaluation is not a new idea. Glaser and Silver (1994) recommend that the performance criteria used in evaluation be evident to students and teachers. The National Council of Teachers of Mathematics (1993) has specified in their assessment standards that students should know what they are to learn and how they will be expected to demonstrate their learning. Moreover, they recommend that both content and performance standards be openly developed and communicated. Those carrying out assessments should provide sample tasks, scoring criteria, and illustrations of student work.

Assessment of a Statistics Unit

Nancy Moffat from the Professional Development Center of Scottsdale, Arizona's school district and Karen Koellner, a middle school teacher of mathematics, have developed and tested a model assessment (Koellner & Moffat, 1995) of the multiple-ability unit on statistics created for CI (Windows on the World, Program for Complex Instruction, n.d.). It was this excellent example that brought me to think of an alternative model of assessment using sociological theory.

Moffat studied the unit on statistics very carefully. She laid out the objectives of the unit as a whole and the objectives of each group task. For example, one objective specified that students will communicate conclusions based on data by forming arguments, by making decisions, and by developing summary descriptions as evidenced in their group discourse, writing activities, and oral presentation to the class. The following are examples of objectives for specific group tasks: design good interview questions; organize and represent data in multiple ways.

For each short-term objective, Koellner and Moffat designed rubrics to be used by the students so that they could assess their own work and see how well they were doing on achieving these objectives. Using these rubrics, students gave a numeric evaluation, from 3–5, to their own individual reports and to the group products. For the criterion, "I will organize and represent the data in multiple ways," the rubrics were as follows:

5. I can develop multiple data organizers which are creative, easy to read, and provide everyone with a place to respond. I can use a variety of plots and graphs for the data set, discuss the impressions given by each, and decide which ones would be most useful in developing the meaning of the information. I can adjust the scale and switch the axis on which the data is labeled to produce the most dramatic results.
4. I can develop data organizers that provide everyone a place to respond. I can transpose this information into several different graphs.
3. I can develop data organizers with assistance that provide everyone a place to respond. I can transpose the data into a bar or circle graph. (Koellner & Moffat, 1995, p. 14)

If students felt they could not score their individual report as a 3 or above, they explained on the back of their paper the nature of the problem they were experiencing in writing. There were no rubrics provided below 3, thus conveying to students the absolute standards they must meet.

The teacher made the objectives clear to the students by giving them a rationale for the activities they were to carry out as well as a specific set of criteria and rubrics for self-evaluation. Students had multiple opportunities to assess individual reports and group presentations. If they were having difficulties, the system allowed for specific feedback from the teacher. The teacher used the same rubrics in assessing written assignments and quizzes.

Theoretically, this example meets the criteria of a soundly based evaluation. Under these conditions, it is not surprising that students achieved spectacular gains from a pre- to a posttest.

Assessment as Professional Development

Once teachers have developed clarity about what students are supposed to be learning and how one can judge the extent to which they have progressed, making up an assessment instrument is neither mysterious nor difficult. They simply choose assessment tasks, much like those the students have carried out, that have the same objectives and can be evaluated with the same rubrics.

Given support by subject matter experts, teachers can benefit from working together to analyze units, develop criteria, and score tests. First, the act of analyzing what they want students to gain from each task should reveal teachers' assumptions about what skills students must have in order to reach these goals. For example, careful analysis of the multiple-ability tasks in the life sciences units reveals that the teachers presume that students know how to construct a carefully labeled diagram. Perhaps a team of teachers working together on the analysis will also plan a simple preparatory exercise to ensure that students have this requisite skill.

Second, for teachers who do not have strong subject matter preparation, it would be particularly good to work together with other experienced teachers and subject matter specialists. They would have the chance to develop a deeper understanding of the individual tasks as well as of the central concepts. Equally important, they would acquire much better ideas about what to say to groups that are foundering or how to respond to group presentations. Having worked out concepts and skills underlying the instruction so that they will be clear to students, teachers will undoubtedly be clearer about this intellectual material.

Third, by scoring tests together, teachers would learn how to look at the results as formative evaluation. When some teachers were more successful than others in producing high scores on particular objectives and tasks, the teachers would discuss particular strategies for orienting the class and for providing feedback that were associated with better results. These discussions might well produce an even sharper focus to the instruction the next time the unit was taught.

Last, teachers who have such a good understanding of the assessment make ideal spokespersons to parents and district officials. They would be able to describe in detail what skills have been acquired and how the tests reflect that learning. They would be able to show improvements with simple measures such as the number and percentage of well-answered items before and after the unit. Even more important, they would be able to document the percentage of students performing well according to specific criteria. This strategy not only should serve educational purposes, but should be adequate to create legitimacy for the curriculum and teaching approach in the minds of parents and school people.

Meeting the Criticisms

How does this proposed method of assessment meet the criticisms developed in this chapter? One criticism had to do with the difficulty of assessing gains in absolute terms. In this proposed model, gains from pre- to posttest should be easily interpretable in absolute terms. For example, for the statistics unit taught by Koellner and Moffat, they will be able to say what percentage of students, before and after the unit, was able, without assistance, to organize data with a place for everyone to respond. For a parent conference, they will be able to describe exactly what the student can do after completing the unit, according to the rubric score he or she received for each item. It would also be possible to look at a summary score and to talk about how well the student had achieved the overall goal of the unit.

A second criticism had to do with the variability in the conditions of testing. In the proposed model, the test would be tightly tied to the grading system, so that students would have some stake in the test. Moreover, insofar as students perceived the evaluations they received as soundly based, they should regard the test as an important evaluation. Theoretically, this should also act to increase student effort.

A third criticism was the central problem of a weak match between curriculum and assessment. Putting the assessment in the hands of the teacher serves to increase the match between the test and the instruction. Integrating assessment and instruction and choosing formats that are more directly aligned with instructional tasks are widely recommended goals (Glaser & Silver, 1994). In addition, the new emphasis in instruction on rubrics and self-evaluation means that the very content of the assessment is part and parcel of everyday activities. The use of rubrics that focus on higher-order skills, as they appear in particular subject matters, handles the problem of assessment of those skills relatively well. As students meet similar rubrics in different tasks, they should develop an awareness of how these skills apply in multiple contexts.

A fourth criticism pointed to the typical lack of awareness in students of the criteria used in the evaluation. Obviously, if students use rubrics to evaluate their own and group products, and if these rubrics are discussed during feedback, most of the students will gain clarity about the criteria. Somewhat less obvious is the way the proposal meets the criticism of cultural capital in interaction with the test itself. If teachers are able to see what underlying knowledge and skills are assumed as they do their initial analyses of the tasks, they should be able to design instruction to fill in some of the missing knowledge for the class as a whole. Individual students in CI can use other group members as valuable resources in making up for missing background knowledge. (It is legitimate to ask for assistance in writing individual reports.) In addition, if students have repeated practice with opportunities for feedback in carrying out tasks similar to those on the test, then the test will not have words and concepts that are entirely new to the students. If the student is struggling with the individual report, the self-evaluation process should be an early warning system for the teacher, indicating the need for individual attention.

SOLVING PROBLEMS OF ASSESSMENT

This chapter started out with the demand for assessment of achievement that will appear as legitimate in the eyes of constituents of the Program for Complex Instruction. If we move away from standardized assessments, how can we solve this problem?

I propose that the need of parents and local school people to know what students have learned, can be met by examining gains in meeting criteria between pre- and posttests in particular classrooms. With some small degree of standardization, wider audiences can find out what students are learning in CI classrooms in different schools and districts. The developer of each multiple-ability unit can include with the materials, rubrics for understanding the big idea underlying the unit, as well as test items. The teacher will combine these rubrics and test items with his or her own rubrics and items for objectives arising out of particular group activities. We can then assess how well students in a variety of settings working with a particular unit grasped the central concepts. A potential drawback of this mode of evaluation across classrooms is that it does not allow for comparison classrooms unless non-CI teachers attempt to meet the same criteria without CI strategies. Evaluation of the proposed model of assessment is a current focus of the Program for Complex Instruction.

Much about the proposed assessment may turn out to be unrealistic when we try it out and evaluate it carefully. Yet, it seems to me that this more theoretical approach uniting assessment and instruction is a significant advance. Of course, this theoretical approach will not be successful without extensive practical experience in working with teachers and classrooms. The proposed solution to the assessment problem would never have been created without the input of talented teachers who have worked closely with us over the years.

CHAPTER 12

The Relationship of Talk and Status to Second Language Acquisition of Young Children

H. Andrea Neves

At the present time more and more children who are learning English as a second language are enrolling in U.S. schools. By the year 2026, language minority students will make up nearly a quarter of our student body. In the state of California alone, these students are projected to increase to 63% of the K–12 student population by the end of the 1990s (Garcia, 1994). How to teach these children English in the most efficient manner is of primary concern to schools. Many limited-English-speaking children who are placed in regular English-speaking classrooms achieve poorly in English as well as in subject matter areas. In many schools, these children are segregated from their English-speaking classmates for bilingual instruction. In other classrooms, non-English-speaking children are "pulled out" of the regular classroom for special lessons in English as a Second Language (ESL) (Nieto, 1992).

Researchers of second language acquisition recognize that social environmental factors are crucial in second language acquisition (Garcia, 1994; Pease-Alvarez, Garcia, & Espinoza, 1991; Villegas, 1991; Wong-Fillmore & Valadez, 1986). They agree that second language learners must be exposed to peers who speak the language and that this exposure can influence the kind of language acquired and the speed with which it is acquired (Hatch, 1977). Children who chose to use the second language more frequently in social settings with speakers of that language acquired it faster (Wong-Fillmore, 1976). Experts recognize that language acquisition occurs when language is used for what it was designed: communication.

THE INSTRUCTIONAL CONTEXT

Educators are concerned with the kind of curricula and classroom instructional strategies that provide an environment conducive to second language learning. Cazden (1979, 1988) suggests that science curricula that focus on experimentation might be the optimum classroom environment for language learning. Here children work together, manipulate objects, and are exposed to clear referents for the nouns and verbs in classroom discourse. Others call for a more responsive pedagogy for academic learning that requires a redefinition of the instructor's role, with an emphasis on discussion in the classroom. Here classrooms are organized to take advantage of natural and spontaneous interactions between teacher and students and among students. In these classrooms, the teachers act as facilitators of learning rather than as transmitters of knowledge (Garcia, 1994).

In the 1970s and 1980s, researchers, for example, Schumann (1976), Wagner-Gough and Hatch (1975), Larsen-Freeman (1976), Seliger (1977), and Krashen (1976, 1981, 1982), began to focus on issues such as native speaker interaction frequency, native speaker/nonnative speaker interaction (children and adults), and instruction as a medium of communication. Their findings indicate that the input to which a learner is exposed is an important variable that influences second language acquisition. The frequency of input, the quality of input, and how that input structures the learner's responses (output) all play an important role.

Wong-Fillmore's (1976) findings indicate that child speech is a better kind of linguistic input than adult speech for the acquisition of a child's second language. In her study of Spanish-speaking children learning English, the strongest motivation for children to learn language was to use it for interpersonal communication. She found that the success or failure of the learners' efforts depended in good part on their ability to establish and maintain social contact with the people who could give them the input and the contexts they needed for learning the new language. In her study, the successful learner gained access to the needed input by seeking out interaction with English speakers and maintaining contact once it was established.

Seliger (1977) showed that "high input generators" are the more successful second language (L2) learners. High input generators are "active learners who utilize the language environment, both formal and natural, for practice by interacting and getting others to use language with them" (p. 274). These learners get both the necessary input and the opportunity for involvement and practice. Given the importance of interaction to the English language development of second language learners, interaction in the context of complex instruction classrooms also should lead to English language development.

In review, this literature strongly suggests that a language-enriched environment provides a context for second language learning. In this chapter, I test the following general hypothesis:

> Interaction in the context of a mixed-language group engaged in a collective task will be associated with English language development for the second language learner.

My hypothesis follows directly from this discussion of the importance of speaking with peers in developing new language skills. I test this general hypothesis in two ways. First, among second language learners, I examine the correlations between their rate of talk in Spanish and English and their gains in English proficiency. Second, I examine the rates of talk and the gains in English proficiency for subgroups of students who differ as to initial proficiency in the two languages.

Many of the children who were in the sample for this study spoke both English and Spanish. The degree of their dual language proficiency must be considered, as numerous studies indicate that the development of competence in a second language is partially a function of the competence already developed in the first language (Cummins, 1979, 1991; Hebert et al., 1976; Ramirez, Yuen, Ramey, & Pasta, 1991; Sarkela & Kuusinen, 1980; Skutnabb-Kangas & Toukomaa, 1976).

METHODOLOGY

For my analyses, I used data collected in the pilot study of the Program for Complex Instruction in the 1979–80 school year, Grades 2–5. The overall design strategy was to analyze weekly observations of selected target children as they interacted with the curriculum, their peers, and adults in the classroom. The curriculum used was *Finding Out/Descubrimiento* (De Avila & Duncan, 1982b), a bilingual Spanish and English, math and science curriculum designed to teach thinking skills. I correlated observational data with language proficiency as measured by scores on the Language Assessment Scales (LAS) (De Avila & Duncan, 1977). This instrument is one of four approved by the State of California for use in assessing dual language (English and Spanish) proficiency.

Setting and Sample

The setting for the study was nine bilingual education classrooms representing five school districts in the area of San Jose, California. The children were largely of Hispanic descent, with a small proportion of Anglo, African-American, and Asian students. Parental background was working class and lower white collar.

Student groups were mixed as to linguistic status with monolingual English speakers, limited-English speakers, Spanish speakers, and mixed-proficiency bilinguals all in the same group. The students could use either Spanish or English in communicating. Because the materials and student communication represented two languages, a second language learner had multiple ways to comprehend what English speakers were saying. The curriculum, *FO/D*, was essentially the same as that described in previous chapters. However, students were not assigned to specific groups, but moved on individually to new learning centers where there were fewer than five students working. Students were told to ask each other for assistance and to give assistance. All teachers involved in the study were bilingual. A set of 99 target children constitute the sample of this study.

Measures

The Target Student Instrument (see Appendix C) was the major source of data. While not specifically designed to measure all possible sources of input, it does provide information on the verbal interactions (in Spanish and English) and behavioral patterns of the target children per 3 minutes of observation (see also Chapter 5 for a detailed description). In this version of the instrument, observers indicated whether Spanish or English was used by each target student. Interaction variables included target child talk in English and Spanish.

I constructed the variable "target child talk in English" by adding together the frequencies for child talk variables: talks about the tasks to other students or adults; requests assistance from either students or adults; offers or gives assistance to other students; talks about nontask-related matters to either students or adults. Mean rates were calculated by dividing total frequencies by the number of observations for an individual student. The variable called "target child talk in Spanish" was constructed in a parallel fashion.

Raw gain scores from the LAS (De Avila & Duncan, 1977) indicated gains in English language proficiency. The LAS is an individually administered test that measures the overall ability to communicate. De Avila and Duncan (1982a) demonstrated the validity and reliability of the individual subscales of the instrument through numerous studies. The LAS is one of the few tests for young children that provides, through the story retelling task, a global measure of the ability to communicate. The publishers were able to establish interrater reliability for the scoring of the story retelling task (which accounts for 50% of the total score).

RESULTS

This analysis omits from the sample children with a pretest score of 75 or over on the English LAS. These children, who are regarded as English proficient, were at the ceiling of the test and could not very well show gain scores. Many students who were not proficient in English on the pretest were also not proficient in Spanish. This seems counter-intuitive in a largely segregated Hispanic setting, but is a well-known finding to those who use the

LAS. Table 12.1 provides some descriptive statistics of the pre- and posttest scores on the LAS as well as the gain scores and the rates of talk in English and Spanish. There is a general upward shift in English proficiency over time for these second language learners, from an average score of 57.67 to 65.17. On the posttest 41% of the children were in the two highest categories of performance. In the context of groups containing English and Spanish speakers, there was talk in Spanish (1.70 times per 3 minutes) as well as in English (2.79 per 3 minutes). However, English talk was much more common than Spanish talk.

Next I examined the relationship between talk and measures of English proficiency. Table 12.2 presents a Pearson correlation matrix of the English and Spanish talk variables, pretest and posttest scores in English, and English gain scores. The correlations between rates of talk in each language and the gain scores provide one test of the general hypothesis.

English language pretest scores and posttest scores are significantly correlated. Evidently, those students who started out high on the pretest ended up high on the posttest. The strong correlation between English posttest scores and gain scores ($r = .52, p < .001$) suggests that children in the 65–74 range were more likely to move into the 85–100 range on the posttest than into lower ranges, where their gains would be smaller. Target child talk in English and English pretest scores were highly intercorrelated.

There is *no association* between children talking in English and gain scores in English. However, there is a statistically significant association between rate of talking in Spanish and gains in English proficiency ($r = .24, p < .05$). Thus, the hypothesis was not supported for the rate of English talk but was supported for Spanish talk. In other words, the more frequently the students spoke in Spanish, the higher were their gains in English language proficiency.

Table 12.1: Descriptive Statistics of Talk Variables, Pretest, Posttest, and Gain Scores on LAS: For Target Students Who Were Not Proficient in English (*n* = 64)

Variable	Mean	SD
Target Child English Talk	2.79	2.07
Target Child Spanish Talk	1.70	1.90
Pretest LAS Spanish	57.67	26.17
Pretest LAS English	52.81	21.54
Posttest LAS English	65.17	24.70
Gains in LAS English	12.36	17.57

Table 12.2: Intercorrelation of Study Variables ($n = 64$)

		1	2	3	4	5
1	Target Child English	1.00	—[a]	.63***	.56***	.007
2	Target Child Spanish		1.00	-.70**	-.45***	.24*
3	Pretest English			1.00	.72***	-.21*
4	Posttest English				1.00	.52***
5	English Gain Score					1.00

[a]Data not available
*$p<.05$; **$p<.01$; ***$p<.001$

The relationship between rate of talking in Spanish and gain score in English suggests that when testing hypotheses about the relationship of talk to gains in English proficiency, one should take into account the initial linguistic status of the child in both languages. I now turn to a second test of the hypothesis that takes into account the child's linguistic status in both English and Spanish.

Relative Language Proficiency in English and Spanish

The simultaneous consideration of proficiency in English and Spanish is based on the assumption that the assessment of both English and Spanish can be made in parallel fashion (that is, proficiency scores are equivalent across the two languages) (De Avila, Cohen, & Intili, 1981). The assessment of linguistic proficiency of target children took place prior to the *FO/D* curriculum. The results of this assessment are translated to a 5-point scale for each language, which produces a 5 × 5 matrix where both languages are considered simultaneously. The procedure for groupings of linguistic categories is based on De Avila and Duncan (1982a). The linguistic categories were the following: English monolinguals ($n = 28$); Spanish monolinguals ($n = 11$); mixed limited ($n = 30$); minimal ($n = 13$); and bilingual ($n = 16$).

Monolinguals showed "native-like" proficiency in one language, with only minimal proficiency in the other. Mixed limited were limited in both languages, but scored at level 3 on the LAS in at least one language. Students who were classified as minimal were considered to be extremely low in both languages. For this study, children classified as bilingual scored 3 in English and 4 or 5 in Spanish, or 4 in English and 3, 4, or 5 in Spanish. The inclusion of individuals who scored 3 in one of the languages meant that there was a lower proficiency level in at least one language; that is, bilinguals are proficient in both languages but not all of them are at the highest levels.

For this second test of the hypothesis, all target students are included. When I divided the sample according to these linguistic categories, there were too few cases within any one category to conduct correlational analysis. Moreover, I could not conduct regressions with this categorical variable. Therefore, I examined the hypothesis using three analytical strategies.

1. An ANOVA that examined the effect of linguistic category on gain scores.
2. Isolation of those subgroups whose gain scores were significantly different from those of other groups.
3. Cross-tabulation of talk rates and gain score rates for each subgroup.

A one-way analysis of variance showed that language group had a statistically significant effect on gains in English proficiency ($F = 4.85, p = .001$). This means that the gains for groups were significantly different despite high standard deviations. Carrying out my second analytical strategy, I determined which language group(s) were different. An a posteriori contrast test, Least-Significant Difference (LSD), showed that the mean for the group of Spanish monolingual children was significantly different from the means of the bilingual group, the English monolingual group, and the group called mixed limited ($p = .05$). The minimal group and the mixed-limited group were both statistically different from the English monolingual group. The English monolingual group was distinctive by virtue of its low gain score, a ceiling effect.

Table 12.3 is the cross-tabulation of rates of talk and gain scores in English proficiency for each linguistic group. Also included in this table are the total rates of talk, which consist of the sum of the rates in each language. Notable in this table is the very large English gain score for the Spanish monolinguals

Table 12.3: Mean Rates of Spanish and English Talk, Gain Score by Language Group

Language Group	n	Spanish Talk	English Talk	Total Talk	English Gain
Bilingual	11	1.14	4.75	5.89	7.25
Minimal	13	1.91	2.89	4.80	12.92
Mixed Limited	31	1.45	4.31	5.77	10.10
English Monolingual	28	.19	5.86	6.05	1.57
Spanish Monolingual	11	4.60	1.38	5.98	21.45

(21.45). The Spanish monolinguals' large gain may be to a certain extent a function of a "floor effect" on the LAS measure. In other words, these children, in comparison to the English monolingual and bilingual children, could make the most gains on the LAS. However, in comparing the Spanish monolinguals with the mixed-limited group, whose mean gain was 10.10, and the minimals, whose mean gain was 12.92, the tremendous gain of the Spanish monolinguals is harder to explain as an artifact of the test. It is twice as great as the average gain for the mixed-limited group.

As would be expected in the hypothesis, the group with the largest gain scores in English had the highest rates of talk in Spanish—the Spanish monolinguals. They had, however, the lowest rates of talk in English. Students in the minimal category had the next highest average gains in English and the second highest rate of talking in Spanish. Thus, this test of the hypothesis also suggests that talk in Spanish, especially for the Spanish monolinguals, was associated with gains in English proficiency. However, the cross-tabulation leaves open the issue of whether those particular Spanish monolinguals who talked more, gained more in English. I retested the hypothesis for the small number of students within each category using correlation. For the Spanish monolingual group, the correlation between total talk and gains in English was significant ($r = .52, p < .05$). There were also positive, albeit not statistically significant, correlations for the bilingual and minimal groups. The number of students within each of these categories is quite small. However, we can compare the average gain scores for Spanish monolingual students who had high and low rates of talk divided according to the median score of 5.75. Here we are comparing six children who had a high rate of talk, with five children who had a relatively low rate. Despite these very small numbers, the average learning gain of the more talkative students among the Spanish monolinguals is an astonishing 33.1, while the average gain of the less talkative students in this category was only 7.40.

The Puzzle of the Minimals

The minimals, for whom neither language was well developed, had the lowest rates of total talk, while the Spanish monolinguals had as high a score on the total talk index as the English monolinguals. To explore the issue of why total talk rates for the minimals was so depressed, the next analysis examined low social status as a possible explanation for low rates of talk. Table 12.4 presents the means, standard deviations, and minimum and maximum scores of the costatus variable by language group. The minimal group had the lowest mean score on the costatus variable (4.77), while the bilinguals had the highest (7.00), followed closely by the English monolinguals (6.75).

Table 12.4: Descriptive Statistics for Costatus by Language Group

Language Group	n	Mean	SD	Minimum	Maximum
Bilingual	16	7.00	2.07	3.00	10.00
English Monolingual	28	6.75	2.15	3.00	10.00
Spanish Monolingual	11	5.82	2.09	3.00	10.00
Mixed Limited	31	5.61	2.20	2.00	10.00
Minimal	13	4.77	2.20	2.00	9.00

A one-way analysis of variance showed that language group had a statistically significant effect on status. An a posteriori contrast test showed that the means for the English monolinguals and the bilinguals were significantly different from the means for the minimals and the mixed-limited group. They were not significantly different from the mean for the Spanish monolinguals. It should be noted that these were all classrooms of the Bilingual Consortium in San Jose, California, where teachers made a tremendous effort to increase the status of the Spanish language. The high status of the Spanish monolinguals may be a consequence of that effort.

DISCUSSION

The data teach a general lesson: It is essential to look at the joint standing of students on two languages when studying the process of language acquisition. Talk rates, English language gains, and the strength of the relationship between these two variables differ by language group. For example, the Spanish monolinguals have higher rates of talk and higher English language gain scores than the minimals and the mixed-limited group. Moreover, they appear to benefit from the talk, as shown by the significant relationship between talk and English language gains. In contrast, the same relationship is not significant for the minimals and the mixed-limited group. The low talk rates of the minimals and to a lesser extent of the mixed-limited group could be explained by their low status or, alternatively, by poor language development, which made it difficult for them to interact. A separate analysis showed that the low total talk rate for this group was not due to particularly low rates of adult initiation toward the children. It is not possible to ascertain from the data which is the better explanation. If this depressed talk rate is a function of the children's low social status, there are ways to treat the problem. If, however, the underlying cause is developmental, no simple classroom intervention is likely to be effective.

The problem with testing any prediction regarding talk is that a minimal talk base rate for gains in language is unknown. We do not know how much talk is needed for gains to take place. It is possible that for some children, growth in English proficiency is not affected by the amount of verbal practice. Also, there is a difference between overt and covert language rehearsal. Krashen (1982) speaks of a silent period where children build up competence in the second language via listening, by understanding the language around them. According to Krashen, speaking ability emerges on its own after enough competence has been developed by listening and understanding. As previously stated, this covert practice is difficult to measure.

Talking in Spanish and Learning English

Perhaps the most striking finding of this study is that monolingual Spanish-speaking children who talk mostly in Spanish show the largest gains in English language proficiency. On the surface this finding would appear to be counterintuitive. However, CI classrooms are linguistically rich settings. The Spanish-speaking children hear both English and Spanish languages in reference to a specific task and a specific set of manipulatives and realia. Chances are that their receptive language developed greatly as a result of the setting.

Research by Cummins (1991) provides further explanation for this finding. Cummins argues that instruction in Spanish, which develops Spanish skills, also develops deeper conceptual and linguistic proficiency that is, in turn, strongly related to the later development of English proficiency. It would seem that knowing one language well helps in the acquisition of a second language. According to Cummins (1979), this "underlying proficiency" makes possible the transfer of cognitive, academic, and linguistic skills across languages. In another analysis of academic achievement (gains on the California Test of Basic Skills), the monolingual Spanish speakers made the largest mean gain in reading comprehension (8.67) as compared with the English monolinguals (6.35), bilinguals (7.58), minimals (7.38) and mixed-limited group (3.85). In summary, based on these results, it would seem that children's facility in Spanish, in conjunction with the CI setting, may be a precursor to their development of English.

The second major finding of this study is that the minimals, who test poorly in both languages, and to a lesser extent the mixed-limited group, make lesser gains in English proficiency than do the Spanish monolinguals; they talk less than others in either language. My analysis, based on the relative language proficiency of the students, indicates that students who are low in both Spanish and English have low status, while monolingual and bilingual students do not. Cummins (1979), using a concept he calls "negative" bilingualism, has tried to explain why the former students have lower rates of talk. He speaks of a threshold of language proficiency that bilinguals must attain before positive consequences of bilingualism can be realized. According to Cummins, results of negative bilingualism are found among language minority students whose mother tongue is gradually being replaced by the dominant language (subtractive bilingualism). In these situations, children develop low levels of language proficiency in both languages. In studies where cognitive advantages have been documented, students continued to develop their mother language while acquiring the second language (additive bilingualism). This "threshold hypothesis" assumes that those aspects of bilingualism that might positively influence cognitive growth are unlikely to come into effect until children have attained a certain minimum or threshold of proficiency in the two languages. Similarly, with a low level of proficiency in both languages, the verbal interaction that these children have with the environment, in terms of both input and output, is likely to be impoverished.

Support for this position also comes from studies by De Avila and Duncan (1982a). In their comparison of monolingual and bilingual students, they found that language minority students who were proficient in both languages performed significantly better on cognitive tasks than partial bilinguals (students who have not yet become proficient in the second language) and those students who were limited in proficiency in both languages.

Limitations of the Study

Before suggesting some implications of this research, it is important to point out certain limitations of the study. The scores from the Language Assessment Scales may be too gross a measure for this type of analysis. The fact that language groups were formed based on cutoff points means that a student may be categorized as minimal, mixed limited, monolingual, or bilingual based on a single point. For future studies, a finer grained analysis would be preferable.

In attempting to demonstrate that "high talkers" within each language group gained more in English language proficiency, I was aware that the size of the sample was extremely small for the number of cells. Such a small sample makes it difficult to show statistical significance in computing correlations. The sample size was also a barrier to some more sophisticated type of multivariate analysis.

IMPLICATIONS

Those who argue that instruction in the mother language will impede English acquisition may not realize that experience or instruction in the first language may actually promote development of both languages, given adequate motivation and exposure to both. It would seem that for these students, the *FO/D* curriculum, which allows for interaction in either Spanish or English, lets them acquire knowledge in subject matter, while exposing them to both languages. The outcome is greater English proficiency.

Another important implication is the need to recognize the necessity of exposing limited- and non-English-speaking children to peers whose English language skills are well developed. Some policy makers recommend that student grouping procedures be based on shared primary or home languages and similar levels of English proficiency. In contrast, results from this research indicate that children who interact in heterogeneous language groups learn English because they are exposed to English-speaking models. I draw this inference from the finding that in the context of mixed-language groups, the rate of talking in Spanish was significantly associated with gains in English language proficiency. Also, for Spanish monolinguals, the rate of total talk was significantly correlated with gains in English language proficiency.

Children who have difficulty in either language should have access to the curriculum in both languages. Classes should be conducted in both English and Spanish in a parallel fashion, in an attempt to ensure that the students understand the assigned tasks. Some students could and did make use of both English and Spanish activity cards. However, this would not guarantee that the students grasped the concepts in either language. The *FO/D* curriculum considers this type of student by presenting subject matter in English, Spanish, and pictograph form.

Finally, children whose language proficiency tests show them to be limited in both Spanish and English need to be studied much more closely. Are these children truly limited in both languages, or is this an artifact of the test? Hayes (1982) states that limited proficiency in both languages exists only as a concept and "observations used to indicate the existence of 'semilingualism' may be the result of limited language proficiency instruments rather than limited language proficiency" (p. 120). My findings indicate that these children are not talking or being talked to very much. Is this because they are in fact, contrary to what Hayes says, truly limited in language? The correlation of observed talk with the test classification suggests that the category of "minimal" is not a mere artifact of the testing situation. Since these children are greatly at risk in the educational system, further research is of critical importance.

CHAPTER 13

Complex Instruction and Cognitive Development

Rachel Ben-Ari

Gliker (1982) argued that Greek philosophy began in the port cities, at the crossroads of cultures, where the Greeks asked interesting and original questions as they compared their cultural practices with those of other peoples. Similarly, the meeting of children of different backgrounds and abilities in the classroom can provoke students to ask interesting and original questions. This assumption that individual differences constitute a valuable resource for intellectual growth underlies the discussion of complex instruction in this chapter.

HETEROGENEITY AND COGNITIVE DEVELOPMENT

In recent years, increased heterogeneity in the characteristics of student populations from kindergarten through university corresponds to the diverse cultural, social, and socioeconomic backgrounds of students, as well as to their different levels of academic achievement. How to provide high-quality education to this diverse student population is the challenge presently facing the educational establishment in many countries.

Some people fear that responding effectively to this challenge is an unreachable goal. Their fears stem, in part, from the belief that providing quality education in a heterogeneous classroom is a zero-sum process by which the teacher deftly maneuvers among the different educational needs of the students—needs that cannot be met simultaneously. Everyday reality in many classrooms, where teachers are unable to fit the level and the pace of instruction to the wide range of previous academic achievement, seems to lend credence to this fear. Many parents worry that students who have been academically successful are no longer intellectually challenged, thereby jeopardizing their future academic success. Furthermore, parents argue that weak students, who cannot keep up with rigorous academic requirements and who need special attention, continue to fall further behind. The conclusion seems inevitable that heterogeneity of the school population makes it difficult, if not impossible, to realize the students' intellectual potential. According to such reasoning, academic heterogeneity of the student population will water down the curriculum, disturb the effective functioning of the school, impede the intellectual performance of individuals, and undermine the pursuit of excellence.

One of the consequences of such public consternation is the demand for homogeneous grouping: ability groups within the same classroom at the elementary level, or inter- and intraschool tracking at the secondary level. In these homogeneous settings, differences among students, considered obstacles to quality education and intellectual progress, are minimized as much as possible. In contrast, complex instruction is predicated on the contention that intellectual heterogeneity is a potentially positive opportunity, which, when realized, leads to progress for all students and for the school as a whole, as well as to the attainment of intellectual and academic excellence.

However, abolishing homogeneous ability groupings or untracking and forming heterogeneous classrooms is not enough to solve the problem. Adequate educational conditions are necessary in order to turn human diversity into pedagogical advantage and a resource for intellectual growth and development. Through restructuring the learning situation, complex instruction establishes the necessary conditions for the cognitive development of students: social interaction and individual autonomy.

SOCIAL INTERACTION AND COGNITIVE DEVELOPMENT

Since the beginning of this century, researchers have advanced models of the contribution of social interaction to cognitive development. Mead (1934) was the first theorist to recognize the origins of cognitive development in the social interactions of infants. Mead argued that before the infant develops symbolic conceptualization, it engages in a "conversation of gestures" with the mother or the caretaker. This primal dialogue becomes the basis for cognition. The three major theories of how social interaction becomes relevant to learning in heterogeneous classrooms and how it contributes to cognitive development are Vygotzky's (1978) *self-regulation*, Piaget's (1954) *socio-cognitive conflict*, and Bandura's (1977) *social learning*.

Self-Regulation

Vygotzky (1978) places the origins of cognition in social interaction. He argues that the acquisition of cognitive skills occurs when children solve problems as they interact with adults or more knowledgeable peers. First as they observe adults and more advanced peers and then as they actively participate in increasingly complex tasks, children become adept at independent problem solving. This process is the transition from other-regulation to self-regulation. According to Vygotzky, talk is the most important mediator in cognitive development. In the transition from the expert giving instructions and providing guidance to final self-regulation, through a stage of inner speech, the child achieves competent functioning. Inner speech decreases over time as the child internalizes the social message and turns it into thought.

Successful self-regulation is contingent upon the existence of a zone of proximal development. Vygotzky created this concept to account for the distance between the child's ability to problem solve individually and his or her potential ability to problem solve with adult or expert guidance.

From this point of view, the optimal learning situation includes the novice, still unable to solve problems independently, and the more advanced peer or adult. The latter uses problem-solving behaviors, experiments with new approaches, and, by assigning responsibility for certain aspects of the task to the novice, encourages him or her to develop cognitive skills. When an adult or a more advanced peer facilitates the functioning of the novice so that his or her functioning is at a higher level than that achieved individually, the process is called "scaffolding." Scaffolding alleviates some of the cognitive burden experienced by the novice and occurs in two ways: First, the adult or the more capable expert assumes responsibility for parts of the problem; second, by supervising the novice's behaviors to see if they fit the task, the expert exerts metacognitive control. Through such metacognitive control, the novice becomes increasingly aware of the mental processes required by the task, thereby activating and practicing them as necessary (Vygotzky, 1962). As the novice develops more and more advanced problem-solving skills, he or she needs less help and is able to solve problems independently (Newman, Griffin, & Cole, 1989).

Vygotzky argues that higher-order, psychological functions develop through social interaction. Adults and more knowledgeable peers broker and foster the novice's development. They manage the environment and demonstrate how to interact with it, explain and give meaning to actions and experiences, call attention to the relevant dimensions of behavior, and illustrate problem-solving strategies. The acquisition of a new skill is not only added knowledge and improved functioning, but also a passage from a dialectic on the outside to an internal world. In other words, new skills help the individual handle the environment.

The Socio-Cognitive Conflict

Piaget (1926, 1968) considers social interaction a central and critical component of cognitive development. He argues that social accommodation is essential for cognitive development during the passage from the preoperational to the concrete, operational stage. As children at the preoperational phase become less egocentric, they recognize the differences and disagreements between their own ideas and those of their peers. They use this intellectual conflict to shape and reshape their thoughts and ideas to reach a more advanced level of cognition.

The encounters among peers make it possible for different ideas to emerge and for conflict to surface. This conflict has external, social aspects and internal, cognitive ones. Cognitive conflict leads to intellectual disequilibrium and to a search for resolution (Doise & Mugny, 1984). Such conflict does not necessarily mean confrontation or opposition, but rather a situation in which the child is open to change and is ready to give up previously held opinions and perspectives and to adopt new ones (Perret-Clermont, 1980). Socio-cognitive conflict occurs when children who are working on a problem together are at different cognitive levels. They approach a problem from different cognitive stances or perspectives, and use different strategies. As children disagree, discuss, explain, and persuade one another, new positions, new ideas, and deeper thinking emerge.

Researchers have documented the relationship between rate of discussion, including agreements and mutual persuasion, and cognitive processes. Light and Glachan (1985) found that children who argued about the appropriate solution to a problem developed more rational processes than children who did not argue or whose discussions focused on issues of power in the group. Bearison, Magzaman, and Filardo (in Rogoff, 1990) studied pairs of children, ages 5–7, who worked collaboratively on spatial problems; they found a relationship between socio-cognitive conflict and changes in relevant cognitive ability.

Social Learning

Social learning theory emphasizes the importance of modeling in cognitive development. According to this theory, children acquire skills through observing and imitating. Unlike the theories of learning discussed above, social learning does not rely on interaction or reciprocity among participants. Children can learn from observing others, who might not be aware that their behavior influenced someone else.

That children learn from watching the behavior of others does not necessarily mean that they will replicate that behavior. Numerous factors affect the performance of a watched behavior: expected consequences (reinforcement or punishment), personal characteristics of the imitator, and personal characteristics of the one imitated, to name a few.

Children prefer to imitate models who are socially accepted. This finding leads to the assumption that social reinforcement leads to imitation

(Bandura, 1977). Cognitive ability is an additional factor that makes children become accepted models for imitation. In support of Bandura's argument, Morrison and Kuhn (1983) found that at age 3 children already imitate competent peers and that the inclination to do so increases with age. Children tend to perform behaviors that have been gained as a result of social learning, even without outside reinforcement. A mechanism of self-regulation or self-reinforcement supports imitation as soon as the children reach a certain level of competence.

Social learning, then, requires relatively little, if any, reciprocity. That is why this approach is particularly useful in early childhood, when the child still lacks the social and cognitive skills for collaboration and cooperation.

INDEPENDENCE AND AUTONOMY:
CONDITIONS FOR COGNITIVE DEVELOPMENT

Children's cognitive development benefits from interaction. Interaction supports multiple perspectives, reveals differences, raises conflict, and forces children to confront complex situations. This confrontation is central to children's cognitive advancement, and teachers should capitalize on this event when it occurs. In order to capitalize on this interaction, it is important to eliminate factors that could potentially delay, limit, or prevent encounters of students with their peers. Adult authority (in this case, the teacher's) could be one such impediment to these encounters.

In support of this claim, Rogoff (1990) argues that children act differently in situations in which adults are in charge compared with situations without adult supervision. Without adult supervision, children are more playful, inquisitive, and divergent in their thinking, and less intent on completing the task. Such playful inquisitiveness is particularly useful for fresh and creative problem solving.

Researchers (Perret-Clermont & Schubauer-Leoni, 1981; Tudge & Rogoff, 1989) consider learning through peer interaction a promising educational approach. Peer interaction motivates students to discover, search, and exchange ideas, and to provide respectful feedback to one another. Kruger and Tomasello (1986) found that children tend to give rationales and to justify with their peers more than with adults. In peer conversations, children improve their logical, analytical abilities and their problem-solving skills (Light & Glachan, 1985). Kruger (in Rogoff, 1990) found that children who discussed moral dilemmas among themselves showed superior moral development in comparison with children who discussed such dilemmas with their mothers. These findings echo the study by French (cited in Rogoff, 1990), who found that the conversations between the children and their mothers were dominated by the mothers and were based on the mothers' opinions, whereas there were more opportunities for mutual involvement in the children's conversations among themselves.

Subbotskii (1987) conducted research in kindergartens where adults, who avoided being authoritative and interfering, imitated child-like behavior: They showed confusion and lack of self-assurance, and made blatant mistakes. In these situations, the children's behavior was more creative, and they acted with greater freedom and independence. This and other (see Rogoff, 1990) research shows that shared decision making among children, under conditions of independence and autonomy, is an important factor in social interaction and is critical to the children's cognitive development. Under such conditions, children are able to pay attention to the arguments of their peers, act in collaboration, and play roles that further problem solving. When children are without direct adult supervision, they can manipulate the rules, explore alternative strategies, and engage in true investigations.

Thus, peer learning without direction and supervision from an "all-knowing adult" creates conditions that are favorable to cognitive development. The responsibility and the need to initiate discussion, to understand, to explain, to confront, and to share with others who are also looking for answers, awaken thinking and investigation. Cognitive development occurs when students have opportunities for relatively independent problem solving, without close guidance and precise directives. In this case, learning is an active process, whereby children can devise solutions, manipulate the environment, pose questions, look for answers, and compare their findings with those of their peers.

To support these processes during instructional time, teachers need to allow children to struggle with the task on their own. Furthermore, teachers can foster cognitive development not only by minimizing supervision and involvement, and by granting independence when children are on task, but also through planned interventions. Teachers need to ask questions that stimulate thinking, raise intellectual conflicts, and assign complex problems. That such stimuli increase interaction and further cognitive development when they are accompanied by minimal teacher supervision and by the teacher legitimizing peer interaction, is the prediction of this study.

Interaction and Autonomy in Complex Instruction

Interaction is the cornerstone for enhancing learning in complex instruction: The instructional goal is to maximize interaction among students in small groups and to minimize direct instruction by the teacher. An analysis of the interaction in CI shows that it includes the conditions for the three learning processes described earlier.

When in heterogeneous groups, the interaction is among children with different ability levels or who are at different levels of cognitive development. In these situations, some children act as experts who have knowledge and skills not yet acquired by others. In such asymmetrical interaction, the experts help the novices and further their cognitive progress. Webb (1989) showed that this process also furthers the learning of the experts.

Interaction among same-age students also creates the symmetrical interaction that Piaget talks about. On the one hand, the connection among same-age students who are working collaboratively on a task and who are supposed to come to an agreement, creates a common denominator for the group; on the other hand, conflict can arise when there are no common understandings and no agreement can be reached. To resolve this conflict, students need to discuss various solutions, argue about ways to develop solutions, and persuade one another—all activities that require the use of cognitive processes that foster development.

Social learning is also apparent in CI settings as a highly valued and central norm. Because of its emphasis on peer interaction, complex instruction is different from many other pedagogical approaches that rely exclusively on the student's individual effort and progress. In CI, modeling is a legitimate way to develop new learning skills and problem-solving strategies. Learning through imitation and transfer from student to student is encouraged in the context of collaborative work, shared deliberations, and mutual assistance. Furthermore, complex instruction supports normative social influences and lateral transmission of values among students. Students less academically successful adopt values that are important for academic success because of their exposure to the values of more academically successful students.

In CI, the teacher is no longer the central figure in the classroom and the sole source of knowledge, feedback, and control. These functions are delegated to the students. The teacher is relieved of having to constantly supervise the students; once the cooperative norms have been internalized, groups are able to work practically without interference. The teacher tries to refrain from interrupting the students' work, but encourages them to support one another as they work on the task. Time can then be devoted to deepening student learning by bringing forth new ideas and by encouraging students to experiment and to be creative and flexible in conceptual and social problem-solving situations. The teacher probes students about their thinking processes, their problem-solving strategies, and their conclusions. She gives the message that there is not necessarily a single solution to a problem, a single opinion that is right or wrong, or a single way to complete the task.

The activity cards, which do not contain detailed and overspecified instructions, but rather general guidelines for completing the task, create some open space in which students can interact. The uncertainty embedded in the activity cards elicits interaction among the students as they clarify and discuss, hypothesize, search for possibilities, and choose successful working strategies. Complex instruction then creates the necessary conditions for the cognitive development of students: social interaction and autonomy of the learner.

Cognitive Development in Complex Instruction

In a study conducted in Israel, my research assistants and I evaluated the effectiveness of CI in facilitating the cognitive development of students. Based on the theoretical framework presented above, we tested a model that related the quantity and quality of interaction among students, the teacher's pedagogical practices, and students' cognitive development.

Trained observers conducted systematic observations in CI classrooms. Using a slightly modified version of the Teacher Observation Instrument (see Appendix B), they recorded frequencies of teacher behaviors and then divided them into two larger categories: "supervisory behaviors" and "behaviors that develop student thinking." The category called "supervisory behaviors" included teachers explicitly facilitating, directing, or helping with student work; providing information; disciplining; and hovering over groups. The second category of behaviors included those teaching behaviors that support the development of student cognitive functioning: stimulating and extending students' thinking, encouraging students to approach problems in new and unusual ways, and talking about multiple intellectual abilities. The distinction between routine and nonroutine behaviors made in Chapters 14 and 15 of this volume parallels these two categories.

Observers used a version of the Whole Class Instrument (see Appendix A) to measure the following aspects of student–student interaction: number of students in *verbal interaction* (talking and manipulating materials together), number of students in *nonverbal interaction* (manipulating together, without talking), and number of students *not in interaction* (working individually, reading, or writing).

We administered the MAN test (Glantz, 1974) to measure the students' cognitive abilities. This test includes subtests that measure different domains of thinking, such as defining, categorizing, classifying, formulating conclusions, and understanding relationships.

Our model predicted relationships between teaching behaviors, student interaction, and change in cognitive ability. In contrast to explanations of cognitive development in terms of the individual characteristics of students, this model is based in the situated and contextual character of cognitive development; that is, cognitive development is affected by the social context in which it occurs. We defined the classroom as the social context and conducted the statistical procedures at the classroom, rather than the individual, level. The social context of learning was indicated by two variables: rate and category of student interaction and teacher's pedagogical practices. We tested the effect of these variables on the cognitive development of students as measured by the MAN test. Students' cognitive skills were assessed at the beginning of the academic year (before the implementation of CI) and at the end of the year. The differences between the pre- and posttest scores on the MAN were the indicators of cognitive development over time.

Our first prediction related to the relationship between interaction and cognitive development. Based on the theoretical framework and the empirical findings reviewed earlier, we predicted that interaction among students would lead to cognitive development; that is, there would be a positive relationship between level of student interaction and the progress on the cognitive test.

The second prediction of the model deals with the relationship between the teachers' pedagogical practices and cognitive development. Based on the theoretical discussion above, one can expect an indirect effect of the teacher's behaviors on the students' cognitive development, a relationship mediated by student interaction. We predicted, then, that the more the teacher's behaviors increase the level of student interaction, the stronger the gains of the students. Our data set permits testing of the alternative and more conventional hypothesis of a direct effect of teacher behavior on student cognitive development.

When the teacher supervises and dictates student behavior through direct instruction, gives information, and interferes with student problem solving, student interaction decreases. When the teacher is the only legitimate source of information and assistance, students will prefer to listen to him because of his role and status. When the teacher is unable to delegate authority, students turn to the teacher for assistance and the peer interaction becomes watered down. We predicted that when the teacher uses direct supervision, students will interact less and manipulate materials, without talking, more.

In contrast, when the teacher does not interfere with the students' problem-solving process, but rather delegates authority, and makes it clear that groups have to complete the task independently, students will use each other as resources. In these situations, interactions become more meaningful and more effective. Furthermore, the teacher can support peer interaction not only through what she does not do, but also through what she does. The teacher who encourages students to think at a high level, to experiment, and to challenge themselves and their peers gives students more opportunities to interact. Thus, we predicted that the more the teacher uses behaviors that develop thinking, the more the students will interact.

Setting and Sample

This study was conducted in Israel, in 36 heterogeneous classrooms in six schools where CI was introduced. The sample included 1,017 students, 503 boys and 514 girls, in Grades 3–5. These students represented a wide range of socioeconomic backgrounds as well as previous academic achievement. Following the model developed at Stanford, the teachers in the sample participated in a 2-week summer workshop conducted at the Institute for the Advancement of Social Integration of the Bar-Ilan University. Also following the Stanford model, the teachers received systematic feedback throughout the academic year from experienced CI trainers.

RESULTS

We predicted that the teacher's influence on cognitive development would be indirect, mediated by students' interaction. The teacher variables were our two categories of teacher behaviors: routine supervisory behaviors, and behaviors that develop and support student thinking. The three student variables were verbal interaction, such as talking and working together; nonverbal interaction, as in working together without talking; and no interaction, in which we recorded students reading or writing individually or working alone. Change in cognitive abilities, as measured by the MAN test, was the dependent variable.

Table 13.1 presents the descriptive statistics of the variables of this study. The teachers in this sample, unlike the average CI teacher in the United States (see Table 14.1), exhibited a relatively low rate of supervisory behaviors, and a relatively high rate of behaviors intended to develop thinking skills. The average percentage of students in verbal interaction was also high by American standards.

Table 13.1: Means, Standard Deviations, and Ranges of Teachers' Behaviors and Students' Activities

Variables	Mean	SD	Range
Teachers' Behaviors			
Supervision	6.86	2.57	2.09–13.11
Developing Thinking	8.74	2.22	5.10–13.56
Students' Interactions (in percentages)			
Verbal Interaction	42.62	13.88	12.50–66.47
Nonverbal Interaction	13.76	6.04	3.75–28.72
No Interaction	13.45	6.36	1.56–29.17

Table 13.2: Interitem Correlations of the Variables of the Study ($n = 36$)

Variables	1	2	3	4	5	6
Teachers' Behaviors						
1 Supervision	1.00	.05	-.33	.44*	-.18	-.02
2 Developing Thinking		1.00	.45*	-.02	-.14	.20
Students' Interactions						
3 Verbal Interactions			1.00	-.42*	-.25	.38*
4 Nonverbal Interactions				1.00	.29*	-.07
5 No Interaction					1.00	-.20
6 Cognitive Growth						1.00

*p < .05

Table 13.2 presents the interitem correlations of all variables, at the classroom level. The only variable significantly correlated with the change in cognitive abilities was the average percentage of students involved in verbal interaction ($r = .38$, $p < .05$). Verbal interaction was also significantly positively related to teacher behaviors that develop thinking ($r = .45$, $p < .05$), and negatively (although not significantly) related to the teacher's supervisory behaviors ($r = -.33$). To analyze the relationship among the variables in a dynamic model of cause and effect, we used the LISREL VII procedure (Joreskog & Sorbom, 1988). The results of this analysis are presented in Figure 13.1.

Figure 13.1 includes two models of teaching: the traditional and the interactive teaching models. According to the traditional teaching model, teacher behaviors in both the supervisory and the developing thinking categories should have a direct effect on the advancement of students' cognitive

Figure 13.1: LISREL—Initial Full Model for All Students

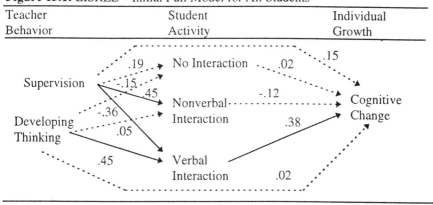

ability. In addition, any experiences with the learning material should have a direct effect on the students' cognitive advancement. In contrast, the interactive model, on which this study is based, states that the teacher's influence is indirect, via student interactions.

The estimation of the full model of all direct and indirect paths produced a chi-square of 7.33 with 5 degrees of freedom, which showed that the replicated matrix did not differ significantly from the original data ($p < .197$) and indicated that the model received empirical verification. However, the adjusted coefficient of best fit was only .74, meaning that there was much residual left.

Testing the model only with the significant path coefficients, as shown in Figure 13.2, led to a better fit estimate (chi-square = 10.66, $df = 12$; $p < .56$), and the adjusted goodness of fit was .85. This model received statistical confirmation. The coefficient of determination of the cognitive ability change was $r^2 = .15$; the coefficient of determination of the verbal interaction by the teacher's categories was $r^2 = .34$ and of the nonverbal, $r^2 = .20$.

The model in Figure 13.2 shows only the significant paths that support the interactive representation of teaching. The direct paths to cognitive change from both categories of teacher behaviors, and from the students' noninteractive behaviors that characterize the traditional teaching model, were not significant.

DISCUSSION

This study shows that advancing the cognitive development of students in heterogeneous classrooms is possible when necessary processes are in place.

Figure 13.2: LISREL—Final Trimmed Model

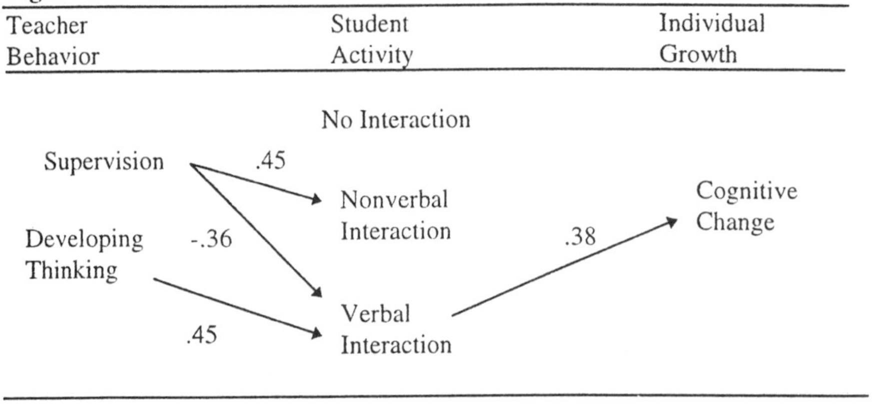

Teacher Behavior	Student Activity	Individual Growth

Supervision .45

No Interaction

Developing Thinking   -.36

Nonverbal Interaction   .38

.45   Verbal Interaction

Cognitive Change

The conceptual basis of complex instruction includes those processes—social interaction and learner autonomy—that lead to cognitive development. Because of the natural variations in the actual implementation of complex instruction by the teachers in the sample, we could examine the effect of the quality of implementation on the cognitive development of students. In those classrooms where the quality of implementation was higher, the gains in cognitive development were higher as well. The quality of implementation was indicated by the use of teacher behaviors that develop and support student thinking and by the level of student interaction.

However, not all interaction was beneficial for the cognitive development of students. The data show that the benefits of social interaction arise only from the verbal interactions: in the discussions, in persuasion, and in experimentation, where students make use of high-level cognitive processes and therefore stimulate their development. Verbal interaction is a useful context for the development and use of cognitive skills, in contrast to nonverbal interaction or individual activity without any interaction. Therefore, the more teachers foster verbal interaction, the greater the cognitive gains of students.

The teacher's behaviors are important in promoting student interaction, as he can enhance or, alternatively, dampen the interaction. The teacher can support interaction through asking meaningful questions, stimulating thinking, and posing intellectual challenges. When the teacher is not the sole source of information, students will turn to one another for information and assistance.

When the teacher intervenes in the groups, she short-circuits the thinking process for the students and eliminates the need for verbal interaction. When it is the teacher who resolves the uncertainty, solves the problem, or helps the students get out of a dilemma, there is no need for the students to turn to one another to solve the task. Indeed, the data showed a positive relationship between supervisory behaviors and nonverbal interaction, and a negative relationship between these behaviors and verbal interaction.

These findings about CI classrooms demonstrate that heterogeneity of the student population, rather than being an impediment for cognitive development, is a positive factor for the development of thinking. Heterogeneity creates variability and differences that lead to intellectual tension and a socio-cognitive conflict. This conflict or tension is resolved through verbal interaction, which in turn leads to the development of thinking.

The implications for teaching and learning in complex instruction and the development of thinking are twofold. First, because of the importance of verbal interaction, groupwork time needs to be maximized. Interaction is also enhanced by appropriate learning tasks that challenge the students' thinking and require them to be resources for one another. Second, because teacher behaviors can enhance or inhibit verbal interaction, teachers who use CI need to learn how to redefine their role, to understand that the hub of teaching and learning is in the student groups, and to recognize the importance and the value of verbal interaction and its effects on cognitive development. Only when teachers internalize these beliefs will they be able to aid their students in fully realizing the potential of interaction.

PART VI

Organizational Theory in Support of Teachers

CHAPTER 14

Teachers as Learners: Feedback, Conceptual Understanding, and Implementation

Nancy E. Ellis and Rachel A. Lotan

I wouldn't have minded if the feedback sessions had been more frequent and earlier in the year. They were extremely useful because they were so specific. I got a very clear picture of what was going on. I now have a much clearer idea of what it is that I said at the beginning of the year and how I've changed. In the beginning, a comment like, "Sally has done thus, thus, thus . . ." would never have struck me as a comment that would fit anywhere. I would never have recognized it as specific feedback. I can see how the same principles apply with us, the teachers, and with the children. That is, the more specific feedback you get, the better you understand. (Sally Patterson*, fifth-grade teacher, May 1985)

In this interview, Sally Patterson revealed that she had gained sophisticated understanding of the importance of specific feedback for students as well as for teachers—crucial elements in CI. Observational data showed that she had successfully translated her understanding to classroom practice: Her rate of giving specific feedback was the highest among the sample of teachers working with the Program for Complex Instruction during the 1984–85 academic year.

In this chapter, we examine the relationships among three aspects of CI: (1) teachers' use of routine and nonroutine strategies in the classroom, (2) systematic feedback to teachers from the staff of the Stanford program, and (3) teachers' conceptual understanding of the theoretical and empirical knowledge base underlying the model. Through this examination, we make three contributions to the research on the implementation of pedagogical innovations such as complex instruction. First, we highlight the significance of systematic feedback to teachers on their classroom practice. Especially

---

*Names used in this chapter are pseudonyms.

important is our insistence on soundly based feedback (Dornbusch & Scott, 1975; Gonzales, 1982), which is grounded on systematic observations of teacher behaviors in classrooms and goes beyond behaviorist models of coaching that fail to relate those practices to the theoretical foundations of the intervention. The specificity of soundly based feedback allows teachers to analyze, reflect, and problem solve on their own classroom practices.

Clarity of criteria and standards is one of the essential features of sound feedback. In CI, the criteria for feedback and standards for implementation are derived from the theoretical framework and the empirical findings. During the summer institute, as described in Chapter 2 of this volume, teachers learn which strategies encourage children to talk and work together, thereby enhancing their learning. Teachers practice these strategies with students; the teachers also are informed about what the standards for quality implementation are in elementary school classrooms.

During the summer institute and during the academic year, members of the Stanford staff provide feedback in nonevaluative, collaborative contexts. Teachers' performance is not a basis for merit pay or any other organizational reward. Ellis (1987) conceptualized this kind of feedback as supportive supervision: well-structured feedback given at regular intervals and focusing on teachers' performance of nonroutine teaching behaviors.

Second, our focus on teachers' conceptual understanding of the body of knowledge underlying an innovation emphasizes the importance of the role of the teacher and of professional development in the change process (see also Lotan, 1985). We argue that when teachers develop a deep understanding of the goal, the theoretical principles, and the research underlying the intervention they are implementing, they will be better able to make it work in their own classrooms.

Finally, we argue that studies of instructional innovations are incomplete without systematic and reliable observational data from the classroom. To gauge the quality of implementation or teachers' use of the innovative strategies, we have monitored and examined the implementation over time, repeatedly, in the classrooms of the teachers using CI.

THEORETICAL FRAMEWORK

Organizational theorists claim that the more complex the worker's task becomes, the more advantageous it will be to use lateral, rather than top-down, channels of communication (Perrow, 1967). The use of lateral communication helps workers by increasing opportunities for them to use each other as information resources. When teachers use a complex classroom technology involving many nonroutine features, they experience higher levels of uncertainty than they would with more routine classroom practices.

Organizational sociologists also theorize that through lateral communication, workers obtain and process information, and gain and provide assistance, thereby lowering their uncertainty and increasing their productivity (Galbraith, 1973). If the theory holds for teachers using a complex technology, then those teachers who talk about their teaching will improve their classroom performance as they gain more knowledge and eliminate uncertainty by collaborating through lateral channels.

March and Simon (1958) argue that in less routine task environments, individuals engage in wider and higher-level search procedures than they do in more routine task environments. Wider search procedures are undertaken when individuals seek information from those in lateral positions; higher-level searches occur when individuals ask experts for information. In the present study, where the task environment of teachers was largely nonroutine, supportive supervisors provided an important arena for collaboration in the feedback sessions with teachers. Supportive supervisors observed teachers and gave them specific, systematic feedback on their implementation of CI. The supportive supervisors were not linked with administrative evaluators in the school organizational hierarchies, but were, experts on the implementation of CI and were able to provide teachers with crucial information. Teachers also were able to inquire freely, exchange information, and problem solve with supportive supervisors.

Increasingly, researchers have documented the importance of lateral communication in educational settings (Little, 1982; Rosenholtz, 1989). In this study, the content of such lateral communication was specific to the implementation of CI and thus immediately relevant to the classroom technology. Conversations were task-oriented since they were based on data collected in the classroom and had to do with identifying ways to help teachers delegate authority, stimulate and extend students' thinking, and treat status problems—strategies closely aligned with the theoretical foundation of CI.

Ellis (1987, 1990) found that, under certain conditions, such collaboration was associated with teachers' use of nonroutine teaching strategies and nonuse of routine strategies in CI. We report the results of Ellis's study in the first hypothesis.

Given a complex instructional technology, supportive supervision will be positively related to the quality of implementation of that technology.

To formulate the second hypothesis, we also draw from organizational theory. Following Scott (1981), Cohen, Deal, Meyer, and Scott (1976), and Perrow (1967), Lotan (1985) conceptualized the three facets of classroom technology as the materials (students and curricula), operations (teaching and learning strategies), and knowledge of the participants. Educational sociologists (Cohen & Bredo, 1975; Intili, 1977) have documented significant relationships between two of these dimensions of classroom technology: the variability of materials and the complexity of operations. Lotan (1985) extended this work to formulate hypotheses regarding the relationship between knowledge and operations, given high variability of materials.

Lotan claims that teachers, like engineers, use two kinds of knowledge: (1) highly codified, regulated, and explicit programs for solving routine problems; and (2) complex, abstract knowledge that enables the participants to make nonroutine, analytical responses by taking into account different alternatives, immediate outcomes, and long-term consequences. The implementation of a new and complex classroom technology based on a body of theoretical and empirical research, is enhanced as teachers develop an understanding of that body of knowledge. Lotan (1985) found that teachers' conceptual understanding of complex instructional technology was positively associated with their implementation of nonroutine teaching strategies. Replicating Lotan's study with this different sample of teachers, our second hypothesis is:

> Given a complex instructional technology, teachers' understanding of the underlying body of knowledge will be positively related to the quality of the implementation of that technology.

In the third hypothesis, we examine the relationship between knowledge and supportive supervision. We argue that teachers' conceptual understanding develops from the following different experiences designed to maximize lateral communication and expert, supportive supervision: (1) the initial institute, with its theoretical and practical components, and the follow-up session; (2) implementation in the classroom; and (3) sound feedback that makes connections between theory and practice. All teachers in the sample for this study participated in the initial institute and the follow-up session; they all implemented CI during the academic year. On the three dimensions mentioned above, the only variation was in the number of feedback sessions in which they participated. Therefore, the third hypothesis is:

> Given a complex instructional technology, supportive supervision will be positively related to teachers' conceptual understanding of the theoretical knowledge base.

METHODOLOGY

For purposes of this study, we used data collected as part of the research of the Program for Complex Instruction during the 1984–85 academic year.

Thirteen teachers in five elementary schools constituted the sample. These teachers all used the *Finding Out/ Descubrimiento* curriculum (De Avila & Duncan, 1982b).

Sources of data were a minimum of 20 classroom observations of each teacher, made with the Teacher Observation Instrument (see Appendix B); questionnaires administered to the teachers at the end of the academic year; structured and open-ended interviews; and records of collaborative meetings between teachers and Stanford staff, who served as supportive supervisors. Selected questions during the interviews with teachers conducted at the end of the academic year were designed to reveal teachers' conceptual clarity and understanding of the basic principles and features of the program (for a detailed description of these interviews and the guidelines for scoring, see Lotan, 1985).

The first hypothesis of the study states that there is a positive relationship between supportive supervision and the quality of the teacher's classroom performance in CI. In the present study, such supportive supervision was provided to the teachers by staff members of the Stanford program. Selected teachers volunteered to receive additional feedback and training by analyzing videos of their students' and their own performances in the classroom.

The frequency of feedback meetings between the teacher and a Stanford staff member indicates the amount of supportive supervision. Although the model of staff development for CI prescribes at least three such meetings during the academic year, in 1984–85 there was considerable variation in the number of such meetings among the teachers in the sample. This variation came about for a number of reasons. First, Stanford researchers were conducting an experiment in which, in addition to the regular feedback, four of the 13 teachers received video feedback focusing specifically on status interventions. (For a detailed description of the use of video to enhance teachers' use of status treatments, see Benton, 1994). Second, initially some teachers felt threatened by the presence of an "outsider" in their classroom and perceived the process as an evaluation of their professional competence. As a result, a few teachers successfully avoided setting up meetings with the staff, and sometimes even canceled meetings already planned. Third, serious shortages of staff members on the Stanford project made them less persistent and consistent in pursuing the teachers and setting up meetings. Thus, one teacher received no feedback before the end of data collection for the present study, six teachers participated in two sessions, three teachers in three, and one teacher participated in four feedback meetings. These numbers include regular as well as video feedback. Measures of frequency of supportive supervision were taken from the records kept by the Stanford staff and were substantiated in debriefing interviews of the teachers.

We categorized teachers' classroom performances in two ways: non-routine behaviors, and routine behaviors that indicate direct supervision by the teacher. Nonroutine behaviors are those behaviors that teachers learn as part of implementing CI: giving specific feedback, treating status problems, and stimulating and extending students' thinking. Routine behaviors are the behaviors to be minimized, particularly at learning centers: telling students what to do, giving information, disciplining. Given the basic differences in the context of instruction during orientation and wrap-up (whole class instruction) and at learning centers (small groups), data were collected separately for these two kinds of situations.

Nonroutine behaviors are those teaching acts in which the teacher engages when she or he has the option to choose from a repertoire of essentially varied behaviors. In CI, the common and familiar repertoire of teacher behaviors has been expanded to include these new strategies in the specific setting of small group instruction. Behaviors are nonroutine when no specific program (as defined by March & Simon, 1958) or preplanned response can be provided for teachers ahead of time. Given the fluidity of the situation and the considerable repertoire of potentially appropriate responses, teachers have to search their minds and make decisions as to which behavior to use. For example, after observing the students at one of the stations, the teacher might decide to extend learning by providing additional examples. He or she might decide to address the group as a whole or to provide feedback to an individual. Or, the teacher might decide to move on to the next center without saying anything at all. The indicators of teachers' use of nonroutine teaching behaviors, taken from the Teacher Observation Instrument, were the following: talking about multiple abilities, giving specific feedback, extending activities, and talking about student thinking.

In contrast to these nonroutine behaviors, some teaching behaviors are more routine in nature, and they are also an essential part of conducting the classroom effectively. However, the teacher needs to minimize these routine behaviors in CI. Research has shown that student interaction (the main predictor of learning) is short-circuited when teachers help students with the task, when they provide too much information, or when they question too often (Cohen, Lotan, & Leechor, 1989). Thus, the indicators of teachers' use of routine teaching behaviors were as follows: facilitating students' work (that is, supervising closely and telling them exactly what procedures to follow or how to approach a problem), disciplining, providing information, and asking questions, when such questioning was accompanied by high rates of supervision.

The first hypothesis of the study translates into the following specific and parallel predictions for learning center time and for orientation and wrap-up:

1. The frequency of feedback meetings between teacher and supportive supervisor will be positively related to the average rate of nonroutine teaching behaviors.
2. The frequency of feedback meetings between teacher and supportive supervisor will be negatively related to the average rate of routine teaching behaviors.

The second hypothesis states a positive relationship between teachers'
understanding of the underlying knowledge base and their classroom performance. We predicted that when the teacher has a better grasp of the theoretical framework and the empirical findings, he or she will minimize the
routine behaviors and will maximize the nonroutine behaviors.

Methodologically, the measurement of teachers' conceptual understanding of this knowledge base presented a serious challenge. Clearly, we could
not administer a test. However, as in a previous study (Lotan, 1985), we
were able to infer conceptual understanding from teachers' answers to certain questions in an open-ended interview. For example, we asked teachers
to consider the following:

> Please think of the child in your classroom who is seen by his
> classmates as slow and who does not have many friends. How did
> this child function during *FO/D*? Do you think the program made him
> feel more competent? What in the program do you think could be
> responsible for helping a child like that? Did you make any special
> effort to help this child during *FO/D*?

The interview, administered to the teachers at the end of the academic
year, had two overt purposes and one covert purpose. It was designed so
that teachers' conceptual understanding could be inferred from their responses
to questions that asked for evaluation of their training and from their responses
to situations that presented them as potential disseminators of information
about CI. Based on the content of these interviews and comparisons with
standards derived from the theoretical formulation of CI, we assessed teachers'
conceptual understanding of the following aspects of CI: (1) goals and scope
of the program; (2) principles of cognitive learning; (3) classroom management in small group instruction; (4) treatment of status problems; (5) the
importance of organizational support for CI. (Guidelines and additional details
for scoring are described in Lotan, 1985.)

Two independent scorers interpreted and coded the content of the interviews. Interscorer reliability was 86%. The scorers were careful to differentiate
between verbal information and cues from which conceptual understanding
of an item could be inferred, and reports about behavioral manifestations,

where conceptual understanding could not be inferred. For example, a teacher who reported refraining from hovering over groups, reported on a behavior. The scorers had no way of knowing whether the teacher was attempting to delegate authority because he or she was told do so by the project staff or because the teacher understood the relationship between such delegation and increased student interaction. However, if the teacher continued and elaborated on how and why delegation of authority was a central feature of CI, conceptual understanding was inferred. Only this latter situation was coded and counted. After coding the content of the interviews, the scorers arrived at a count of the total number of times a particular item was mentioned, as well as the total number of items to which references were made. The overall sum of items marked indicated the breadth of the teacher's understanding, that is, the overall grasp of the theoretical underpinnings of CI. The measure of relative frequency of any particular item indicated the depth of that teacher's understanding. For this study, we added the total number of items mentioned, weighted by the relative frequency, to indicate the teacher's overall understanding.

The predictions for the second hypothesis, separately for learning center time and for orientation and wrap-up, are:

3. Teachers' overall understanding of the knowledge base of CI will be positively related to the rate of nonroutine teaching behaviors.
4. Teachers' overall understanding of the knowledge base of CI will be negatively related to the rate of routine teaching behaviors.

The third hypothesis deals with the relationship between supportive supervision and the teachers' overall conceptual understanding. The following prediction is derived from the third hypothesis:

5. The frequency of feedback meetings between the teacher and the supportive supervisors will be positively related to the teacher's overall conceptual understanding of the program.

RESULTS

Table 14.1 shows the descriptive statistics of the variables in the study. The mean value of the variable of teachers' overall conceptual understanding was 94.82, and the standard deviation for that variable was 26.68. There was a considerable range in this variable, as indicated by the minimum and maximum values. The descriptive statistics ($x = 1.77$, $sd = 1.17$) of the next variable, frequency of feedback, reflects the variation in the number of feedback meetings for the teachers in the sample.

Table 14.1 also shows the average rate per 10 minutes of observation of selected teaching behaviors. Among these behaviors, the highest average rate was for direct supervision at learning centers (x = 21.2, sd = 12.46). The lowest average rate was for nonroutine behaviors during orientation and wrap-up (x = 6.49, sd = 3.51). In general, the average rates of nonroutine behaviors were lower than those of behaviors classified as supervisory.

Table 14.2 shows the strength of relationships among the variables of the study. All the relationships between frequency of feedback and teaching behaviors were in the direction predicted and were statistically significant. Frequency of feedback and direct supervision at learning centers and during orientation and wrap-up were both significantly negatively related: $r = -0.53, p < .05$ and $r = -0.65, p < .01$, respectively. Frequency of feedback and non-routine behaviors at learning centers and during orientation and wrap-up were both significantly positively related: $r = .57, p < .05$ and $r = .68, p < .01$, respectively.

The relationships between teachers' overall understanding and teaching behaviors were in the predicted direction. However, only the relationship between overall understanding and nonroutine behaviors at learning centers achieved statistical significance, $r = .55, p < .05$.

Table 14.1: Descriptive Statistics of Variables of the Study

Variable	Mean	SD	Range	n
Overall conceptual understanding	94.82	26.68	49–161	11
Frequency of feedback	1.77	1.17	0–4	13
Direct supervision at learning centers	21.20	12.46	10.42–44.27	13
Direct supervision orientation/wrap-up	12.55	5.61	6.43–25.43	13
Nonroutine behaviors at learning centers	7.17	2.68	3.50–12.25	13
Nonroutine behaviors orientation/wrap-up	6.49	3.51	3.09–13.29	13

Table 14.2: Correlation Matrix of Variables of the Study

		1	2	3	4	5	6
1	Overall conceptual understanding	1.00					
2	Frequency of feedback	.62* (11)	1.00				
3	Direct supervision at learning centers	-.36 (11)	-.53* (13)	1.00			
4	Direct supervision orientation/wrap-up	-.20 (11)	-.65** (13)	.40 (13)	1.00		
5	Non-routine behaviors at learning centers	.55* (11)	.57* (13)	-.17 (13)	-.52 (13)	1.00	
6	Non-routine behaviors orientation/wrap-up	.43 (11)	.68** (13)	-.28 (13)	-.35 (13)	.47 (13)	1.00

*$p<.05$ (one-tailed); **$p<.01$ (one-tailed)

There was also a statistically significant positive relationship between the frequency of feedback meetings and teachers' overall understanding ($r =$ .62, $p < .05$), meaning that those teachers who participated in more feedback meetings also showed a better understanding.

DISCUSSION

Results of the data analysis showed significant relationships between supportive supervision and teaching behaviors, and between supportive supervision and knowledge, as predicted in the first and third hypotheses, respectively. The data, then, support the contention that when classroom technology is complex, sound feedback becomes necessary to promote and maintain quality implementation. Both the technology and the content of the supportive supervision described in this study were quite different from many simplistic instructional innovations or certain current models of coaching. As presented in this study, the feedback to the teachers was highly structured, task-oriented, and performance-specific. The innovation was complex, and the teachers' behaviors, highly nonroutine. It could well be the case that other, less complex and less deep-reaching educational innovations do not need such an elaborate support system to be well implemented or to survive.

Results for the second hypothesis were in the predicted direction, but only the relationship between conceptual understanding and nonroutine teaching behaviors at learning centers reached statistical significance. Thus, teachers' conceptual understanding of the underlying body of knowledge seems particularly relevant to the implementation of nonroutine behaviors during learning center time. It is precisely at this time that decision making is most challenging because the teacher needs to "think on her feet." In contrast, orientations and wrap-ups are more easily planned and thought out ahead of time. We speculate that more routine strategies, which can be planned ahead for orientations and wrap-ups, can be employed by teachers without so great an overall understanding of the theoretical bases of the program.

The existence of a well-defined and immediately relevant body of knowledge that underlies this complex technology is of particular importance. Unlike many educational innovations, CI has a solid theoretical basis that is supported by educational research. It includes definitions of social science concepts as well as predictions and explanations of relationships among these concepts in classroom settings. The body of knowledge posits general pedagogical rules and principles and the conditions for their applications.

EXAMPLES FROM CASE STUDIES

In this section, we turn to the teachers' interviews to find out what they said about the feedback they received from supportive supervisors. Ms. Patterson, quoted at the beginning of this chapter, best exemplifies the predicted results. She was observed and received feedback in four formal sessions. Her implementation in the classroom was exemplary. She had the highest-ranking scores on nonroutine teaching behaviors and overall understanding of the program. She ranked lowest and second lowest, respectively, on routine teaching behaviors during orientations and wrap-ups.

Ms. Patterson's explicit comparison between her own learning and that of her students is one example of her understanding of the theoretical knowledge base of CI. Observational data show that she implemented the program successfully. The connections between her theoretical knowledge and successful implementation illustrate the second hypothesis of the present study: Teachers' understanding of the underlying body of knowledge is positively related to their classroom performance. The third hypothesis of the study is illustrated by Ms. Patterson's attribution of her knowledge and "clear picture of what was going on" to feedback sessions.

Consistent with the predictions of the present study but at the other end of the scale, Mrs. Valenza's story was not a tale of success. She participated in only one feedback session, her overall understanding of the program was low, and her performance of routine teaching behaviors at learning centers was higher than any other teacher's. Mrs. Valenza's mean score on routine behaviors at learning centers was 44.3, more than twice the sample mean of 21.2. At the end of the year, she commented:

> Jane [the supportive supervisor] said I was supervising kids a lot. After our first [feedback] session I tried not to do that a lot. But Jane understood that one student needed more help from the teacher than the other students. The time I spent directly supervising them was well-spent time. Once Jane showed me the percentage graphs, she understood why I had to supervise so much. Especially since I have a second grade. After Jane understood the conditions, I don't think there were any problems. I know she wanted me to do more. She suggested a couple of things, like: let the aide do more questioning, stand back, and watch kids in their roles, give specific feedback. I think I'll use those suggestions next year. (Interview with Mrs. Diane Valenza, May 1985)

Mrs. Valenza seemed to resist acting on the feedback based on the summary graphs of her teaching behaviors. Jane tried to show her that she was giving students too much help and supervising too directly. Mrs. Valenza had ready excuses for refusing to take suggestions and ingratiated herself by resolving to follow more of Jane's suggestions next year. Blaming the grade level she taught and a student who needed extra help, she failed to recognize principles that applied to her own learning processes. Observers in Mrs. Valenza's classroom noted that she frequently apologized because her second graders didn't "get" the science concepts they explored, even when she gave explicit help and instruction. She didn't seem to understand that a goal of the program was to encourage students to ask questions, observe, and discover independently.

Ms. Patterson's and Mrs. Valenza's experiences illustrate predictions based on the hypotheses in this study. Ms. Escher illustrates other, more puzzling findings. Ms. Escher participated in three feedback sessions, two of them based on videotapes of her teaching. Classroom observations disclosed her as a highly skilled teacher who used many of the program's recommendations frequently. She ranked second highest in the use of nonroutine teaching behaviors (x = 11.2 at learning centers; x = 7.6 at orientation and wrap-up). Surprisingly, she had the lowest score on overall understanding of the program. Although Ms. Escher focused on negative information she received in feedback sessions, she acknowledged the practical assistance provided through the feedback. She explained:

Many times I got caught up with facilitating and helping too much. It was helpful for [a colleague] to observe me to remind me to stay in my role. I think the purpose of the feedback is to help us to be aware of our mistakes and help us improve on them and to help us know what we're doing right. What was useful? Pointing out the positive things and negative things. Seeing things I wasn't even aware of. Everybody hates to know they're doing something wrong or negative. In the long run it was good. Once in a while when I had a good day, no one was there. (Interview with Ms. Ellen Escher, June 1985)

Ms. Escher complained that Felicity, her classroom aide, liked to "hover" over students while they worked. She said she had "tried to talk to Felicity, but she's established in her ways." Ms. Escher was self-critical and mentioned habits she tried to eliminate, such as facilitating, hovering, or helping students too much. She often asked the children stimulating questions, extended activities, and talked to them about multiple abilities and thinking processes. In the context of trying to model teaching behaviors for her aide to adopt, she may have been able to "step outside" her own perspective and see herself objectively. Although she did not have a thorough understanding of the knowledge base itself, the feedback sessions may have given her enough information and visual imagery to enable her to act in a recommended way without being well grounded in the theory.

What can we learn from the individual cases? Considered as a pair who were alike in successful implementation and receiving greater amounts of feedback, Ms. Patterson and Ms. Escher were both eager to implement the program well. Ms. Patterson was a teacher-leader, who conducted observations of other teachers and gave them feedback, worked closely with her aide to develop teaching skills, and wrote grant proposals to pay for science lab materials. Ms. Escher was attentive to the behavior of another teacher she admired and whose implementation of the program was excellent. Like Ms. Patterson, Ms. Escher was excited about the program, but unlike Ms. Patterson perhaps she relied more on observation and copying models than on understanding of the program for successful implementation and nonroutine decision making.

Mrs. Valenza's low scores on all measures seem to be self-explanatory. What prevented her from gaining knowledge about the program? Mrs. Valenza excused herself and her students, convinced that they needed lots of extra help and extensive direct instruction. She postponed ("until next year") changes in her own action, as recommended by the supportive supervisor. Was there a cultural gap, a key misunderstanding, fatigue with "new programs every year," or an inability to accept the supervisor's critique constructively?

IMPLICATIONS

Feedback appears to be an important condition for successful implementation of all aspects of CI. Furthermore, after the staff developers leave the schools and teachers continue providing such feedback to one another on a collegial basis, the quality of implementation is maintained (Lotan, 1990). Overall understanding, closely associated with the frequency of feedback sessions, was more closely related to the more difficult aspects of implementation but less closely related to elimination of routine behaviors. Performance of more complex instruction may require conceptual understanding, but elimination of old habits may require more than that.

Organizational support such as the soundly based feedback included in the model of professional development of complex instruction is essential for the successful implementation of sophisticated instructional programs involving nonroutine teaching strategies. School boards and administrators may consider the expense of providing feedback as impractical in the context of perennial lack of resources. Although teachers' apparent compliance can be obtained by mandate, teachers' understanding and long-term adoption of new, complex programs may be obtained only by ensuring teachers' understanding of programs and providing regular and systematic feedback, especially during the early stages of implementation. Complex instructional programs attempted with sufficient organizational support will have excellent chances for quality implementation and long-time survival.

CHAPTER 15

Principals, Colleagues, and Staff Developers: The Case for Organizational Support

Rachel A. Lotan, Elizabeth G. Cohen, and Christopher C. Morphew

As technology in the classroom becomes more differentiated and complex, new organizational arrangements at the school are necessary to support the change in instruction. In complex instruction, where each group is working on a different task with a different set of materials and manipulatives, the teacher prepares for and monitors a highly complex situation. Teachers need substantive and practical help with delegating authority, with nonroutine decision making, and with strengthening their subject matter expertise.

In this chapter, we present evidence of the connections between organizational support for the teachers and their ability to implement CI after the initial summer workshop. During that year, the staff developers work in concert with the team of teachers and administrators from each school to provide the necessary support for teachers learning the new strategies. Previous research indicates that the impact of the staff developer in the first year of implementation is considerable (see Chapter 14). In this chapter, we show how the influence of the principal and that of colleagues relates to the implementation of CI in the context of the staff developer's work with the teachers.

TECHNOLOGICAL COMPLEXITY AND ORGANIZATIONAL SUPPORT

We start from the fundamental organizational proposition that uncertain and complex changes in the technology of work will require changes in organizational arrangements. The general hypothesis is that teachers who experience favorable support from staff developers, principals, and colleagues will show superior implementation to that of teachers who experience less support. We use organizational theory to unpack the notion of organizational support by developing a set of specific propositions concerning the ways in which support relates to implementation. The three major dimensions of support are: (1) soundly based feedback for the teachers, (2) adequate resources and coordination of those resources at the school level, and (3) an organizational climate of expectations that teachers will persist with the implementation of the technology over time.

Soundly Based Feedback

In Chapter 14, Ellis and Lotan argued that if teachers are to master an uncertain and nonroutine technology like complex instruction, they will require highly specific feedback that they regard as soundly based. They related the frequency of such feedback to the quality of implementation and to the teachers' conceptual understanding of the knowledge base underlying CI. In this chapter, we also take into account the teachers' perception of the soundness of the feedback provided to them by the staff developers.

Despite the efforts to provide sound feedback, teachers vary in how soundly based they *perceive* the feedback to be. Some teachers do not participate in three feedback meetings as recommended by the program. Some teachers are not completely clear about the criteria, and others might feel that the staff developer did not get an adequate picture of the implementation in their classroom. Thus, a study of the perceptions of teachers enables us to test the following proposition:

> Feedback that is perceived as soundly based is related to better-quality implementation of uncertain and complex technology than feedback that is perceived as less soundly based.

Resources and Coordination

Classroom technology that requires curricular materials and manipulatives (e.g., test tubes, magnets, audiotapes, costumes, art supplies) for six different groups in simultaneous operation, makes obvious demands on school resources. First, someone must purchase or gather, organize, store, and replenish these materials and manipulatives. Second, teachers require adequate furniture and space suitable for groupwork as well as for storage. Finally, although time is one of the scarcest resources in schools, teachers must have time to plan, prepare, meet, and solve problems that arise in connection with the implementation of the technology.

At the school level, providing resources for a team of teachers requires coordination. For example, teachers who use *Finding Out/Descubrimiento* (De Avila & Duncan, 1982b) need to have a wide array of materials; they need a budget to acquire these materials and organizational help to manage, store, and effectively share them. The principal often delegates the task of providing such organizational help to a resource teacher, to a complex instruction trainer who is on site, or to one of the CI teachers on the team. Similarly, if teachers are to have release time or a common preparation period, the principal needs to coordinate the schedule. He or she also needs to set up a budgeting system whereby teachers can replenish the perishable goods (e.g., sugar, oranges, raisins) necessary for some of the activities.

At the middle school, acquiring and managing manipulative materials is frequently a tradition in the science department. However, no such tradition exists in the social studies or the mathematics departments. Even if teachers and department chairs assume these newly created responsibilities, administrators at the school level must still allocate the necessary budget, coordinate the effort, and understand the importance of this supportive task.

When classroom technology is more complex and uncertain, the principal can no longer coordinate by rules and schedules. Face-to-face coordination is more effective. If the principals attend the summer institute with the teachers, become well informed about complex instruction, and frequently visit the teachers' classrooms, they can talk with the teachers, see what the problems are from close-up, and discuss what they can do to help. Yet, principals vary in the time or the motivation they have to carry out these functions that are tightly related to instruction. Variability among principals permits the test of the second proposition:

> Teachers who report more resources and more coordination of those resources will have more successful implementation than those who report fewer resources and less coordination.

An Organizational Climate of Expectations

Sometime between the end of the initial 2-week workshop and the first feedback session, some teachers find the implementation of complex new strategies difficult and discouraging. In this period of transition, the new methods might appear as less effective than the old, even unnecessarily taxing. Because they assume that they might be found lacking in their professional competence, some teachers are suspicious of the feedback sessions and try to postpone them as long as possible or avoid them altogether.

At this juncture, a strong organizational climate of expectations encourages and helps these teachers to persist in their efforts. The expectations of the staff developer from outside the school will not be sufficient. When colleagues and principals make it clear that, despite the difficulties, teachers are expected to persist with the implementation and the feedback process, they will be more likely to keep going and continue to attempt the most challenging, nonroutine features of the new approach.

Sociologically, when considering these expectations, we are talking about *organizational sanctions*. In schools, being the loosely coupled organizations that they are, no one gives direct orders to teachers. The principal shows that he or she expects teachers to follow through on implementation by his or her efforts to become knowledgeable about complex instruction, by including it in school goals, and by visiting the classrooms. Colleagues communicate expectations for follow-through of implementation in grade level or departmental meetings, in informal conversations about what worked and what didn't, and in making specific plans about how and when to use certain units or materials.

A climate of expectations is not independent of coordination of resources. Certainly, a principal who is sufficiently well informed to conduct face-to-face coordination with teachers is, at the same time, communicating expectations concerning the importance he or she places on the program. In addition, the principal indicates his or her intentions and commitments by thoughtfully providing organizational help as well as a budget for materials.

In some schools where individual teachers implement CI, the principal and some faculty may not be fully committed to it. Often, teachers try to implement several innovations at the same time, significantly increasing the demands on their time, effort, and personal as well as school resources. Some principals do not define their role as including deep concerns about instruction. Thus, variability on these dimensions permits the test of the third proposition:

> Organizational sanctions in the form of expectations for implementation will be positively associated with better-quality implementation.

STUDIES OF ORGANIZATIONAL SUPPORT

The design of studies at both the elementary and the middle school levels related questionnaire responses from the teachers to observational and questionnaire measures of implementation. Teachers answered questionnaires at the end of the first year of implementation. Indicators of organizational support were teachers' perceptions, which varied among teachers in the same school and among teachers from different schools and departments.

Description of the Samples

The sample for the elementary schools contained 36 teachers who taught Grades 2–5 in 11 schools in the Sacramento, Fresno, and San Francisco areas in California. All teachers had participated in similar summer workshops and follow-up activities during the 1987–88 academic year; all teachers used *FO/D*. Questionnaires were administered in June 1988. Using the Whole Class and the Teacher Observation Instruments (see Appendices A and B, respectively), observers conducted observations in the classrooms throughout the academic year.

The middle school data came from classroom observations (with the Whole Class and the Teacher Observation Instruments) and two similar questionnaires administered to teachers in June 1992 and June 1993. The sample contained 34 teachers who taught seventh and eighth grades at six middle schools in the San Francisco Bay Area. They taught social studies, mathematics, and science, using multiple-ability units that fit the state curriculum guidelines and were specifically designed for CI. Included in the middle school sample were some teachers who were in their second year of implementation.

Measurement

Questionnaires administered to the teachers provided data on teachers' perceptions of soundness of feedback, on resources and the level of coordination, and on the climate of expectations and their perceptions of the principal's knowledge, behavior, and expectations. Data on implementation, the dependent variable, were gathered using the Whole Class and the Teacher Observation Instruments (see Appendices A and B, respectively). To measure teachers' perceptions of the soundness of the feedback, all questionnaires contained three items (see also Chapter 14). At the elementary level, the index of soundly based feedback combined the Likert responses to the following three items:

1. How clear were the criteria upon which this feedback was based?
2. To what extent was this feedback sufficiently specific so that you knew how to improve the implementation of complex instruction in your classroom?
3. To what extent do you feel that the observer(s) got an adequate picture of the implementation of complex instruction in your classroom?

At the middle school level, this index was multiplied by the number of feedback sessions in which each teacher participated.

Indicators of resources and coordination, the second source of organizational support, include a number of items on organizational help, release time, and the adequacy of materials and space. The organizational help item asked teachers how satisfactory assistance from the school was in helping them to acquire and organize materials for the multiple-ability curricula. Release time was a dummy variable, with the availability of this resource given a value of

"1." We had asked teachers about release time to plan and prepare for CI during a regular school day. At the elementary level, an index of materials, derived from teachers' rating of the supply and availability of curricular materials, nonconsumables, and consumables, was also an indicator of resources. The overall index of resources combined the index of materials, the availability of release time, and the adequacy of space for use with CI.

To measure the climate of expectations, the third source of organizational support, three items appeared on all the questionnaires.

1. The principal expected me to follow through and implement complex instruction this year.
2. Other complex instruction teachers at my school expected me to follow through and implement complex instruction this year.
3. The staff of the Stanford Program for Complex Instruction expected me to follow through and implement complex instruction this year.

The index of a climate of expectations consists of the sum total of the Likert-type responses to these three items.

The index of principal knowledge, behavior, and expectations is a combination of three items appearing in almost identical form on all the questionnaires.

1. The principal expected me to follow through and implement complex instruction this year.
2. How often did the principal or other administrators from your school visit your classroom in order to observe the implementation of complex instruction?
3. How well informed do you think your principal or other administrators in your school are about complex instruction in your classroom?

This index is a mix of coordination and organizational expectations. Visits from the principal often were the occasion for invaluable face-to-face coordination simultaneously with the communication of expectations.

Dornbusch and Scott (1975) argue that soundly based evaluation elicits greater effort from actors. In the research on complex instruction, we have often attempted to measure teachers' effort. Initially, we asked teachers how many hours they spent planning for implementation, organizing materials, and giving feedback on individual reports. However, this measure did not show significant relationships to any of the dependent variables. We concluded that there were other factors that affected the time teachers spent on these activities. In a further attempt to measure effort, we asked the middle school teachers how much they worried about and worked on identifying multiple abilities and on convincing students of the relevance of these abilities to groupwork; we also asked them a similar question about how much they focused on assigning competence to low-status students.

Several measures indicated the quality of implementation. The percentage of students talking and working together, calculated from the Whole Class Instrument, is an indicator of how well the teacher is able to delegate authority and to foster interaction. Because special features of middle school classrooms (aside from teacher behavior) affected student interaction, we included two additional measures of quality of implementation in the middle school data. The first measure, the percentage of teacher's nonroutine behaviors, comes from the Teacher Observation Instrument used while students were working in small groups. This index combines the frequencies of treating status problems, making connections, and stimulating higher-order thinking. The index represents the percentage of total teacher talk in any of these three categories, that is, the nonroutine behaviors during learning center time. The second measure of nonroutine behavior is the average rate at which the teachers used status treatments (talked about multiple abilities and assigned competence) over a period of 10 minutes.

In addition to these measures of the quality of implementation, at the elementary level we also documented the amount of time spent and the number of *FO/D* units covered: the quantity of implementation. For a measure of implementation time, teachers estimated the average number of minutes per week children were at learning centers. Teachers also checked off a list of *FO/D* units they had implemented, thereby creating a measure of the number of units covered.

RESULTS

We first present the intercorrelations of measures of organizational support and implementation for the two studies. Simple correlations provide the first estimate of support for the three propositions. The matrices also indicate important control variables that affect implementation. The multivariate analyses that test the propositions then follow.

Intercorrelations

In Table 15.1, we present the matrix of intercorrelations for the elementary school data. With respect to the first proposition and as in previous studies (see Chapter 14), there is a statistically significant correlation ($r = .37$, $p < .05$) between the index of sound feedback and the percentage of students talking and working together. For the second proposition, there are some significantly positive associations between resources and coordination,

Table 15.1: Intercorrelations of Organizational Support Variables and Implementation: Elementary School

	1	2	3	4	5	6	7	8	9
1 % Talk	1.00								
2 Number of Units	.02	1.00							
	(30)								
3 Implementation Time	-.08	.45**	1.00						
	(30)	(33)							
4 Sound Feedback	.37*	.15	.04	1.00					
	(30)	(31)	(31)						
5 Materials	.22	.05	.36*	.26	1.00				
	(30)	(34)	(33)	(31)					
6 Resources	.35*	.03	.29*	.48**	.68***	1.00			
	(30)	(33)	(33)	(31)	(33)				
7 Organizational Help	.11	-.01	-.02	.30*	.54***	.63***	1.00		
	(30)	(34)	(33)	(31)	(34)	(33)			
8 Climate of Expectations	.47**	.09	.26	.10	.33*	.22	.41**	1.00	
	(27)	(27)	(27)	(27)	(27)	(27)	(27)		
9 Principal Knowledge, Behavior, Expectations	.33*	.51**	.19	.13	.29	.26	.29	.59***	1.00
	(30)	(33)	(33)	(31)	(33)	(33)	(33)		

*p<.05; **p<.01; ***p<.001

and measures of implementation. The index of resources is significantly related to percentage of students talking and working together ($r = .35, p < .05$) and to implementation time ($r = .29, p < .05$). The index of adequacy of materials is also related to the amount of implementation time ($r = .36, p < .05$). The index of climate of expectations correlated with the percentage of students talking and working together ($r = .47, p < .01$), giving some support for the third proposition. The knowledge, behavior, and expectations of the principal (an index reflecting both coordination and expectations) also correlates with the percentage of students talking and working together ($r = .33, p < .05$) and with the number of units covered ($r = .51, p < .01$).

In the middle school data (see Table 15.2), there is a significant negative relationship between the percentage of students disengaged and the dependent variables of the percentage of students talking and working together, and the percentage of nonroutine behaviors ($r = -.61, p < .001$ and $r = -.34, p < .05$, respectively). As described in Chapter 10, a number of classrooms in this middle school sample had severe management problems. Thus, in further analyses, we controlled for percentage of students disengaged. In this analysis, we also controlled for whether the teacher was in her second year of implementation.

The index of resources is significantly related to the number of units completed ($r = .58, p < .001$) and to implementation time ($r = .51, p < .001$), which is also significantly related to the index of the principal's knowledge, behavior, and expectations ($r = .38, p < .01$).

Multivariate Analyses

In this section, we report on a series of regressions of implementation on organizational support factors, typically two such factors at a time. Turning first to the impact of the feedback, Table 15.3 presents the regression analyses of the percentage of students talking and working together on measures of the perceived soundness of feedback at the elementary and middle school. The elementary school regression also includes the index of climate of expectations as a predictor variable.

For the elementary school, the index of perceived soundness and specificity of the feedback is a statistically significant predictor of the percentage of students talking and working together (Beta $= .36, p < .05$). This effect is independent of the effect of the climate of expectations which is also a significant predictor (Beta $= .43, p < .05$). In other words, in the classrooms of teachers who perceive their feedback as more specific and soundly based, the percentages of students interacting on task were higher than in classrooms of teachers who did not have such favorable perceptions of the feedback. Independent of this effect, the more the teachers reported expecta-

Table 15.2: Intercorrelations of Organizational Support Variables and Implementation: Middle School ($n = 53$)

	1	2	3	4	5	6	7	8	9
1 % Talk	1.00								
2 Number of Units	.34*	1.00							
3 Implementation Time	.08	.66***	1.00						
4 Sound Feedback	.09	.05	.21	1.00					
5 Materials	.11	.27	.12	.07	1.00				
6 Resources	.08	.58***	.51***	.23	-.28	1.00			
7 Organizational Help	-.17	.21	.31*	-.02	.00	.19	1.00		
8 Climate of Expectations	-.06	.27	.23	-.07	-.17	.30*	.69***	1.00	
9 Principal Knowledge, Behavior Expectations	.18	.25	.38**	-.26	-.34*	-.09	.07	.14	1.00
10 % Disengaged	-.61***	-.34*	.00	.11	-.28	-.04	.18	-.08	-.04

*p<.05; **p<.01; ***p<.001

Table 15.3: Relationship of Soundly Based Feedback to Percentage of Students Talking and Working Together: Elementary and Middle School (Dependent Variable = % Students Talking and Working Together)

Predictors	B	Beta	t	p (one-tailed)
Elementary School (n = 24)				
Constant	-.46 (14.98)[a]	.00	-.31	.382
Sound Feedback	2.08 (1.02)	.36	2.03	.028
Climate of Expectations	1.90 (.79)	.43	2.42	.013
$R^2 = .335$				
Middle School (n = 53)				
Constant	38.37 (2.12)[a]	.00	18.07	.000
Second Year Teacher[b]	7.38 (2.39)	.34	3.90	.002
% Disengaged	-.50 (.10)	-.54	-5.12	.000
Feedback Index[c]	0.13 (.07)	.21	2.00	.025
$R^2 = .48$				

[a]Standard errors in parentheses
[b]Dummy Variable: 2nd year = 1; 1st year = 0
[c]Summed index of 3 questions on perceived soundness X number of feedbacks

tions for implementation, the higher were the percentages of students interacting in their classrooms.

The middle school index of sound feedback, which includes the number of feedback meetings the teacher attended, is also a significant predictor of the percentage of students talking and working together (Beta = .21, $p < .05$). The effects of sound feedback, although not apparent in the correlation matrix, show up in this regression, when we controlled for the percentage of students disengaged and whether the teacher was in her second year of implementing. The percentage of students disengaged had a strong negative effect on the percentage of students talking and working together. Second-year teachers were significantly more successful in enhancing their students' talking and working together than were first-year teachers.

What were the effects of variables measuring resources and coordination in the multivariate analyses? For the elementary school data, a path model (Figure 15.1) illustrates the positive effects of resources and organizational help on the two indices of quantity of implementation. All the path coefficients in this model are statistically significant. The index of resources is a direct precursor of the amount of implementation time. Teachers' perceptions that they received satisfactory help with their materials is a predictor of reports of adequate resources.

Figure 15.1: Organizational Support and Quantity of Implementation:
Elementary School

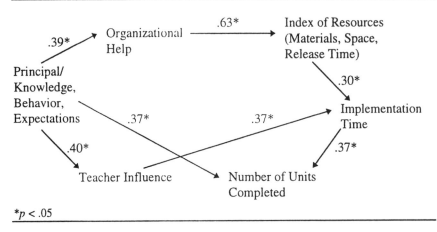

*p < .05

This particular path model shows a series of direct and indirect effects
of the index of principal knowledge, behavior, and expectations. Teachers
who gave a higher rating to their principals are the same teachers who
reported receiving more satisfactory organizational help. Informed principals who work with teachers and convey expectations are also the ones
associated with more units completed. Teachers who reported knowledgeable, active principals also reported a greater sense of their own influence,
which, in turn, has a direct effect on implementation time.

In the middle school data, we observed a similar pattern of the independent effects of organizational help and an informed, active principal
on teacher behavior (see Table 15.4). The dependent variable in this
regression is the percentage of teachers' nonroutine behaviors. Table
15.4 shows significant Beta weights for organizational help (Beta = .26,
$p < .05$) and for the principal's knowledge, behavior, and expectations (Beta
= .33, $p < .01$).

For the third indicator of implementation in the middle school data,
release time is a significant predictor of the rate of status treatments (see
Table 15.5). The more release time the teachers received, the more frequently
they implemented status treatments. The other significant predictors in this
regression are the index of sound feedback, whether the teacher is in the
second year of implementation, and the index of teacher effort in implementing the status treatments. Not surprisingly, the more teachers work and
worry about status treatments, the more they implement them.

The multivariate analyses just presented provide considerable evidence
in support of the proposition on organizational sanctions. At the elementary

Table 15.4: Regression of Nonroutine Behavior on Adequacy of Organizational Help and Principal Knowledge, Behavior, and Expectations: Middle School ($n = 51$) (Dependent Variable = % Non-Routine Behavior)

Predictors	B	Beta	t	p (one-tailed)
Constant	16.89 (3.57)[a]	.00	4.74	.000
Organizational Help	.66 (.35)	.26	1.97	.030
% Disengaged	-.16 (.09)	-.24	-1.77	.042
Principal Knowledge, Behavior, and Expectations	0.82 (.33)	.33	2.51	.008
$R^2 = .25$				

[a]Standard errors in parentheses

school level, the climate of expectations had a direct impact on the percentage of students talking and working together (see Table 15.3). The path model predicting the quantity of implementation showed a number of direct and indirect effects of the principal's behavior and expectations on the number of units covered. It should be recalled that principal expectations is one of the three items making up this index. The index of principal knowledge, behavior and expectations proved to be a powerful predictor of nonroutine behaviors at the middle school level (see Table 15.4).

DISCUSSION

The analysis shows good support for the importance of sound and specific feedback, of resources and coordination, and of a climate of expectations

Table 15.5: Regression of Rate of Status Treatments on Release Time, Soundly Based Feedback, and Teacher Effort on Using Status Treatments: Middle School ($n = 53$) (Dependent Variable = Rate of Use of Status Treatments)

Predictors	B	Beta	t	p (one-tailed)
Constant	-.84 (.34)[a]	.00	-2.44	.010
Teacher Effort	.15 (.04)	.41	3.67	.001
Sound Feedback	.01 (.01)	.24	2.21	.016
Release Time	.73 (.15)	.53	4.95	.000
Second-Year Teacher	.36 (.21)	.20	1.75	.044
$R^2 = .50$				

[a]Standard errors in parentheses

for successful implementation. Building on the findings of Ellis and Lotan (see Chapter 14), these results show that as important as the sheer number of feedback meetings is to the implementation of nonroutine behaviors, the perception by teachers that the feedback is soundly based and specific is equally powerful.

These findings support the utility of the rational perspective in organizational theory. Although we agree that schools exhibit many features of loose-coupling, we also argue that when teachers attempt to implement complex technology, schools need to become more tightly coupled. Moreover, if sociologists want to document rational connections between structure and technology, it is necessary to pick organizational arrangements that are very close, in time and in space, to specific features of the technology. By moving carefully from detailed knowledge of the challenges of implementation of this technology to the specific kinds of organizational support necessary to meet those challenges, we have been able to find solid support for three propositions relating complexity of technology to organizational arrangements.

These findings also illustrate the practicality of a theoretical model. When the principals and colleagues paid attention to the new technology, devoted resources and organizational attention to it, and coordinated those resources so that they were delivered to the classroom as needed, implementation flourished. To be sure, in some schools of our sample, teachers did not give a good, or even satisfactory, report on coordination and resources. However, there were many schools with relatively high values on these indicators, and teachers in these schools did better with implementation.

Differences Between School Levels

The effects of feedback were consistent, regardless of school level. However, we have reported some differences in the way that the organizational context affects the classroom at the two levels of schooling. How seriously should we take these differences? Some of the differences were due to problems of measurement of quantity of implementation at the middle level. Other differences were due to the special effects of peer group dynamics on the amount of observable student interaction among middle school students. The relationship of peer and academic status, discussed in Chapter 6, was a predictor of percentage of students talking and working together. Since this statistic varied among classrooms, it probably accounted for the differences among classes taught by the same teacher. Also, the levels of disengagement were higher in the middle school than in the elementary school, with serious disengagement in some classrooms reducing the amount of task-related interaction.

Undoubtedly, there are some true differences in the organizational context at the two levels. Middle schools appear to be even more loosely organized than elementary schools. Teachers at the middle school reported lower levels of support on all measures than teachers at the elementary level. However, it is of great interest that the middle school principals who were strong and active instructional leaders had important effects on the implementation of complex instruction. In the elementary school data, the general level of cooperation reported for teachers in the school as a whole was a positive predictor of the percentage of students talking and working together. No such relationship was found at the middle school. With departments and teams, it is not clear that teacher collaboration is a characteristic of an entire middle school. When departments and teams are allowed to set their own goals, the middle school may be very loosely coupled (Lee, 1995).

Importance of the Principal

The centrality of the role of the principal to successful innovation is a truism in the literature on school change. However, this literature is often not very precise about what the principal *does* that is effective in implementing change. According to the analyses reported in this chapter, there are two separate dimensions to the role of the principal: provision of resources and coordination, and instructional leadership. Strange as it may seem to those unacquainted with the behavior of school administrators, many principals take up innovations with enthusiasm and commitment, but with little follow-through. They do not worry about the teachers having the proper curriculum materials or the time to plan with other teachers. Other principals allocate the resources, but spend little or no time and effort coordinating them so that teachers actually benefit from them in a timely fashion.

Instructional leadership is a related, yet different, dimension. When principals attend workshops and make themselves expert in the innovation, they are in a far better position not only to coordinate but to help the teachers solve instructional problems and to insist that they follow through with the new strategies. Principals who have integrated the new methods of teaching with overall school goals, goals shared by the teachers, are in the strongest position to foster implementation (Lee, 1995).

In the Principal's Words

Mrs. Marlene Sipes, the principal of one of the middle schools in our sample, echoed our findings in talking about the role of the Stanford staff developers and teacher colleagues at her school.

First off, the fact that [Stanford's] support is in place, that the teachers know that the Stanford staff are coming out, it just gives that structure, so that they say "I need to be doing this." The other thing is, we have teams of teachers so that the teachers can support each other and they can work together to get ready for Stanford coming out, to get their lessons ready, and I think that helps also. So it gives a sense of structure, they know that they're coming just about once a month, they know that they will be getting feedback from them, they know that they've got to get a lesson ready. It forces them to implement the concepts and implement the curriculum. When they come out, it is a pleasurable experience for the teachers. They don't see it as somebody checking up on them or evaluating them. They see it as somebody there to support them, give them feedback. As we are getting things from them to help us provide better instruction and more appropriate curriculum for our kids, we're also helping Stanford learn about how children learn and how teachers teach.

The principal continued by describing her own role in supporting complex instruction:

One role that I played is just letting my staff know that I was supportive of this, this was a vision of mine. I set that tone, and then provided a lot of opportunity for dialogue, in staff development days as we began getting ready, about the components of complex instruction. So that was one way. Then, of course, in addition, I've got to find ways to support Diane and Marlene, to free them up to be teacher-leaders, so I set monies aside for that. They were the ones who wrote the sixth-grade curriculum, and I certainly don't expect them to do all that on weekends, so we provide for these times substitutes for them to come in and they are working in here down the hall. I provide space for them to work together, provide materials for them, they have a computer down there, so I support them in that kind of way. And then I mentioned the collaboration time for staff. And I try to get into the classrooms as much as I can and just champion the whole cause. It's exciting to see, it's always exciting to see complex instruction lessons. There are times when I talk to communities. We made a presentation at our board meeting about complex instruction, our relationship with the staff at Stanford. I talk about it at open houses, back-to-school night, and parent meetings of any sort. I write about it in our newsletter—just to keep people in the community informed that this is happening. (Interview, June 16, 1992)

CONCLUSION

A strong implication of the studies we reported in this chapter is that those working with demanding educational innovations would do well to select their schools for implementation carefully. A loosely coupled school will provide little support for the new technology. A principal who rarely visits classrooms, who is unwilling to attend staff development meetings, and who is unable to marshal necessary resources is like the proverbial "bad news" for the innovator. In contrast, a school where both the teachers and the principal feel influential in making decisions about instruction, a school marked by a high level of teacher collaboration with each other and with the principal, is much more likely to make the changes in instruction and to provide the necessary support for teachers during that critical first year of mastering new ways to teach.

CHAPTER 16

Linking Sociological Theory to Practice: An Intervention in Preservice Teaching

Patricia E. Swanson

The extent to which teachers use sociological theory to create more equitable classrooms rests on their understanding of the relevant theories and their application. Because teachers choose the learning tasks, define the organizational structure of the classroom, and shape its evaluation systems, it is they who must translate theory into practice. This chapter outlines findings from the study of a teaching intervention designed to assist preservice teachers in understanding and using principles from expectation states theory (Berger, Cohen, & Zelditch, 1972) to treat status problems in the classroom.

Teacher education is increasingly under critique as beginning teachers say there is little relation between the theory and research presented in university coursework and the realities of classroom life (Goodlad, 1990; Lanier & Little, 1986). Simultaneously, educational researchers argue that the knowledge base of teaching is increasingly complex (Shulman, 1987) and that teachers must learn not just to reflect on experience, but to incorporate into classroom decisions thoughtful analysis of relevant theory and research (Gage & Berliner, 1989).

Research from the Program for Complex Instruction at Stanford University documents both the importance of the teacher's theoretical understanding in treating status problems (Ellis & Lotan, 1991; Lotan, 1985; Swanson, 1993) and the efficacy of status treatments in equalizing student interaction during groupwork (Cohen & Lotan, 1995; see Chapters 5 and 6, this volume). These findings have clear implications for teacher education and lead to the question of how best to embed sociological theory into university coursework for teacher preparation. What instructional strategies are best employed in the university classroom to assist beginning teachers in seeing the relevance of theory and its link to student behavior? How, and to what extent, can beginning teachers learn to use formal sociological theory to analytically solve classroom status problems? While this study focuses on one sociological theory and its classroom application, it provides critical insights into the necessary features of university coursework that seeks to prepare teachers to reflect on formal theory when responding to complex and nonroutine classroom situations.

THEORETICAL FRAMEWORK FOR THE TEACHING INTERVENTION

In this study I analyzed a teaching intervention that combined extensive discussion of expectation states theory with the use of video vignettes designed to both model the status treatments and provide practice opportunities for beginning teachers to identify and treat classroom status problems.

The videotaped vignettes were used in two very distinct ways. Following introductory theoretical lectures, participants were divided into two groups. In one group, the tapes were used as a behavioral model for the learner to follow; in the other, the tapes were used to assist the learner in linking concepts from the theory to the status vignette and using theoretical knowledge to design an appropriate status treatment.

The instructional strategies employed for use with the videotapes stem from distinct theoretical frameworks. The first, behavioral modeling, rests on the principles of abstract modeling discussed by Bandura (1977). The learner's attention is drawn to the behavioral features of the status treatment, the treatment is modeled, and the learner is given opportunities to practice and receive feedback.

The second strategy rests on concepts from organizational theory, specifically the work of Perrow (1967). Perrow proposes that when organizational workers are faced with complex, nonroutine problems (e.g., status problems), they implement a search procedure. Increasing the knowledge of the worker increases the reliability of the analytic search procedure. I used Perrow's concept of analytic search in designing the second instructional strategy. The tapes were used as a vehicle to assist teachers in linking back to analytically search the theory in order to treat status problems. In this study, analytic search was defined as those instances in which the learner mentally links back to the theory, reviews it, and utilizes it in order to problem solve or implement new behaviors. I predicted that analytic search of the theory would enhance the learners' theoretical understanding, and that theoretical understanding would be essential for implementation of the status treatments.

I hypothesized that teachers' conceptual understanding of expectation states theory would be related to their ability to implement the status treatments (Hypothesis 1). In addition, I predicted that teachers who had opportunities to analytically search the theory during the interactive tape sessions would demonstrate both stronger implementation (Hypothesis 2) of the status treatments and enhanced conceptual understanding of the theory (Hypothesis 3).

PROCEDURE

The study was conducted in five preservice courses at two urban California State Universities (n = 112 subjects). Prior to the teaching intervention, teacher candidates completed a background questionnaire and several preassessment measures. These instruments were designed to assess teaching experience, beliefs about students and the nature of intelligence, and how teacher candidates interpreted groupwork problems prior to the intervention.

Subjects from participating preservice courses were divided into two groups for each of three instructional sessions (see Figure 16.1). The sessions, which both groups attended, began with introductory lectures on expectation states theory and the status treatments. Following the lectures the groups split for interactive sessions using the videotapes. While the same vignettes were used in each group, the tapes were discussed using very different strategies.

In the first group (called *modeling only*), teachers viewed and discussed the video vignettes, focusing on the behavioral features of status problems and status treatments, with no explicit linking to the theoretical knowledge base. For example, when discussing a group of seventh-grade boys participating in a groupwork activity involving setting priorities, subjects were asked to observe participation and influence, and identify the specific behaviors that indicated low status. They practiced identifying specific steps for treating status when observing the modeling vignettes, and they were asked to practice the status treatments by following those steps.

The second group (called *modeling with analytic search*) combined the abstract modeling intervention with extensive discussion of the theory. In contrast to the step-by-step behavioral procedures used in the first group, participants in the *modeling with analytic search* group were repeatedly asked to link the modeled behavior to relevant principles from expectation states theory. Rather than simply identifying those behaviors that indicated low status, this group was asked to analyze what status characteristics appeared to be operating in the group and to link those characteristics to students' expectations for competence and subsequent behavior. When observing the modeling vignettes, participants in the second group were asked to identify essential theoretical components of the treatments rather than procedural steps. When practicing the treatments, they were encouraged to include those components rather than follow a specific procedure. In this group, subjects

Figure 16.1: Study Sessions

PREASSESSMENT SESSION
Teacher Background Form: *Beliefs, Teaching Experience*
Vignette Preassessment: *Cognitive Predisposition*
(whole class, 60 minutes)

TEACHING SESSION 1
Lecture: *Expectation States Theory*
(whole class, 45 minutes)
Interactive Tape Session
(divided groups, 45 minutes)

Modeling Only   Modeling with Analytic Search

TEACHING SESSION 2
Lecture: *Multiple Abilities Status Treatment*
(whole class, 45 minutes)
Interactive Tape Session
(divided groups, 45 minutes)

Modeling Only   Modeling with Analytic Search

TEACHING SESSION 3
Lecture: *Assigning Competence Status Treatment*
(whole class, 45 minutes)
Interactive Tape Session
(divided groups, 45 minutes)

Modeling Only   Modeling with Analytic Search

OUTCOME SESSION
Outcome Assessment: *Conceptual Understanding and Implementation*

---

were repeatedly asked to link back to the theory and to use it to solve classroom status problems.

Following each of the three teaching sessions, subjects were asked to reflect on the session in a written journal entry. During the final session, an outcome assessment was administered. The test included open-ended questions designed to assess both conceptual understanding of expectation states theory and implementation of the status treatments. Most questions required subjects to reflect on written or video vignettes. For example, questions used to measure conceptual understanding required subjects to rank status orders, identify status treatments and their purposes, and discuss theoretical principles such as status generalization or the relevance bond. To measure implementation, or how well the subjects *used* the status treatments, subjects were asked to respond to written and video vignettes and to write exactly what they would do or say in response to the problematic situation. For example, after viewing a groupwork vignette in which a low-status student is excluded from a math task even though he is making excellent suggestions, subjects were asked to write exactly what they would say and to whom in order to treat the status problem. While clearly it would have been preferable to measure implementation of the status treatments through actual classroom behavior, the use of written and video vignettes provided a controlled setting in which to examine subjects' responses.

Scoring rubrics were created for measures of conceptual understanding and implementation. Subjects' answers were scored according to the quality and number of relevant theoretical components included in their answers. Scoring reliability (over 85%) was established for each instrument, and a detailed analysis of the outcome measure was completed in order to understand those aspects of the theory and its application that were problematic for subjects.

ANALYSIS OF THE OUTCOME ASSESSMENT

Subjects' scores on both conceptual understanding and implementation demonstrated a wide range of understanding and expertise. On questions assessing conceptual understanding, most subjects demonstrated knowledge of essential theoretical concepts such as status generalization and status orders. They were able to identify high- and low-status students from groupwork vignettes and label the different status treatments modeled by teachers. Most could identify the purpose of the assigning competence treatment; however, many had difficulty discussing the purpose of the multiple-ability treatment or explaining how teachers create a mixed set of expectations for competence. While subjects generally understood the link between status and group participation, they frequently ignored the ultimate effects of status on student learning.

Responses to vignettes measuring implementation, in which subjects were asked to treat actual status problems, again demonstrated a wide range of skill. When implementing the multiple-ability treatment, most subjects were able to analyze a multiple-ability task and identify the necessary abilities for students; however, they struggled with those components of the status treatment designed to equalize student status by creating a mixed set of expectations for each student's competence. Rather than conveying the message that no one student would have all the abilities, but each student would have some, they would state that "not everyone is good at all these abilities," which in fact implies that some people *are* good at all the abilities. Others stated, "No one has all these abilities, but everyone is good at *something*." Unfortunately, being "good at something" does not convey the message that each student has important *intellectual* abilities. There is no reason to assume that these statements would change students' perceptions of their peers' intelligence.

Several subjects during the teaching sessions commented that they felt the message embedded in the multiple-ability status treatment was simply not correct. They argued that some students did have all the intellectual abilities necessary to do most tasks, and that to state otherwise would be wrong. Whether through omission, difficulties with syntax, or differing beliefs about student intelligence, most subjects were unwilling or unable to include in their multiple-ability treatments those components designed to create a mixed set of expectations.

Subjects appeared more comfortable with assigning competence to low-status students. On the outcome measure, most could identify low-status students for treatment and explain what the students were doing successfully. They struggled, however, to identify the intellectual ability demonstrated by the low-status students' performance.

It is interesting to note that experienced teachers often comment that assigning competence to low-status students is very difficult. Low-status students often represent severe behavioral and academic challenges to the teacher, and it is difficult to move beyond these perceptions and recognize the intellectual abilities these students bring to a groupwork task. In comparison, when working from video vignettes, subjects in this study found it relatively easy to identify positive performances by low-status students. Unlike the classroom teacher, they were not struggling to look beyond existing knowledge of the students' academic skills or behavior.

ANALYSIS OF HYPOTHESES: THE RELATIONSHIP BETWEEN CONCEPTUAL UNDERSTANDING, IMPLEMENTATION, AND THE ANALYTIC SEARCH TREATMENT

The first hypothesis predicting a positive relationship between subjects' conceptual understanding and implementation was tested using Pearson pairwise correlation. The second and third hypotheses predicting the positive impact of the analytic search treatment on both implementation and conceptual understanding were examined using *t*-tests to assess group differences between the *modeling only* and the *modeling with analytic search* treatments.

The correlation between outcome assessment scores of conceptual understanding and implementation was positive and highly significant ($r = .484, p < .01, n = 90$). Teacher candidates' conceptual understanding of the theory was instrumental in their ability to treat status problems.

The impact of the analytic search treatment is considerably less clear. Table 16.1 provides descriptive statistics by group on outcome measures of conceptual understanding and implementation, as well as results of *t*-tests for significant group differences.

The analytic search treatment had no appreciable effect on subjects' conceptual understanding and a significant negative impact on implementation when compared with outcome scores from the *modeling only* group. The treatment did not enhance subjects' conceptual understanding and appears to have interfered with their implementation of the status treatments.

Interpretation

What caused the unexpectedly poor performance of subjects in the *modeling with analytic search* group? To answer this question, it is necessary to re-examine the teaching sessions.

Both groups received intensive exposure to expectation states theory, and both groups viewed the status vignettes during the interactive tape sessions. However, the analytic search treatment provided subjects with addi-

Table 16.1 Comparison of Average Group Scores on Dependent Variables

VARIABLE/ Treatment	range of scores	GROUP 1 modeling only			GROUP 2 modeling with analytic search			t-statistic p-value
		n	M	SD	n	M	SD	
CONCEPTUAL UNDERSTANDING	0–44	45	18.56	4.90	48	18.71	4.41	$t = 0.16$ ($p = .438$)
IMPLEMENTATION	-4–28	46	11.98	4.43	53	10.32	5.08	$t = -1.72$ ($p = .045$)
Multiple Ability Treatment	-2–14	49	5.98	2.24	55	5.31	2.64	$t = -1.39$ ($p = .084$)
Assigning Competence Treatment	-2–14	48	6.04	3.87	53	5.06	3.17	$t = -1.41$ ($p = .082$)

Note: All *p*-values represent one-tailed significance tests.
  Possible range of scores for each variable is noted after the variable name.

tional opportunities, through prompts and questions, to reflect on, or analytically search, the theory. In contrast, facilitators in the *modeling only* group avoided reference to the theory and focused participants on behavior. In spite of these structural differences, it appears that the *modeling only* group also searched the theory and used it to solve status problems. A comparison of one of the interactive sessions illustrates this point.

In the first interactive tape session, the participants discussed two vignettes showing status problems during groupwork. In the *modeling only* group, they discussed the vignettes in light of student participation and influence. They were asked to identify the specific behaviors that indicated high and low status in the group. In contrast, the *modeling with analytic search* group was asked to analyze the power and prestige order of the student groups and discuss the status characteristics and associated expectations they suspected were operating in the group.

In retrospect, it seems clear that both sets of questions initiate an analytic search of the theory. In the modeling group, subjects were prompted to use student behavior as evidence for their status ranking, while the analytic search group was asked to use specific concepts from the theory. Both are valid strategies for identifying a status order; the former is more concrete, the latter more abstract.

The *modeling only* treatment was originally designed not to stimulate thoughtful analysis, but to provide a procedure to teach subjects to replicate behavior. This was a naive assumption. Both groups had to think. It is not possible to identify a status order or do a status treatment without careful analysis. A teacher candidate's journal entry from the *modeling only* group clarifies this point: "I was thinking how you could just give us advice on group learning from your conclusions . . . but instead you show situations and get us thinking about the problems ourselves" (10211, journal, October 30, 1991).

This teacher clearly did not feel that she had been given a rote recipe delineating how to identify status problems. She saw the purpose of the interactive session as to "get us thinking about the problems ourselves." While her group was not prompted to think back to the theoretical lecture they had just heard, it is highly probable that they did. They may not have used the theoretical language of status characteristics and expectations when they discussed the vignettes, but they used the theory enough to identify the status order in each vignette, an analytic task.

Teachers in the *modeling with analytic search* group repeatedly were asked to use theoretical terms when discussing the vignettes. Use of these terms was designed to enhance access to the theory. This conscious effort to use theoretical language kept their discussion at a more abstract level than in the *modeling only* group. Unfortunately, neither raising the level of abstraction nor increasing subjects' use of theoretical language implies analytic search. The concept was misapplied. Indeed, it is possible that the formal, technical language used in the analytic search treatment had the effect of making an already complex set of ideas more difficult to understand.

What, then, triggered analytic search of the theory? It appears to have been the video vignettes. The tapes provided concrete situations for participants from *both* groups to refer to the theory and use it to problem solve. One subject from the analytic search group showed in his journal how a groupwork vignette from a science activity on chemical change, triggered an analytic search of the theory.

> The concept of getting low-status students to become participants in group activities is a very useful one. Recognizing who they are was a real revelation to me. Seeing them frozen out by their peers was a shock, but easily understood.
>
> The cures or techniques to get them some + status is more difficult. In tonight's film Millie certainly deserved recognition and praise, to get the plus that was needed.
>
> John is a tougher problem, and our group thought he said toward the end that the sugar had gone away. If he did, he also deserves a much needed + from the teacher. (10214, journal, November 13, 1991)

This beginning teacher used the tape as a base for linking back to the theory in order to analyze and treat status problems. He moves from discussing the concept of low status to a concrete situation in which he watches low-status students "frozen out by their peers." This situation then prompts him to turn back to the theory to problem solve, suggesting that Millie's and John's actions provided the opportunity for the teacher to give them some much needed "+ status."

The difference between the two treatment groups proved to be superficial in terms of its effect on conceptual understanding. It was not the questions, the prompts, or the abstract theoretical language that stimulated analytic search of the theory. It was the tapes. Both groups received initial exposure to the theory in the introductory lectures, and the two groups had equal opportunities to view the tapes. Consequently, they had equal opportunities to use theory. I believe this accounts for the lack of significant differences in conceptual understanding between the groups.

The negative impact of the analytic search treatment on implementation may be attributed to three factors: time constraints during the interactive tape sessions, too few practice opportunities, and too much information presented without the mental scaffolding provided by practice.

The teaching sessions were always rushed. Facilitators and subjects from both groups frequently commented that there was insufficient time during the interactive sessions to discuss the ideas presented. These time constraints were particularly severe in the *modeling with analytic search* group, where theoretical discussion often cut into time to practice the status treatments.

One student from the analytic search group expressed both frustration and faltering confidence in his ability to implement due to insufficient time and practice.

> These are new concepts for me and I felt [the experimenter] had too much to present in too short a time. We had [to] rush-rush at each step of the analysis. Only one group spoke on their project [a multiple-ability orientation]. They did better than we would have. (10214, journal, November 7, 1991)

Concrete practice opportunities to cognitively rehearse and to present the status treatments, are an essential component of abstract modeling. Subjects in the *modeling only* treatment group had less to discuss and more time to practice; consequently, their implementation scores were significantly higher than those in the analytic search treatment.

Finally, the *modeling with analytic search* treatment was far more intellectually demanding than the *modeling only* treatment. The modeling group received specific instructions on how to implement the status treatments. In contrast, the components used in the analytic search group required more open-ended problem solving. This left more room for creativity and more room for error. To use these abstract components, teachers needed to be given more, not less, time for practice and feedback. Practice and feedback provide the necessary mental scaffolding for the learner to gain a deeper understanding of the underlying concepts and their application.

This analysis of the treatment groups offers several insights. First, the tapes provided invaluable opportunities for both groups to practice analytic search of the theory. While it was essential that subjects reflect on the major ideas discussed in the theory, it was not necessary that they use abstract theoretical language to do so.

Second, when time is limited (and it usually is), modeling is an exceptionally strong strategy to assist learners in the implementation of new complex behaviors. Given the time constraints of the teaching sessions and limited practice opportunities, the detailed instructions that participants in the *modeling only* group received, provided the necessary specificity for adequate implementation.

ADDITIONAL ANALYSIS OF THE DATA

Additional analysis was conducted to determine the effect of a number of variables with clear potential to influence subjects' scores on conceptual understanding and implementation. These variables included attendance, academic writing ability, teaching experience, beliefs about students and the nature of intelligence, and a measure designed to assess how subjects interpreted groupwork problems prior to the intervention. Attendance was recorded during each of the teaching sessions. Academic writing ability was measured using three open-ended questions from the outcome assessment, which were scored for general coherence as well as grammar and syntax. The remaining variables were calculated from two instruments administered prior to the teaching sessions: the teacher background form and the vignette preassessment measure. On the teacher background form, subjects were asked a number of questions concerning their prior teaching experiences. These questions were compiled to form a five-point scale ranging from a score of one, indicating fewer than 10 days of student teaching, to a score of five, indicating more than one year of full-time teaching. Subjects were also asked to complete a series of 17 Likert-scale questions relating to their beliefs about students and the nature of intelligence. These questions focused primarily on the degree to which subjects viewed intelligence as multidimensional, or composed of many different abilities, and subject to improvement with time and practice. I included these questions because I felt that teacher candidates who viewed intelligence in this way would be more comfortable using the multiple-ability treatment and more likely to see intellectual abilities in students lacking traditional academic skills.

In contrast to the Likert-scale beliefs questions, the vignette preassessment measure required subjects to respond to a series of written and video vignettes in which they were asked to interpret and respond to student groupwork situations. The vignette preassessment was designed to capture the degree to which subjects analyzed groupwork problems sociologically and to ascertain whether subjects were able to notice the intellectual contributions of low-status students. I called this tendency to interpret groupwork problems sociologically, cognitive disposition, and it proved to be one of the most interesting variables in the study.

For example, in one question from the vignette preassessment, teacher candidates were asked to view a tape showing a group of third graders building a straw structure. In the vignette, one student, Juan, stood slightly apart from the group alternately watching or quietly disengaged and playing with a straw. Subjects were asked why they thought Juan was not participating. While many attributed his behavior to lack of *individual* motivation or to shyness, others noted that the *group* made no room for Juan at the table. They ignored him and seemed to feel he had nothing to offer the group. Subjects whose answers reflected this dimension of *group analysis,* rather than strictly focusing on the individual, were viewed as having a cognitive disposition to view groupwork problems sociologically. The cognitive strategies they used in interpreting the vignette would allow them to easily see status problems.

Other written vignettes examined cognitive disposition to recognize the intellectual abilities that low-status students display. One vignette provided examples of two third-grade worksheets. Each worksheet contained a diagram and a written explanation showing how to make a complete electrical circuit. One worksheet, Norma's, included an excellent diagram that showed two different ways to connect the circuit; however, her written explanation was poor, with many grammatical and spelling errors. The second worksheet, Angela's, had an adequate diagram and a well-written, although not detailed, explanation. Subjects were asked to assess which student had a better understanding of the scientific concepts.

Subjects who were able to note the scientific understanding embedded in Norma's diagram, in spite of her poorly written explanation, were considered to have a cognitive disposition to recognize the intellectual abilities that low-status students often display when given a multiple-ability task.

Detailed analysis of each of the variables described in this section showed three with significant correlations to subjects' scores on the outcome assessment: teaching experience, academic writing ability, and cognitive disposition. It is interesting to note that neither attendance nor teacher candidates' beliefs about intelligence showed significant correlations to conceptual understanding or implementation. It is possible that attendance was not a significant factor due to a degree of redundancy in the teaching sessions; however, the lack of any relationship between the beliefs questions and outcome scores is perplexing. Teacher candidates appear to have answered the Likert-scale beliefs questions normatively. It is possible that they had been exposed to the idea of multiple intelligences in their coursework and consequently attempted to choose what they perceived to be the "right" answers rather than choosing answers that accurately reflected their own beliefs. Tables 16.2 and 16.3 provide descriptive statistics and intercorrelations for each of the variables significantly correlated to conceptual understanding and implementation.

Most subjects had some degree of classroom experience and adequate writing skills. However, to the degree that variation existed, these variables were significantly correlated to outcome assessment scores on conceptual understanding and implementation. Subjects' wide range of scores on cognitive disposition demonstrate considerable variation in how subjects inter-

Table 16.2: Descriptive Statistics: Variables Correlated to Conceptual Understanding and Implementation

Variable	score range	n	M	SD	Min.	Max
Teaching Experience	1–5	93	3.32	1.18	1	5
Cognitive disposition	-2–8	95	4.06	1.84	0	8
Academic Writing	0–6	96	5.38	0.72	3	6
Conceptual Understanding	0–44	93	18.63	4.63	9	29
Implementation	-4–8	99	11.09	4.83	0	23

preted groupwork situations prior to the intervention. The strong positive correlation between cognitive disposition and conceptual understanding suggests that this variable played an important role in determining how subjects came to understand expectation states theory.

Analysis of the Path Model

Regression analysis was used to determine the relative effects of each of the independent variables on scores for conceptual understanding and implementation. Conceptual understanding, as predicted, proved to be a mediating variable with respect to implementation. When conceptual understanding was regressed on teaching experience, academic writing ability, and cognitive disposition, each had a significant independent effect. These variables had no direct effect on implementation. In contrast, the analytic search treatment showed no significant relationship to conceptual understanding, but had a direct negative impact on implementation.

Table 16.3: Intercorrelations: Variables Correlated to Conceptual Understanding and Implementation

Variable	1	2	3	4	5
1. Teaching Experience	1.00	—	—	—	—
2. Cognitive Disposition	-.025	—	—	—	—
3. Academic Writing	-.260*	.294**	—	—	—
4. Conceptual Understanding	-.274*	.372**	.298**	—	—
5. Implementation	-.261*	.138	.228*	.484**	—

Note: Asterisks indicate 2-tailed significance tests. $*p < .05$ $**p < .01$

Figure 16.2: Path Model—Relationship of Independent Variables to Conceptual Understanding and Implementation

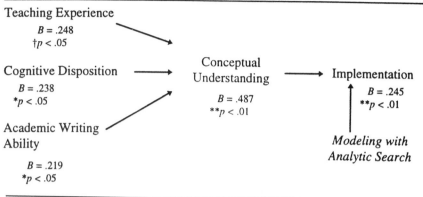

Note: *p indicates a one-tailed probability test; †p indicates a two-tailed probability test

Figure 16.2 illustrates the relative effects of each of the independent variables on conceptual understanding and implementation. The strongest factor affecting implementation of the status treatments was conceptual understanding of expectation states theory. Teaching experience, academic writing ability, and cognitive disposition each, in turn, shaped outcome scores on conceptual understanding.

The effect of writing ability on conceptual understanding is predictable since understanding was measured on a written test; however, the negative impact of teaching experience is perplexing. It is possible that teacher candidates with more classroom experience (as instructional assistants or teaching on emergency credentials) had less recent experience in academia than those who moved directly from undergraduate studies into a fifth-year credentialing program. These more experienced teacher candidates may simply have been out of practice academically and may have struggled with the technical vocabulary and the extensive writing required on the outcome assessment. Tentative support for this argument is provided by the negative correlation between teaching experience and academic writing ability ($r = .-260$, $p = .019$).

Cognitive disposition proved a particularly robust measure. Subjects' responses to vignettes on the preassessment measure showed the cognitive strategies they used to interpret groupwork problems prior to the intervention. These initial strategies played an important role in how teacher candidates came to understand expectation states theory. The following section examines the unique characteristics of this variable.

Cognitive Disposition

The impact of cognitive disposition on conceptual understanding is fascinating from two perspectives: its predictive power and its ability to change.

The predictive power of cognitive disposition is particularly striking when compared with the more traditional Likert-scale beliefs questions included on the teacher background form. Teacher candidates tended to answer these questions normatively, and their answers showed no relation to their responses on the outcome measure. The weaknesses in the beliefs questions emphasize the strengths of the vignette preassessment. The vignettes captured the interaction between beliefs and cognitive strategies and consequently were a strong predictor of conceptual understanding. Two examples from the vignette preassessment demonstrate the strength of this measure. The first focuses strictly on cognitive strategies, the second on the interaction between beliefs and cognitive strategies.

In the first vignette, as described previously, a group of third-grade students are building a straw structure. One student, Juan, stands at the edge of the group, playing with a straw and watching intently, but is unable to get close enough to the structure to participate. Subjects were asked to give reasons for Juan's lack of participation in the activity.

> One subject listed a string of possibilities: He is new to the class. He doesn't communicate well with the other children. He feels excluded from the group. He has problems outside of the classroom (at home, etc.). He's not as outgoing as the other kids. He doesn't speak English. He doesn't want to be rejected. He's shy. He's afraid of failing. (10311)

This subject focused entirely on the personality and characteristics of the one excluded student. Her cognitive strategy for analyzing the vignette focused on information about the individual, not the group. Teachers who look only to the excluded individual to define a status problem come up with very different strategies for addressing the problem. These strategies usually rest on raising the self-esteem of the individual rather than changing the group's perceptions. This cognitive disposition leads teachers to attend to information that will not assist them in understanding or treating status problems.

The second example contrasts two subjects' responses to Norma's and Angela's worksheets on completing a circuit. Reduced copies of the two worksheets are provided in Figure 16.3.

Subjects were asked to decide which student had a better grasp of the concepts and to explain their choice. One subject wrote the following:

Figure 16.3: Student Worksheets

Name Norma
Date _____

How did you make your circuit?

Draw

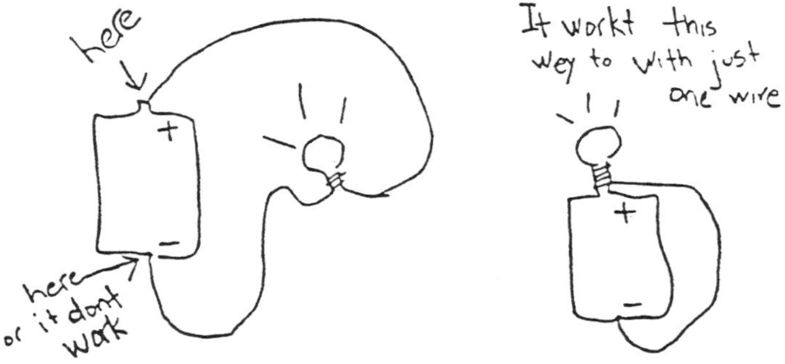

here
it won't
work

Explain

It had to tuch both
ends of the batry

Name _____
Date Sept 30, 199_

How did you make your circuit?

Draw

It workt this
wey to with just
one wire

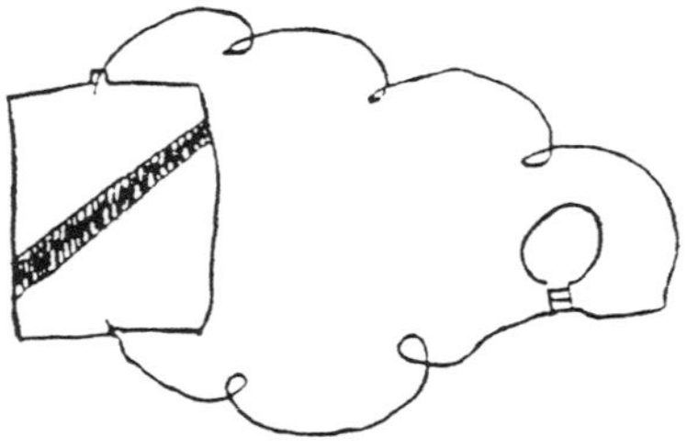

Explain

To make a complete circuit you have to
have a battery wires and a light bulb you have
to attach one end of the wire to the light bulb
and the other end to the bottom of the battery
You have to attach the other wire to the light
bulb end the top of the battery you have to
be carefull they touch or it should light up
the light bulb

255

Angela has a better grasp of the important concepts because she specifically tells how the hook-up should be done. This way would be a complete circuit. . . . I would compliment Angela on the completeness of her answer to encourage the behavior and thought processes in the future. I would also compliment Norma on hers but w/ the addendum, "You're on the right track!! Explain a little more to me." Hopefully this would encourage her to "run" with her idea, that it is valid as long as she justifies it. What's impt. [*sic*] here is to encourage her that she definitely is *not* wrong. (10217)

Another subject responded in this way:

Norma [has a better grasp of the concepts]—because she included the positive and negative charges in her diagram and presented two possibilities. . . . Angela's meticulous drawing with the curly-Q's in the wires could indicate lack of comprehension of the principle. . . . Norma needs encouragement of what she's good at. Grammar and neatness on these kinds of assignments should be ignored. (10107)

These two teachers thought in different ways about Norma's intellectual ability and had different priorities in terms of the purpose of the lesson. More important, they attended to very different information in the vignette, and their responses indicate different cognitive strategies for addressing the situation.

The first teacher attributes tremendous importance to writing ability. Because Angela can write about the circuit, this teacher assumes that her understanding is superior. She indicates that she would encourage Angela's "thought processes" and tell Norma she's "on the right track." She ignores Norma's diagram, which shows the positive and negative ends of the battery, and misses the fact that Norma demonstrates superior application of electrical principles by showing two ways to connect the circuit. While she wishes to encourage Norma, her response does not indicate that she considers Norma particularly intelligent. She sees writing ability as an indicator of intelligence and uses this information to shape her response to the situation.

The second teacher attends to very different information. Ignoring Norma's lack of writing ability, she notes that Norma has labeled the positive and negative ends of the battery and demonstrated two ways to complete the circuit. She focuses on the demonstration of scientific understanding rather than written form. This teacher believes that Norma is intellectually capable. She is cognitively disposed to attend to the content of Norma's diagram rather than to her written explanation. She uses different information than the first teacher to shape her response.

The vignette preassessment instrument captured a rich variety of information relevant to how subjects came to understand the theory. Beliefs about students and their intellectual capacity were nested in subjects' responses to the vignettes. However, it was the different kinds of cognitive strategies that subjects displayed that were of the greatest interest. These existing dispositions to organize and process information in different ways played an important role in subjects' ultimate understanding of the theory and its classroom application.

A second interesting feature of cognitive disposition was its ability to change as subjects learned to attend to new information during the teaching sessions. The following excerpts from one teacher's vignette preassessment and her outcome test illustrate both the predictive power of cognitive disposition as well as the fact that it changes with new information.

On the preassessment instrument, this teacher provided the following interpretation for Juan's lack of participation in the groupwork activity:

> Juan may be bored with this particular activity, he may not know what the task is, or have other things on his mind such as family concerns, etc. He may also feel "uncomfortable" with the students in his group. . . . He might think that he may ruin the structure by having it fall apart, or he may fear what the other kids might say about where he places his straw. (20127)

This teacher ignores the group's behavior toward Juan. Her interpretation focuses on Juan and the difficulties he may be experiencing. On the outcome instrument, this same teacher watched a different vignette of a seventh-grade boy, Will, excluded from a groupwork activity. While the circumstances in the vignette were quite similar, she used very different information to interpret and respond to the groups behavior. Asked to explain her rationale for which student she chose to assign competence to, she now responded:

> I chose Will because he was the one who was "ignored" by the other two. Those who are "ignored" may be seen as incompetent, and it's best if the teacher doesn't allow such "leaving out" of people to continue since it might damage the person's self-esteem. (20127)

This time she did not put the entire burden on Will, but rather looked to the group. It is interesting to note that she saw the consequence of Will's exclusion as damaging to his self-esteem rather than as affecting his learning opportunities. Her understanding of status problems and their consequences is incomplete. Nonetheless, she has learned to analyze the group sociologically. Because of this she will be more likely and more able to treat status problems in the future.

Findings from this study indicate that while cognitive disposition predicted conceptual understanding of the theory, it was nonetheless possible to change cognitive disposition. Exposure to sociological theory enabled teachers to attend to new information during groupwork, to interpret this information differently, and consequently to respond in new ways.

IMPLICATIONS FOR TEACHER EDUCATION

Three issues emerge from this study that carry powerful implications for teacher education. First, the power of the video vignettes as both a research and a teaching tool; second, the role of practice and feedback in learning to implement new and complex classroom strategies; and finally, the utility of addressing cognitive disposition rather than confronting beliefs in teacher education.

The video vignettes proved to be a powerful instructional tool. They provided models to assist beginning teachers in their implementation of the status treatments. More important, they allowed participants to respond to concrete classroom situations and practice treating status problems. The tapes helped teachers link formal theory to classroom practice.

The tapes did not allow for subterfuge. The responses to the tapes brought the learners' beliefs and cognitive strategies to the surface and opened them up for discussion and analysis. This made the vignettes not just a powerful teaching tool, but a strong research instrument.

A second important implication stems from a comparison of the implementation scores of the two groups. The *modeling only* group, which had slightly more time for practice and feedback, showed significantly stronger implementation than the *modeling with analytic search* group. It is essential to note that both groups received intensive introductory lectures on the theory and that conceptual understanding was the strongest predictor of implementation. However, it was not necessary to place continued emphasis on technical theoretical discussion during the interactive tape sessions. Rather, the learners needed time for practice and feedback.

A final implication for teacher educators emerges from the analysis of data concerning the relationship of subjects' beliefs and cognitive disposition to their conceptual understanding and implementation. Likert-scaled questions designed to directly measure subjects' beliefs about students and the nature of intelligence showed no relation to subjects' understanding of the theory or their ability to implement status treatments. When subjects were asked directly how easily they could rank their students by intelligence, or whether they thought students who did not do well in school might have other intellectual strengths, they tended to answer normatively. Beliefs are difficult to bring to the surface, particularly if subjects, in this case students, suspect that their beliefs may not be shared by the instructor. Reformers often argue that the key to changing teaching practice is to change teachers' beliefs. Data from this study suggest a different strategy. Beliefs are easily hidden and resistant to change. Cognitive disposition is not. Cognitive disposition, as measured by the vignette preassessment, showed how teacher candidates viewed a classroom situation, what information they used, and how they used that information. Their beliefs were embedded in their interpretations. Cognitive disposition was strongly related to how teacher candidates came to understand the theory and ultimately how they implemented the status treatments. New knowledge can affect the information learners attend to and how they use that information. For the teacher educator, this implies that rather than confronting teachers' beliefs directly, it is more productive to provide them with a knowledge base and concrete practice opportunities in which to interpret classroom situations in new ways.

CONCLUSION

Creating more equitable classrooms rests in large part on the knowledge and skills of teachers. This study demonstrates that there is a place for sociological theory in the classroom. It can guide classroom practice in the most challenging situations.

The strength of the modeling intervention cannot be overlooked. However, modeling alone was not sufficient to help teachers address status problems. If beginning teachers are to know when, how, and, most important, why to implement the status treatments, the treatments must be learned in conjunction with the knowledge base from which they are derived.

CHAPTER 17

Organizational Factors and the Continuation of a Complex Instructional Technology

Rene F. Dahl

One of the most enduring dilemmas faced by those who work in schools is how to institutionalize effective instructional practices. This problem, extensively documented in the literature, continues to be a concern for school personnel who want positive instructional programs to survive over time. In this chapter, I examine the survival of a complex instructional program that makes unique demands on the organization. The guiding question for this study was, What organizational conditions must be in place if a complex instructional program is to continue over time?

Conducted during the 1986–87 academic year, the study examined the continuation of *Finding Out/Descubrimiento* (De Avila & Duncan, 1982b). The teachers in this sample had participated in the summer institute and began implementation a minimum of 3 years prior to the beginning of this study. The uniqueness of this study lies in its use of sociological theory to explain the phenomenon of program continuation.

This chapter includes a discussion of the theoretical framework used in the study; descriptive findings of how well the *FO/D* curriculum continued over time; the role of the teacher, school, and district in program survival; the results of tests of several formal hypotheses drawn from organizational theory; and several cross-organizational level analyses of specified district, school, or classroom level indicators.

THEORETICAL FRAMEWORK

Two models of organizations provided the theoretical framework for this study, the institutional and rational models. I explain them briefly here to provide the reader with a context with which to understand the hypotheses and findings of this study.

Institutional Theory

According to Meyer and Rowan (1977), the institutional model of organizations has been used increasingly to explain the structure and processes of schools. The authors claim that organizations that exist in institutionalized environments are highly dependent on these environments for acceptable accounts to legitimate their activities. Thus, schools abide by institutionalized rules that define what a school is, because it is important to their survival. In turn, they are funded, thereby ensuring their own survival. Schools, therefore, must be open and responsive to environmental demands and must structurally reflect what society believes schools "should" look like. Typically, it is the responsibility of organizational elites, or managers, to interact with and negotiate the environment(s) in order to maintain and increase the organization's legitimacy. This means that the managers' time and energy are focused outward rather than inward on the work of the organization. In the case of schools, then, superintendents interact with governing and regulatory bodies, with funding sources such as foundations and government staff, and with any actor with the ability to affect the schools' legitimacy. Moreover, any program that increased a district or school's legitimacy would receive support and resources from organizational elites. Meyer, Scott, and Deal (1981) go so far as to claim that schools succeed or fail based on their conformity to institutional rules rather than on their technological efficiency and performance. In this study, I examined the relationship between a district's perceptions of legitimacy of the program and the program's continuation in order to test the following hypothesis:

> The continuation of a complex technology will be related positively to the degree of perceived legitimacy of the technology by organizational elites.

For this proposition, program continuation was measured as formal existence (i.e., whether the program existed) as well as the quality and extent of continuation.

Rational Theory

I used a second model of organizations, rational theory, to examine some of the internal processes and structures of schools. The rational model emphasizes the importance of coordination and control of the technical core as a critical ingredient for organizational effectiveness (Thompson, 1967). Perrow (1967) claimed that complex technology, characterized by high levels of interdependence and task uncertainty, pushed an organization toward interdependent work arrangements, while Thompson (1967) added that organizations with interdependent workers have an increased need for coordination.

When principals coordinate, they are expected to focus their efforts on bringing together grade level curriculum, resources, time, teaching schedules, and classrooms. The staff of the Program for Complex Instruction mandated principal coordination in the first year of implementation, which pushed the school toward increased staff interdependence. Even though the teachers were facing uncertainty in the classroom, this uncertainty also imposed certain expectations on the principal (Dahl, 1989).

The following theoretical proposition was derived from the rational organizational model:

> Given a complex technology that mandates coordination and control, coordination will be positively related to the continuation of the technology.

For this proposition, program continuation was measured as both quality and extent of continuation.

In the next section, I discuss how continuation was measured and present the descriptive findings regarding how well *FO/D* continued over time.

CONTINUATION MEASURES

Three program continuation measures were used; the first measure was formal continuation. This measure only was used to test the hypothesis on legitimacy and continuation.

For the second measure, quality of implementation, I used the following indicators derived from the Whole Class Instrument (see Appendix A): percentage of students talking and working together, percentage of students disengaged, and use of multiple materials and learning centers. These indicators measured delegation of authority, teacher's classroom management, and the level of differentiation of the technology in the classroom, respectively. In addition, I used a summary measure of quality of implementation (see Dahl, 1989, for a full discussion of measures).

Indicators for the third measure, quantity of implementation, included the number of months per school year that the curriculum was used, the number of days per week it was used, and the total number of *FO/D* units the teacher used during the school year.

THE STATUS OF PROGRAM CONTINUATION:
INITIAL FINDINGS

Sixty-one teachers met the criteria for the study, which meant that they had received their CI training 3 years or more before the study was conducted. Of those 61 teachers, 32 (52%) reported that they were still using *FO/D*. Nineteen teachers (31%) were not using *FO/D*; 10 teachers (16%) could not be located. The teachers were organized into four cohorts according to the year in which they received CI training at Stanford University (see Table 17.1).

Thirty-three percent of the 51 teachers who reported data had 14 or more years of teaching experience at the time they were surveyed for this study, while 28% had 11–13 years of experience. Only one teacher had taught for less than 4 years. Grade levels ranged from kindergarten to sixth grade, and most classrooms were designated as English-speaking only, although some of the teachers spoke Spanish to their students, as needed.

Twenty-six schools in eight districts were represented in this study. All of the schools except two were located in urban areas. Data collected from the schools indicated that on average, 46% of students were of Latino descent, while on average, students of Asian and South Pacific Island descent represented 10%. Almost half of students in the schools qualified for Chapter 1 funds, and half were in free lunch programs.

Reasons for Continuation or Discontinuation

The two most frequent reasons that teachers articulated for continued implementation of *FO/D* were (1) the program worked for students, and (2) students like the program. One teacher stated, "Of all my training, *FO/D* put all the pieces together . . . it really works and I get excited watching the kids learn." Another teacher said, "*FO/D* is great," and continued that "its link with survival is its cooperative learning component." Still another teacher said that she liked the math units and her students liked the entire program.

Table 17.1: FO/D Teachers by Training Cohort, 1982–1986

Cohort	Year Trained	*n*	Continuing Sample	Not Continuing Sample	Not Located
I	1982–83	17	10	4	3
II	1983–84	11	1	7	3
III	1984–85	18	13	3	2
IV	1985–86	15	8	5	2
TOTALS		61	32	19	10

The biggest barrier to program continuation was teacher turnover. When asked why they stopped implementing the program, the 19 teachers who had discontinued cited numerous reasons, including becoming an administrator, being transferred to non-*FO/D* schools and grade levels, not enough school support, implementation was too demanding, dislike of the program, and use of another science program.

Closer analysis revealed an important finding: Of the 19 teachers who stopped using the program, 17 (89.5%) did so for organizational reasons such as transfers, promotions, and assignments to new positions. Only two of the teachers stopped implementing the program for reasons that were solely "within their control." In other words, only two teachers (10.5%) could have continued the program but chose not to.

Classroom Implementation

To determine what classroom implementation looked like 3 or more years after training, I collected observation data in classrooms of 21 of the 32 teachers who were still using *FO/D*. Data were collected during five visits to each classroom over a span of 4 months. Two observations were collected per visit, for a total of 10 observations per classroom.

Observational data show that the teachers still using *FO/D* 3 years after training were implementing the program successfully. Classroom observations of these teachers indicated that sound implementation in the first year meant sound implementation in subsequent years. In other words, when teachers successfully implemented *FO/D* in their first year, in which they received specific feedback and organizational support, they continued to implement the program successfully 3 years or more after training. I determined this by comparing the teachers' first-year implementation and subsequent implementation data with quality control standards developed by the Program for Complex Instruction at Stanford University.

The teachers in this study were impressive on the major indicator of quality of implementation, students talking and working together, which provides evidence that the teachers delegated authority to students. Only one classroom fell below the first-year quality control standard of more than 30% of students talking and working together.

More problematic were the teachers' ratings on classroom management, as measured by students who were disengaged from the academic task. Seven of 21 classrooms had higher than the 6% quality control standard for students disengaged, although 4 of those 7 classrooms were just over 6%, at 6–7.8%. When compared with first-year implementation data, 12 classrooms showed an increase in their percentage of students disengaged. Of these 12 classrooms, 3 had had the highest rates of percentage disengaged during their first year of implementation. This finding suggested that when class-room management problems were not solved adequately early on, they continued to plague teachers and in some cases grew worse in subsequent years of implementation.

For quantity of implementation, findings showed that teachers used the *FO/D* curriculum less frequently than the standards recommended by the Program for Complex Instruction. On average, teachers implemented the program between 4 and 5 months during the school year, compared with the recommended 8–9 months. In addition, teachers used the curriculum 1–2 days a week, versus the recommended 4 days a week, and they completed between two and seven curriculum units out of the 17 that were available for use.

School Support and the Principal's Role

Data on school level factors were collected by a questionnaire distributed to principals. Principals identified specific tasks in which they engaged during the school year to help teachers implement *FO/D*. The question used to obtain these data was as follows:

Please put a check beside any of the following tasks that you have done this year:
—— Arranged for appropriate *FO/D* classroom
—— Arranged for storage of supplies and materials
—— Provided time for teachers to observe and give feed back to one another
—— Provided time for teachers to meet
—— Met with *FO/D* teachers to develop plans for next year
—— Arranged for a classroom assistant in each *FO/D* classroom
—— Provided time for *FO/D* teachers to develop new curriculum
—— Developed a school-wide plan regarding which grade level taught what *FO/D* units

The data showed that principal involvement varied considerably, both by principal and by year of implementation. Even though principals were strongly encouraged to be involved in numerous ways during the first year of implementation—from attending the training sessions, to securing resources and supplies, to arranging for teachers to observe one another during imple-mentation, to coordinating room schedules – their involvement in the year of my study ranged from complete support to no involvement at all.

Some of the principals who were supportive in the first year perceived their roles differently in subsequent years. Some of these principals relied on *FO/D* trainers to fulfill the functions that they themselves had carried out the first year, while others continued to perform those duties beyond the first year of implementation. Overall, the data showed that the type of support provided by principals was not stable from year to year, even with the same principal.

To determine whether principal turnover had an effect on program continuation, I used the sample of 35 teachers who taught in the same school during the entire time they used *FO/D*. Then I determined how many principals each teacher had at her school. Twenty teachers, or 57%, reported working with only one principal, while 15 teachers, or 43%, had two principals. Of the 20 teachers who had one principal, 14, or 70%, continued to use *FO/D*, while 10 teachers, or 67%, with two principals continued to use *FO/D*. I used analysis of variance to determine whether there were district effects regarding principal turnover. The F ratio of 8.29 was statistically significant at $p < .001$, which indicated that the district was a source of variation regarding principal turnover.

District Support

Data on district level support were obtained from a questionnaire that was distributed to the person identified as the most knowledgeable about *FO/D*. In the third year and beyond, the ideal district continued to provide funding for the program. One example was the expense of training *FO/D* trainers. Often schools did not have the resources to fund trainers, so by providing resources to develop its capacity to expand the program, the district demonstrated a commitment to the program. The items on the questionnaire that related to program support were: "Is your district planning to train any new *FO/D* trainers for next year?" with "Yes," "No," and "Don't Know" response choices. The follow-up question was, "If yes, to what extent will the district provide funding for these trainers to attend training?" These response choices were "Great," "Moderate," "Slight," and "Not at all." Three of the eight districts (37.5%) in this study provided some funding for trainers.

To determine how *FO/D* was coordinated at the district level and by whom, the following question was asked, "Is there a position in your district designated specifically to coordinate *FO/D*?" The response choices were "Yes" and "No." The follow-up question was, "If yes, please explain." None of the districts designated a district level position solely for *FO/D*. Instead, this responsibility fell to managers in charge of other programs, such as language development and bilingual education, mentor teacher, and elementary instruction. One district did not designate anyone to oversee the program, but instead shifted the responsibility to mentor teachers at the school level.

Most district level staff indicated that their role in relationship to *FO/D* was primarily financial, while others saw their responsibilities as providing human resources, evaluating the program, encouraging teachers to use the program, sponsoring *FO/D* training within the district, preparing and distributing materials, giving feedback, and problem solving regarding program expansion.

Data on 51 teachers in eight districts indicated that two districts had a higher proportion of teachers who stopped using *FO/D* than those who continued. In two other districts, approximately half of the teachers continued and half did not, while in the remaining four districts, all the teachers continued using *FO/D* 3 or more years after training.

To determine whether the district was a factor in the continued use of *FO/D*, I used a chi-square test, resulting in a likelihood ratio chi-square value of 21.940, with $df = 7$, $p < .01$. This finding indicated that there was a statistically significant relationship between the district in which a teacher worked and whether she continued to implement *FO/D*.

When I examined the number of schools in which a teacher taught— one school or two or more schools—the data showed that of the 51 teachers in the total sample, 35 of them (69%) taught *FO/D* in only one school. Eleven teachers (22%) taught *FO/D* in two or more schools. Of those 11, 8 (73%) were from one district. Data were missing for 5 teachers.

Looking more closely at only the teachers who continued with *FO/D*, 24 of 35 teachers (69%) taught only in one school. By comparison, of the 11 teachers who taught in two or more schools, 6, or 55%, continued to implement *FO/D*. An analysis of variance test was performed to determine whether there was more variation across districts than within them. The *F* value was 2.08, indicating that districts were not a source of variation regarding teacher movement.

In summary, the district in which one taught had a major influence on the continuation of *FO/D* in several ways. Although the finding was not statistically significant, the data indicated that teachers who taught in only one school were more likely to continue *FO/D*, 75% versus 55% for teachers who taught in more than one school. Principals in some districts were shifted around more than principals in other districts, which also influenced the continuation of *FO/D*.

HYPOTHESIS TESTING

In this section, I report the outcome of the two hypotheses on factors affecting program continuation: legitimacy and coordination.

Legitimacy

Working with the theoretical proposition on the importance of the district's perception of legitimacy for program continuation, I predicted that the continued formal existence of a complex instructional program would be positively associated with the degree of perceived program acceptance by district level administrators. I also predicted that the extent to which a complex instructional program continued over time would be positively associated with the degree of perceived program acceptance by administrators.

While Meyer and Rowan's (1977) formulation typically applies to perceptions of actors and institutions external to the organization that are located in the organization's environment(s), their model has been utilized here because I conceive of the district as the environment for the schools. District level administrators make decisions about which programs help them to meet various state guidelines and mandates, and those decisions often influence funding decisions. Therefore, district level perceptions can influence the survival of a program. The other theoretical framework discussed earlier, the rational model, does not address perceived legitimacy as a concern of organizational managers, but focuses on the internal processes and structures of the organization.

The indicator for perceived legitimacy was an index of three items from the district questionnaire. The first item asked if the *FO/D* program helped the school to meet any state educational requirements or regulations. The second item asked whether the *FO/D* program was mandated in the district. The third item in the index was used to determine the extent to which district personnel were aware of the program. The responses were coded as: Most very aware = 5 to Most not aware = 1. Because the three items had different scales and ranges of responses, they were standardized by transforming them into z scores. The alpha for the index was .67.

To test the first hypothesis, each teacher was assigned his or her district's legitimacy score. Formal continuation was assessed by responses from teachers or their principals on whether a teacher was using the program 3 years or more after training. Teachers who continued using *FO/D* were coded "Yes = 2" and those who stopped were coded "No = 1."

Pearson product moment correlation was used to determine the strength of association between legitimacy and formal continuation, resulting in a Pearson r of .26, $p < .05$, which indicated a positive, statistically significant relationship between legitimacy and formal continuation. These findings must be read with caution, however, because of the small number of districts in the sample.

A test of the hypothesis regarding legitimacy and extent of continuation, as measured by number of *FO/D* units completed, resulted in a Pearson r of .44, $p < .01$, indicating a positive, statistically significant relationship between district legitimacy and extent of program continuation. Once again, these findings must be read with caution because of the small number of districts in the sample.

In further analysis of legitimacy and number of *FO/D* units completed, I conducted a regression analysis that controlled for grade level and adequacy of resources (see Table 17.2). Both of these variables could have provided alternative explanations for the findings. Thus, it was necessary to control for their possible effect. The standardized coefficient of .49 for the legitimacy variable changed little from the previous analysis (r = .44, p < .01) and was statistically significant beyond p < .05, indicating that higher levels of legitimacy were related to an increased number of *FO/D* units completed. Both grade level and adequacy of resources also showed positive relationships to number of *FO/D* units completed, with standardized coefficients of .34 (p < .02) and .30 (p < .03), respectively. This indicated that grade level and level of resources also influenced the number of *FO/D* units completed. The results of the analysis indicated that the model was statistically significant at p < .001.

Coordination

Using the proposition on the importance of control and coordination at the school level, I predicted that principal coordination would be positively associated with both the quality and extent of program continuation. The indicator for coordination was an index comprising five items taken from the principal questionnaire that were designed to determine which tasks the principal carried out to help teachers manage the increased demands for coordination and interdependence while using the *FO/D* curriculum. Responses to items selected for the index were intercorrelated with each other and included: arranged for storage of supplies and materials; provided time

Table 17.2: Regression Analysis of Prgoram Legitimacy and Number of FO/D Units Completed, Controlling for Grade Level and Adequacy of Resources

Variable	Standard Coefficient	Standard Error	t	p (one-tailed)
Constant	.00	.43	2.49	.01
Legitimacy	.49	.05	3.44	.00
Grade	.34	.07	2.17	.02
Resources	.30	.15	1.94	.03

Dependent Variable: Units $n = 23$
R^2 =.59

for teachers to observe and give feedback to one another; arranged for a classroom assistant in each *FO/D* classroom; provided time for *FO/D* teachers to develop new curriculum; and developed a school-wide plan regarding which grade level taught what *FO/D* units. The alpha for the index was .71. The range of values was 5–10, with a mean of 7.42 and a standard deviation of 1.53. Each teacher was assigned his or her principal's coordination value, meaning that a school level variable was, in essence, treated at the individual level. This cross-level analysis was used because of the small sample size and because other techniques such as hierarchical linear modeling are not applicable to this sample size.

To test the hypothesis on coordination and quality of continuation, partial correlation was used, holding constant first-year implementation. This control on first-year implementation was designed to control for the variability in the quality of implementation during the first year. There was a positive, although not statistically significant, relationship between coordination and two of the quality measures.

To test the hypothesis regarding coordination and extent of continuation, I used partial correlations, holding constant first-year implementation, which resulted in a positive correlation between the number of *FO/D* units completed and coordination at $r = .39, p < .05$. In further analysis of coordination and number of *FO/D* units completed, I controlled for grade level and adequacy of resources, again because these two variables could have provided alternative explanations for the findings. The results of this regression analysis showed a positive, statistically significant relationship beyond the $p < .05$ level, between number of *FO/D* units completed and principal coordination, with a standardized coefficient of .33. In other words, the more a principal created a supportive work environment by coordinating resources and finding ways to support teachers, the more units the teachers completed. The standardized coefficient for grade level was .46, significant at $p < .01$, indicating that grade level did influence the number of *FO/D* units completed. The overall model was statistically significant at $p < .001$ (see Table 17.3).

DISCUSSION AND INTERPRETATION OF FINDINGS

A test of the hypothesis regarding legitimacy and formal continuation had a positive, statistically significant finding, albeit to be read with caution because of the small number of districts (8) in the sample. Institutional theory provides a useful explanation of this finding. Schools try to maintain their legitimate status by adopting instructional programs that are agreed upon in the larger environment as proper, acceptable, and worth doing. If organizational elites devote their time and energy to interacting and negotiating with the environment in order to maintain or increase the district's legitimacy, it

Table 17.3: Regression Analysis of Coordination and Number of FO/D Units Completed, Controlling for Grade Level and Adequacy of Resources

Variable	Standard Coefficient	Standard Error	t	p (one-tailed)
Constant	.00	.77	-.46	.33
Coordination	.33	.09	1.98	.03
Grade	.46	.20	2.67	.01
Resources	.23	.20	1.31	.10

Dependent Variable: Units　　　n=23
$R^2 = .45$

is important for them to reassure the external environment that they are, in fact, using acceptable forms of instruction. From this perspective, it is sufficient to say that a program exists, without the added concern of how well it works.

The institutional model may also explain the finding that differentiation, or number of *FO/D* units a teacher used, had a positive relationship to legitimacy. This differentiation was a highly visible aspect of the curriculum, which included multiple learning centers, instructional tasks, and roles. With legitimacy as a primary concern of organizational managers, this prominent feature provides "evidence" that acceptable forms of instruction are being used by the district. Again, program effectiveness would not be relevant from this perspective. The lack of focus on program effectiveness can also explain the lack of support for other hypotheses regarding legitimacy and quality of continuation.

The positive relationship between principal coordination and extent of continuation, as measured by *FO/D* units, suggested that principals who coordinated certain features of the school helped to create a favorable work environment for teachers, thus making it easier for them to use more *FO/D* units during the school year. This finding was supported by the rational theory of organizations, which emphasizes the importance of coordinating the technical core for organizational effectiveness. In this case, coordination created favorable conditions at the school, such as organizing supplies and materials, which, in turn, influenced the teachers' ability to use the *FO/D* curriculum.

Tests of the hypotheses indicated that principal coordination was not related to the quality of program continuation, as had been predicted. Even under the conditions of a complex and differentiated technology with demands for control and coordination, the organization did not produce coordination responses similar to those found in technical organizations.

Meyer and Rowan (1977) claimed that coordination does not take place in schools because attempts to coordinate instructional matters would reveal inconsistencies in school policies and programs, leading to conflicts or loss of legitimacy. Meyer, Scott, and Deal (1981) assert that instructional programs are performed beyond the purview of managers, goals are ambiguous, and individuals are left to work out technical interdependencies informally.

The lack of association between coordination and the quality continuation measures may also indicate that once teachers had a strong understanding of the program, the principal's role changed, or became less important to what happened in the classroom (Dahl, 1989). It may be that teachers asked for less assistance from principals or that principals turned their attention to other demands in the school once the program was implemented. This finding highlights the resiliency of teachers who continued to use the program in spite of the low levels of organizational support they received, as evidenced by the fact that only one teacher in the sample cited "not enough support" as a reason why she stopped using the program.

The findings may also indicate that coordination was too far removed from the technical core to influence the quality of implementation. They suggest loose-coupling between the various levels of the organization, where factors at one level do not directly influence what occurs at other levels. In other words, organizational influences such as coordination, or even legitimacy, that did not directly affect teaching were simply too far away from the classroom to make a difference. What factors, then, did affect classroom teaching, or the technology?

One such factor is collegial feedback, as shown in a study, conducted with the same sample of experienced CI teachers used in this study, in which Lotan (1989) found a strong, positive relationship between quality of implementation, as measured by the number of students talking and working together, and collegial feedback. Specifically, Lotan found that the more frequently the teacher received soundly based collegial feedback, the higher the percentage of students talking and working together in her classroom. Lotan argued that such in-depth discussions about implementation helped to clarify a teacher's understanding of her work and also helped her to develop strategies for managing the classroom, which, in turn, resulted in more effective implementation.

In an additional correlational analysis of Lotan's (1989) data, I found a negative relationship between classroom management problems and feedback ($r = -.46, p < .05$), when controlling for first-year implementation. This finding showed that the more feedback a teacher received, the less likely she was to have classroom management problems, and indicated, once again, that collegial feedback influenced what occurred in the classroom.

Rational theory can explain the relationship of feedback to quality of continuation. Feedback is related directly to teaching—it is part of the technical core and thus influences what occurs there. Conversely, legitimacy is only related to the symbolic nature of the technology. Coordination helps to create favorable work conditions for program implementation, but neither factor influences the technology itself.

DISTRICT, SCHOOL, AND CROSS-LEVEL ANALYSES

The previous analyses were conducted at the classroom level, with the district and school as contextual variables. I also analyzed the data at the district, school, and cross-organizational level to determine if the district or school in which the teachers taught influenced whether they continued teaching *FO/D*. As stated earlier, these findings must be read with caution, and perhaps heuristically, because of the small sample size for districts and schools.

I did not find any school level variables that mediated between the district and the classroom levels. I did, however, find two important effects of the district on the principal's coordination. These two district effects were (1) a favorable effect on coordination of the use of district resources ($r = .49$, $p < .05$), and (2) an unfavorable effect of principal turnover on coordination ($r = -.33$, n.s.). The second effect, while not statistically significant, might have become so with a larger sample. At the school level, the principal's coordination was positively related to the average number of units covered ($r = .40$, $p < .05$).

CONCLUSION

The purpose of this study was to examine organizational conditions and features of schools that contributed to the continuation of a complex instructional technology. Using two theoretical models of organizations, I examined three types of continuation: formal continuation, or whether the program continued; quality of continuation; and extent of continuation.

The descriptive findings indicated that the program was being implemented successfully by teachers 3 years or more after they learned to use it, despite low overall levels of organizational support, as measured by principal coordination. The biggest barrier to program continuation was teacher turnover, even when the turnover occurred for positive reasons such as promotions. Principal turnover had a negative effect on program continuation. Some districts moved principals around more than others, which, in turn, was shown to influence program continuation. It was possible to predict, by district, whether a teacher continued to implement the program.

Both the rational and institutional models of organizations were useful in understanding program continuation more fully. Legitimacy, an indicator drawn from institutional theory, explained features at the district level that related to program continuation. While coordination was drawn from rational theory, it reinforced the institutional perspective of schools, versus the rational view, indicating that coordination was still too far from the technology to influence it in a substantive way. The rational model of organizations explained effects on continuation that occurred in the technical core based on collegial feedback.

Even though teachers continued to implement the *Finding Out/Descubrimiento* curriculum successfully 3 or more years after training, it is incumbent on districts and schools to provide teachers with organizational support to implement complex instructional programs. In addition to carrying out specified tasks at the school level to create a favorable work environment for implementation, schools and districts must find ways to reduce principal and teacher turnover and to encourage collegial feedback among teachers.

PART VII

Conclusion

CHAPTER 18

A Viewpoint on Dissemination

Nikola N. Filby

Regional educational laboratories like Far West Laboratory (FWL), where I have worked for over 20 years, are intended to provide a bridge between research and practice. If universities and research centers conduct research, adding to the knowledge base about effective schooling practices, then laboratories work with regional educators to help them locate, implement, and institutionalize those practices. Thus, in the simple, linear view, research leads to school improvement.

Reality is seldom so simple or linear, and impact is harder to achieve. Much has been written about the gap between researchers and practitioners, about the disparity between controlled laboratory settings and messy, complex, real-world classrooms, about the need for more interactive and less linear models of Research, Development, Dissemination, and Utilization (RDD&U). Quite often, research is seen as irrelevant (according to practitioners) or is bewilderingly and unwisely ignored (according to researchers).

The history of complex instruction has been different. This 20-year research and development process has led to insights and materials that are sought after by practitioners. In this chapter, I reflect on the nature of the research, development, and dissemination process as it has evolved over the history of the Program for Complex Instruction. I will look at both the history of the program, as described in this book and elsewhere, and the results of the process—the complex instruction program for the middle school. My lens in looking at the process and the program is a practical one: What makes the program powerful and useful for teachers? How did it get that way?

IMPACT IN ARIZONA

The analysis draws not only on the research base but also on my own experiences in assisting with program implementation. For the past 5 years, I have worked with two districts in Arizona—Tempe and Scottsdale—to help them implement the program in middle schools. From a beginning with 38 teachers from eight schools, the program has steadily grown. Each summer a new group of teachers has been trained. At this point, all nine of the middle schools are participating. Over 170 teachers have been trained and most are implementing. Each school has sent teachers to be trained as trainers so that they can extend and support the program at their schools, with a total of 16 trainers now certified. Along the way, my Arizona colleagues and I have added new features to the program, such as performance-based assessment techniques, multiple intelligences resources, and new professional development support strategies, including action research and case discussions. (Some of these features have been incorporated into the Stanford program, as they reflect common needs, especially for assessment.) The trainers hope to provide services beyond their two districts in the near future.

While no formal evaluation of the program has yet been conducted, the growth of the program in the two districts is clearly a function of its perceived usefulness and impact. Principals and teachers who were not part of the first wave were drawn to the program by what they saw and heard from their colleagues. In a year-end activity listing their successes, teachers mentioned the following:

> Everyone had an equal opportunity to participate.
> Students needed to rely on each other for information.
> The CI activities gave the opportunity for certain students to emerge as leaders.
> Learning stayed with students.
> Student enthusiasm was high.
> I saw many "resource" students experiencing learning and success with the groupwork.
> It brought out positives and talents in kids.
> Discipline problems decreased; truancy went down.
> Grades went up. (Teacher Year-End Reports, May 1993)

These comments and other reactions from teachers during workshops and school visits begin to indicate what practitioners find so appealing. While they hope for increased achievement, they are even more directly motivated to reach children and involve them successfully in classroom activities. In part, this is a management issue; when children are on task, they are not causing problems. But more deeply, teachers want students to be drawn in, productively engaged, and successful. In other forms of groupwork, this may or may not have happened. Often, low-achieving students remain relatively uninvolved and unproductive.

Complex instruction provides teachers with a new way to think about this problem and a new set of tools. Teachers learn to "think like a sociologist," to understand how the expectations of peers may influence a student's behavior, and how to change those expectations. This new approach to the problem is what seems to have the greatest appeal, especially for teachers who may already have had a lot of cooperative learning. While teachers retain their psychological lenses, citing "improved self-esteem" as an outcome of the program, they also learn to see classroom interaction differently. In workshops, teachers are taught the underlying theory, and they receive it well because it offers a new answer to an important, practical problem.

The program itself has evolved over time to include a number of specific elements or tools. It includes engaging, multiple-ability curriculum; groupwork management tools through roles and norms; status treatments; and teacher support through observations and feedback. Initially, teachers find this somewhat overwhelming, saying things like, "Now I know why it's called complex instruction." But they also appreciate the comprehensiveness of the program. While they may have familiarity with some of the components, which is reassuring, they say that they have seldom found anything that pulls the pieces together so thoroughly.

RESEARCH AND DEVELOPMENT PROCESS

What is it about the process of research and development that has led to this outcome? In Chapter 1, Cohen summarizes the background and development of the program (see also Cohen, 1993). In these accounts, it is apparent that there has been consistent dedication to two things: theory and application. The first study, in 1972, examined whether the theoretical description of status generalization would predict behavior in an experimental setting. The purpose of the study was to test the theory in specific scope conditions. Additional studies followed, including experimental studies of various interventions aimed at changing behavior.

Cohen (1993) describes this early phase not as "basic science: the production and evaluation of knowledge claims," but as "applied science: the discovery of new uses for knowledge claims" (p. 386). This identification says at least as much about the motivation of the researchers as it does about the nature of the research at this early stage when the theory itself was still being tested and developed, when surely they were "evaluating knowledge claims" (p. 386). According to Cohen, the orientation of the program at that point was "a search for practical problems that status characteristic theory could solve" (p. 386). Even though the work was still in experimental settings at this point, it is significant that the researchers moved quickly to interventions and saw their work as solving problems rather than building theory or adding to the knowledge base. In effect, at this early stage, the program goal seemed to be to demonstrate that there is nothing so practical as a good theory.

Cohen credits her graduate students, "dedicated educators," with the move out of the laboratory into normal classrooms. By the mid-1980s, interventions in real classrooms were being tested. This led to a host of new problems, solutions, and empirical studies, which are chronicled in the chapters of this book. With the goal of helping *teachers* to create the conditions under which students would interact more equally, program staff have been led into curriculum development and staff development, along with an expanding array of instructional interventions.

Cohen (1993) identifies this phase as "engineering: the solution of technical problems where the problem to be solved is regarded as given" (p. 386). The problem to be solved was creating more equal participation in regular classrooms, but the technical subdimensions of that problem were many, and they unfolded progressively in successive rounds of engineering. The curriculum had to be one that embodied multiple abilities. "Although there is no tradition of sociologists working in the area of curriculum, we were forced to include changing the curriculum as a program goal" (p. 400). The classroom management system had to be developed to create and sustain appropriate small group work. The status treatments had to be ones that teachers could safely and effectively use in the classroom, leading them to focus on combining treatments for greater effect, instead of isolating treatments to study experimentally.

In this engineering phase, the way that the program staff framed problems and looked for solutions was again influenced by their strong belief in the value of theory. For instance, they interpreted the relationship between students talking/working together and student achievement as a phenomenon explained by organization theory, which posits the value of lateral communication among workers in dealing with uncertain tasks (see Chapter 3). This formulation led the staff to develop and test a management system in which teachers delegated authority to students and supported lateral communication in a variety of ways.

The CI program brought the same problem-solving orientation and use of theory to the issue of how to get teachers to use these new methods. Staff have developed both an intensive training program, with modeling and guided practice, and feedback procedures based on observation of teachers in their own classrooms. Again, they can cite both theoretical rationales for their procedures and evidence from empirical studies that the procedures work.

It is interesting that program staff view this line of work as various forms of research. Another alternative would be to label it "development." Indeed, this noun creeps into both my language and theirs, but with a small "d," not as Development, in the linear Research-Development-Dissemination-Utilization sense.

In a briefing paper for the Office of Educational Research and Improvement, Hood and Hutchins (1993) review the history of research-based development in education. In the early 1970s, the phrase "educational research and development" was common parlance. University-based R&D centers were funded. Up to 40% of education R&D funds went to development, which was defined as: "the repeated and systematic testing and improvement of some education product or curriculum" (Gideonse, 1969, pp. 128–129). While research produces "refined knowledge," development produces "usable products."

By this definition, at least the "engineering" phase of complex instruction could be called development. Clearly, it has involved the systematic refinement of a product so that it can be used effectively by teachers. The choice of labels may reflect underlying assumptions about purpose. The purpose of development is generally to create a product that can then be disseminated broadly. The purpose of engineering remains one of inquiry—to find out how to solve practical problems effectively. Inquiry is the fundamental scholarly process, and this program is university-based.

It is clear that the quality of complex instruction has benefited from this scholarly process of engineering. The relentless pursuit of a better product, solving new problems as they arise, and showing outcomes are all aspects that could be short-circuited if the process were seen as product development and the product were to be rushed to market. It is probably no accident that other examples of in-depth engineering/development, such as Success for All from Johns Hopkins, also came from a university environment.

On the other hand, Hood and Hutchins (1993) chronicle the decline in explicit attention to development, and this also has disadvantages. While R&D remains a common term, the development part has been less funded and less clearly conceptualized over the past 2 decades. By the 1990s, less than 15% of education R&D dollars were spent on development (Vinovskis, 1993). The problem with this is that it may deflect attention from exactly the kind of in-depth engineering that strengthened complex instruction. If research, with a goal of knowledge production, is viewed in an undifferentiated way, then people may not understand the need for the practical problem solving represented by engineering; they may not fund it; and they may have unrealistic expectations for the transferability and applicability of research. In bridging between research and practice, practical problem solving is essential, whether it is called engineering or development.

DISSEMINATION

These subtle distinctions and thorny issues have implications for dissemination as well—getting the program out to the field and in use by practitioners. Certainly the history of complex instruction, and our experiences with educators in Arizona, contain some lessons about dissemination.

As part of their comprehensive engineering/development effort, the CI staff incorporated a number of components to train and support teachers in learning to use the program. The initial 2-week training includes teaching the underlying theory, modeling lessons, and practicing components and whole lessons. The follow-up support includes observations and feedback by an "expert" for a full year. These are pieces that have proven necessary to help teachers learn a demanding innovation. They are not always easy to sell to people who want the program. In particular, the follow-up support piece is a target for negotiation. Districts may not believe that they have the financial resources to pay for this in-depth support. Moveover, establishing the program at a new site may require new models, or it may take a while to develop the expertise to provide the desired support.

Another important issue in dissemination has been that of curriculum availability and fit. At the middle school level, curriculum units have been developed in several subject areas, but with special attention to the California frameworks and topics covered at specific grade levels in California. In Arizona, the match is not the same. Some subjects in some grade levels have units available; others do not. This becomes particularly problematic when many teachers in a school are trained. Maybe one grade level can use the poetry unit, but not all of them can use it (at least not without modifications and extensions, which are now underway).

A less readily apparent issue around curriculum is the general approach to curriculum and instruction. CI units are built around "big ideas," use open-ended tasks, and depend on the teacher to make connections and stimulate higher-order thinking. Such an approach is consistent with the constructivist approach now advocated by learning theorists. It is consistent with the spirit of state and national curriculum frameworks. But it is not necessarily well understood or practiced by educators. Hence, there may be major issues around helping teachers value and succeed at a very different approach to instruction. These issues sometimes get lost in the scope of the program as a whole, with its greater explicit attention to status issues and equal participation. In other words, teachers do not come to the program because of the curriculum, but they need to understand the curriculum approach in depth in order to direct participation toward the content outcomes they desire.

These issues with curriculum—both fit to subject areas and the need for in-depth understanding of the curriculum potential—are ones that we have continued to struggle with in Arizona. We have tried various formats for curriculum writing and adaptation, but we have yet to find the best one or to support teachers fully as they learn to use specific units well. The Stanford CI program staff have likewise encountered these issues in their work with other groups as well as with us. They are now designing an advanced professional development strand that will focus on curriculum and assessment.

These two problematic issues in dissemination are mentioned briefly as background for a larger issue—the nature of dissemination itself. In the simple, linear view, dissemination involves getting the product out to consumers, generally with a limited amount of on-site support. Our dissemination process in Arizona has been different. For the past 5 years, I have been acting as a multifaceted technical assistance provider, superlinker, and coach to the two districts implementing the program. From initial contacts, providing awareness workshops, and facilitating negotiation and decision making, I have continued to be involved in a variety of ways. I have conducted CI training and assisted new trainers in planning and carrying out training. I have visited school sites and consulted with individual teachers and teams. I helped maintain a link between the districts and Stanford, including participation in training-of-trainers sessions, which I am now authorized to conduct myself in Arizona, but with continuing input from Stanford staff. I met with district staff to discuss next steps with the program, prepare budgets, and plan and conduct additional training sessions. I helped them look for new sources of curriculum and develop their own units. Over time, my goal has been to develop the districts' capacity to continue the program on their own and even to train teachers in other districts. But it has taken the 5-year time span to approach this goal. In one of the two districts, it was only in the third year of training that they had internal resources and expertise to provide the full observation and feedback for teachers. Someone needed to maintain the vision, support internal advocates, and continue the dialogue to help the district move ahead. My multifaceted support role was critical.

This kind of intensive dissemination assistance seems particularly appropriate to a regional laboratory culture and mission, at least as interpreted at Far West Laboratory (FWL) and our sister institution, the Southwest Regional Laboratory (SWRL; now united with us as WestEd). SWRL has supported the dissemination of the Success for All program from Johns Hopkins with a similar intensity, although the specific activities differ (Dianda, 1995; Long, 1995). In part, this is the result of a laboratory's commitment to both research and practice. We take an inquiry stance ourselves in a number of ways. We value the research base of the program, are reflective in our implementation, and understand the key components of the program, but we also know from research on the change process about the complexities of local adaptation. We are committed to making a difference in practice and know that we have to stay with it to help schools deal with all the local decisions about implementation. Some of these decisions also mean adding to the program itself.

While laboratories can do this on a selective basis, setting up pilot or demonstration projects, they do not have the funding to provide this kind of support on a widespread basis. Unfortunately, neither does anyone else. Dissemination theory and research recognize the need for sustained assistance and (increasingly) for dealing with the larger system context for program implementation. "Coaching" is becoming popular, but funding remains uncertain.

Cohen and Lotan have appreciated the thoroughness with which FWL undertook its task. In some ways, we have filled a gap that they perceived. Cohen (1993) asked "when does the researcher let go?" (p. 414). From their own research as well as knowledge of the field, they were concerned about fidelity of implementation as well as school organizational issues that threaten institutionalization. They decried the absence of trained "educational engineers" (p. 415), people who assisted in change efforts with the same problem solving and systematic study that they do themselves as program developers. FWL's role, while admittedly less formally researched, has been somewhat of this sort. Without this level and type of assistance, they fear that complex instruction is not commercially viable in a market where educators are more apt to want to buy a product, cut a few corners, and put it in place.

Perhaps there is some hope in the increasing attention to systemic reform. One interpretation of systemic reform is to look for more comprehensive solutions, to take into account more aspects of the teaching–learning process and context, and to pursue reform more deeply. These factors should encourage appreciation of complex instruction, with its multifaceted approach to curriculum, instruction, and teacher training. Systemic reform could also provide better environmental conditions, as when schools (like one in Tempe) embark on the Accelerated Schools process and find in complex instruction the instructional component that operationalizes their developing philosophy.

There is also hope in the more sophisticated understanding of RDD&U processes. It is increasingly apparent that the simple, linear view is inadequate. Hood and Hutchins (1993) write about the "nesting" of RDD&U, in which the processes may occur together or in various combinations over the course of a longer cycle. Research on change processes moves us toward a view of schools as learning organizations in which a continuous improvement orientation provides a foundation for specific implementation efforts. Throughout these more complex processes, there is both the opportunity and the need to embed more systematic forms of inquiry.

In the end, this history of complex instruction shows both the potential of engineering—the use of theory to solve practical problems—and the limitations to our broader views of RDD&U processes and structures, in which inquiry processes need to be embedded at multiple points. The opportunities for researchers with a practical bent are limitless.

Whole Class Instrument

Part I

Teacher Name: _____ Date of Obs. _____

Total # Adults in Classroom: _____ Time of Obs. _____

Total # Students in Classroom: _____ 1st or 2nd Obs. _____

Observer Name: _____ Unit: _____

# of Different Group Tasks Used: ____ Grade:_____ Per. _____

Part II

Type of Activities Used in Small Groups

Small Groups	Talk or Talk/Manip. "O"	Manip. Materials "O"	Read/ Write "O"	Look/List. On-Task "O"	Disen-gaged	Waiting for Adult	N for rows
1							
2							
3							
4							
5							
6							
7							
8							
9							
N for columns							

Total N in Small Groups =

Part III

Not in Small Groups with Assigned Tasks:

a. In Group, Listening to Teacher : _____

b. In Transition (on Business) : _____

c. Waiting for Adult : _____

d. Wandering, Fooling Around, Disengaged : _____

e. Other Academic Activity : _____

Total N, NOT AT CENTERS : _____

Please put a star * if adult is working with students in place where you have coded students

APPENDIX B
Teacher Observation Instrument

Teacher _____   Orientation   Yes ___ No ___
Date _____ Period _____   Wrap-up   Yes ___ No ___
Observer _____   Learning Stations Yes ___ No ___
                                      Time at Start of Obs. _____

Categories	Number of Instances	Total	%
1. Facilitates Students' Work			
2. Disciplines (Student or Class)			
3. Informs/Instructs/ Defines			
4. Asks Factual Questions			
5. Stimulates Higher-Order Thinking			
6. Makes Connections			
7. Gives Specific Feedback to Individual or Group			
8. Talks About Multiple Abilities			
9. Assigns Competence			
10. Talks About Roles			
11. Talks About Cooperation			
OVERALL TOTALS			

UNIT: _____

COMMENTS:

APPENDIX C
Target Student Instrument

Student ID# _____ Unit ID# _____ Teacher ID# _____
Role _____ Read/Write _____ Composition _____
Observer ID# _____

		Minute 1		Minute 2		Minute 3		
Coding Category		1–30	31-60	1–30	31-60	1–30	31-60	Total
T.S. Talk								
A	Offers/Gives Assistance							
B	Requests Assistance							
C	Talks Like a Facilitator							
D	Task-Related Talk							
E	Nontask-Related Talk							
T.S. Behavior								
F	Works Alone							
G	Works with Others							
H	Behaves Like Facilitator							
I	Look/Listen							
J	Waits for Adult							
K	In Transition							
L	Other Academic Work							
M	Disengaged							

Codes: For Talk: T = Teacher; M = Male; F = Female; G = Student Group; S = Self.
For Behavior = Use Hash Marks

References

Armento, B. J., Nash, G. B., Salter, C. L., & Wixson, K. K. (1991a). *Across the centuries*. Boston: Houghton Mifflin.

Armento, B. J., Nash, G. B., Salter, C. L., & Wixson, K. K. (1991b). *A more perfect union*. Boston: Houghton Mifflin.

Bandura, A. (1977). *Social learning theory*. Englewood Cliffs, NJ: Prentice-Hall.

Benton, J. (1994). *Treating status problems in the classroom: Training teachers to assign competence to students exhibiting low-status behavior in the classroom*. Unpublished doctoral dissertation, Stanford University.

Berger, J. B., Cohen, B. P., & Zelditch, M., Jr. (1966). Status characteristics and expectation states. In J. Berger & M. Zelditch, Jr. (Eds.), *Sociological theories in progress* (Vol. 1, pp. 29–46). Boston: Houghton-Mifflin.

Berger, J. B., Cohen, B. P., & Zelditch, M., Jr. (1972). Status characteristics and social interaction. *American Sociological Review, 37*, 241–255.

Berger, J. B., & Conner, T. L. (1974). Performance expectations and behavior in small groups: A revised formulation. In J. Berger, T. L. Conner, & M. H. Fisek (Eds.), *Expectation states theory: A theoretical research program* (pp. 85–109). Cambridge, MA: Winthrop.

Berger, J. B., & Fisek, M. H. (1974). A generalization of the theory of status characteristics and expectation states. In J. Berger, T. L. Conner, & M. H. Fisek (Eds.), *Expectation states theory: A theoretical research program* (pp. 163–205). Cambridge, MA: Winthrop.

Berger, J. B., Fisek, M. H., Norman, R. Z., & Zelditch, M., Jr. (1977). *Status characteristics and social interaction: An expectation-states approach*. New York: Elsevier.

Berger, J. B., Rosenholtz, S. J., & Zelditch, M., Jr. (1980). Status organizing processes. Annual Review of Sociology, 6, 479–508.

Berger, J. B., Wagner, D. G., & Zelditch, M., Jr. (1985). Introduction: Expectation states theory: Review and assessment. In J. Berger & M. Zelditch, Jr. (Eds.), *Status, rewards, and influence* (pp. 1–72). San Francisco: Jossey-Bass.

Bianchini, J. (1995). *How do middle school students learn science in small groups? An analysis of scientific knowledge and social process construction*. Unpublished doctoral dissertation, Stanford University.

Bianchini, J., Holthuis, N., & Nielsen, K. (1995, April). *Cooperative learning in the untracked middle school science classroom: A study of student achievement*. Paper presented at the annual meeting of the American Educational Research Association, San Francisco.

Braddock, J. M. (1990). *Tracking: Implications for student race-ethnic subgroups*. Baltimore: Johns Hopkins University, Center for Research on Effective Schooling for Disadvantaged Students.

California State Department of Education (1988). *History–social science framework for California Public Schools*. Sacramento: Author.

California Test of Basic Skills. (1982). Monterey, CA: CTBS/McGraw-Hill.

Cazden, C. B. (1979). Curriculum/language contexts for bilingual education. In *Language development in a bilingual setting* (pp. 129–138). Los Angeles: National Dissemination and Assessment Center.

Cazden, C. B. (1988). *Classroom discourse: The language of teaching and learning.* Portsmouth, NH: Heinemann.

Cohen, B. P., & Arechavala-Vargas, R. (1987). *Interdependence, interaction and productivity* (Working Paper 87–3). Stanford: Stanford University, Center for Sociological Research.

Cohen, B. P., & Cohen, E. G. (1991). From groupwork among children to R&D teams: Interdependence, interaction and productivity. In E. J. Lawler, B. Markovsky, C. Ridgeway, & H. Walker (Eds.), *Advances in group processes* (Vol. 8, pp. 205–226). Greenwich, CT: JAI Press.

Cohen, E. G. (1982). Expectation states and interracial interaction in school settings. *Annual Review of Sociology, 8,* 209–235.

Cohen, E. G. (1984). Talking and working together: Status, interaction and learning. In P. Peterson, L. C. Wilkinson, & M. Hallinan (Eds.), *Instructional groups in the classroom: Organization and processes* (pp. 171–187). Orlando, FL: Academic Press.

Cohen, E. G. (1986). *Designing groupwork: Strategies for heterogeneous classrooms.* New York: Teachers College Press.

Cohen, E. G. (1993). From theory to practice: The development of an applied research program. In J. B. Berger & M. Zelditch, Jr. (Eds.), *Theoretical research programs: Studies in the growth of theory* (pp. 385–415). Stanford: Stanford University Press.

Cohen, E. G. (1994a). *Designing groupwork: Strategies for heterogeneous classrooms* (2nd ed.). New York: Teachers College Press.

Cohen, E. G. (1994b). *Status treatments for the classroom* [Video]. New York: Teachers College Press.

Cohen, E. G., & Bredo, E. R. (1975). Elementary school organization and innovative instructional practices. In J. V. Baldridge & T. E. Deal (Eds.), *Managing change in educational organizations* (pp. 133–149). Berkeley: McCutchan.

Cohen, E. G., Deal, T. E., Meyer, J. W., & Scott, W. R. (1976). *Organization and instruction in elementary schools.* Stanford: Stanford University Center for Research and Development in Teaching.

Cohen, E. G., & De Avila, E. (1983). *Learning to think in math and science: Improving local education for minority children* (Final Report to the Walter S. Johnson Foundation). Stanford: Stanford University School of Education, Program for Complex Instruction.

Cohen, E. G., Lockheed, M., & Lohman, M. (1976). The Center for Interracial Cooperation: A field experiment. *Sociology of Education, 49,* 47–58.

Cohen, E. G., & Lotan, R. A. (1990). *Final report to Pacific Gas and Electric.* Stanford: Stanford University School of Education, Program for Complex Instruction.

Cohen, E. G., & Lotan, R. A. (1994, April). *Complex instruction and status problems in the untracked middle school.* Paper presented at the annual meeting of the American Educational Research Association, New Orleans.

Cohen, E. G., & Lotan, R. A. (1995). Producing equal-status interaction in the heterogeneous classroom. *American Educational Research Journal, 32*, 99–120.

Cohen, E. G., & Lotan, R. A. (1997). Operational status in middle grades: Recent complications. In J. Szmatka, J. Skvoretz, & J. Berger (Eds.), *Theory development and theory growth*. Stanford: Stanford University Press.

Cohen, E. G., Lotan, R. A., & Catanzarite, L. (1988). Can expectations for competence be treated in the classroom? In M. Webster, Jr. & M. Foschi (Eds.), *Status generalization: New theory and research* (pp. 27–54). Stanford: Stanford University Press.

Cohen, E. G., Lotan R. A., & Holthuis, N. (1995). Talking and working together: Conditions for learning in complex instruction. In M. T. Hallinan (Ed.), *Restructuring schools: Promising practices and policies* (pp. 157–174). New York: Plenum Press.

Cohen, E. G., Lotan, R. A., and Leechor, C. (1989). Can classrooms learn? *Sociology of Education, 62*, 75–94.

Comstock, D. E., & Scott, W. R. (1977). Technology and the structure of subunits: Distinguishing individual and work group effects. *Administrative Science Quarterly, 22*, 177–202.

Cook, J. T., & Brown, J. S. (1994). *Two Americas: Comparisons of U.S. child poverty in rural, inner city and suburban areas*. Medford, MA: Tufts University School of Nutrition, Center on Hunger, Poverty, and Nutrition Policy.

Cossey, R. (1997). *Mathematics communication: Issues of access and equity*. Unpublished doctoral dissertation, Stanford University.

Cummins, J. (1979). Linguistic interdependence and the educational development of bilingual children. *Review of Educational Research, 49*, 222–251.

Cummins, J. (1991). Interdependence of first and second language proficiency in bilingual children. In E. Bialystok (Ed.), *Language processing in bilingual children* (pp. 70–89). New York: Cambridge University Press.

Dahl, R. F. (1989). *Organizational factors affecting the continuation of a complex instructional technology*. Unpublished doctoral dissertation, Stanford University.

De Avila, E. A., Cohen, E. G., & Intili, J. K. (1981). *Improving cognition: A multicultural approach* (Final Report to NIE, Grant #NIE-G-78, MICA Project). Stanford: Stanford University School of Education.

De Avila, E. A., & Duncan, S. (1977). *Language assessment scales, level I* (2nd ed.). Corte Madera, CA: Linguametrics Group.

De Avila, E. A., & Duncan, S. (1982a). *A convergent approach to oral language assessment: Theoretical and technical specifications on the language assessment scales (LAS) Form A*. San Rafael, CA: Linguametrics Group.

De Avila, E. A., & Duncan, S. (1982b). *Finding out/descubrimiento*. San Rafael, CA: Linguametrics Group.

De Avila, E. A., & Pulos, S. M. (1978). Developmental assessment by pictorially presented Piagetian material: The cartoon conservation scale. In G. I. Lubin, M. K. Poulsen, J. F. Magary, & M. Soto-MacAlestor (Eds.), *Piagetian theory and its implications for the helping professions* (pp. 124–139). Los Angeles: University of Southern California.

Dembo, M., & McAuliffe, T. (1987). Effects of perceived ability and grade status on social interaction and influence in cooperative groups. *Journal of Educational Psychology, 79,* 415-423.

DeVries, D. L., & Edwards, K. J. (1977). Student teams and learning games: Their effects on cross-race and cross-sex interaction. *Journal of Educational Psychology, 66*(5), 741–749.

Dianda, M. (1995). *Annual report on program adoptions and successes: The implementation of Success for All.* Los Alamitos, CA: Southwest Regional Laboratory.

Doise, W., & Mugny, G. (1984). *The social development of the intellect.* Oxford: Pergamon Press.

Dornbusch, S. M., & Scott, W. R. (1975). *Evaluation and the exercise of authority.* San Francisco: Jossey-Bass.

Ehrlich, D. E. (1991). *Beyond cooperation: Developing science thinking in interdependent groups.* Unpublished doctoral dissertation, Stanford University.

Ellis, N. (1987). *Collaborative interaction and logistical support for teacher change.* Unpublished doctoral dissertation, Stanford University.

Ellis, N. (1990). Collaborative interaction for improvement of teaching. *Teaching and Teacher Education, 6,* 267–277.

Ellis, N., & Lotan, R. A. (1991, April). *Looking in Mirrors: Teachers looking, seeing, knowing.* Paper presented at the annual meeting of the American Educational Research Association, Chicago.

Entwisle, D., & Webster, M., Jr. (1974). Raising children's expectations for their own performance: A classroom application. In J. Berger, T. L. Conner, & M. H. Fisek (Eds.), *Expectation states theory: A theoretical research program* (pp. 211–243). Cambridge, MA: Winthrop.

Epstein, J. S., & Karweit, N. (1983). *Friends in school: Patterns of selection and influence in secondary schools.* New York: Academic Press.

Foot, H. D., Chapman, A. J., & Smith, J. R. (1980). Patterns of interaction in children's friendships. In H. D. Foot, A. J. Chapman, & J. R. Smith (Eds.), *Friendship and social relations* (pp. 267–289). New York: Wiley.

Fry, L. (1982). Technology-structure research: Three critical issues. *Academy of Management Journal, 25,* 532–552.

Gage, N., & Berliner, D. (1989). Nurturing the critical, practical, and artistic thinking of teachers. *Phi Beta Kappan, 71,* 212–214.

Galbraith, J. (1973). *Designing complex organizations.* Reading, MA: Addison-Wesley.

Gamoran, A. (1989). Measuring curriculum differentiation. *American Journal of Education, 60,* 129–143.

Gamoran, A., & Berends, M. (1987). The effects of stratification in secondary schools: Synthesis of survey and ethnographic research. *Review of Educational Research, 57,* 415–435.

Garcia, G. (1994). *Understanding and meeting the challenge of student cultural diversity.* Boston: Houghton-Mifflin.

Gardner, H. (1983). *Frames of mind: The theory of multiple intelligences.* New York: Basic Books.

Gideonse, H. D. (1969). *Educational research and development in the United States.*

Washington, DC: U.S. Office of Education, National Center for Educational Research and Development.

Glantz, J. (1974). *Logic processes in psychological light*. Ramat-Gan, Israel: Bar-Ilan University Press.

Glaser, R., & Silver, E. (1994). Assessment, testing, and instruction: Retrospect and prospect. In L. Darling-Hammond (Ed.), *Review of Research in Education, 20*, 393–419. Washington, DC: American Educational Research Association.

Gliker, Y. (1982). *The rise of Greek philosophy* [in Hebrew]. Tel Aviv: Matkal, Misrad ha-bitahon.

Gonzales, J. (1982). *Instructor evaluations and academic effort: The Chicano in college*. Unpublished doctoral dissertation, Stanford University.

Goodlad, J. I. (1990). *Teachers for our nation's schools*. San Francisco: Jossey-Bass.

Graham, S. (1994). Motivation in African Americans. *Review of Educational Research, 64*, 55–117.

Grant, L. (1983). *Sex roles and statuses in peer interaction in elementary school*. (ERIC Document Reproduction Service No. ED 214 677)

Graves, N., & Graves, T. (1991). Candida Graves: Complex teamwork in action. *Cooperative Learning, 12*, 12–16.

Hallinan, M. T. (1976). Friendship patterns in open and traditional classrooms. *Sociology of Education, 49*, 254–265.

Hallinan, M. T. (1977). *The evolution of children's friendship cliques*. Chicago: Spencer Foundation. (ERIC Document Reproduction Service No. ED 161 556)

Hallinan, M. T., & Tuma, N. B. (1978). Classroom effect on change in children's friendships. *Sociology of Education, 51*, 270–282.

Harwood, D. (1989). The nature of teacher–pupil interaction in the active tutorial work approach: Using interaction analysis to evaluate student-centered approaches. *British Educational Research Journal, 15*, 177–194.

Hatch, E. M. (1977, February). *An historical overview of second language acquisition research*. Paper presented at the First Annual Second Language Research Forum, University of California at Los Angeles. (Eric Document 184297)

Hayes, Z. (1982). *Limited language proficiency: A problem in the definition and the measurement of bilingualism*. Unpublished doctoral dissertation, Stanford University.

Hebert, R., et al. (1976). *Summary: Academic achievement and language instruction among Franco-Manitoban pupils* (Report to the Manitoba Department of Education). Saint-Boniface, Man.: College universitaire de Saint-Boniface, Centre de recherches.

Heller, H. C., & Kiely, M. L. (1997). Hum Bio: Stanford University's human biology curriculum for the middle grades. In R. Takanishi & D. A. Hamburg (Eds.), *Preparing adolescents for the 21st century*. New York: Cambridge University Press.

Hoffman, D. E. (1973). *Students' expectations and performance in a simulation game*. Unpublished doctoral dissertation, Stanford University.

Hood, P. D., & Hutchins, C. L. (1993). *Research-based development in education: Its history and future*. San Francisco: Far West Laboratory for Educational Research and Development.

Humphreys, P., & Berger, J. (1981). Theoretical consequences of the status characteristic formulation. *American Journal of Sociology, 86,* 953–983.

Intili, J. K. (1977). *Structural conditions in the school that facilitate reflective decision-making.* Unpublished doctoral dissertation, Stanford University.

Johnson, D. W., & Johnson, R. T. (1994). *Learning together and alone: Cooperative, competitive, and individualistic learning* (4th ed.). Englewood Cliffs, NJ: Prentice-Hall.

Joreskog, K. G., & Sorbom, D. (1988). *LISREL VII: A guide to the program and its applications.* Chicago: SPSS.

Kepner, D. (1995). We're in all this together. In J. H. Shulman, R. A. Lotan, & J. A. Whitcomb (Eds.), *Groupwork in diverse classrooms: A casebook for educators* (pp. 71–78). San Francisco: Far West Laboratory for Educational Research and Development.

Kerckhoff, A. C. (1986). Effects of ability grouping in British secondary schools. *American Sociological Review, 51,* 842–855.

Koellner, K., & Moffat, N. (1995). *Informed social participation: Survey, design, data collection and statistical analysis to examine social issues of today.* Unpublished paper, Scottsdale Arizona School District.

Krashen, S. (1976). Formal and informal linguistic environments in language learning and language acquisition. *TESOL Quarterly, 10*(2), 157–168.

Krashen, S. (1981). Bilingual education and second language acquisition theory. In *Schooling and language minority students: A theoretical framework* (pp. 125–134). Sacramento, CA: Department of Education, Office of Bilingual Bicultural Education.

Krashen, S. (1982). *Principles and practices in second language acquisition.* Oxford: Pergamon Press.

Kruger, A. C., & Tomasello, M. (1986). Transactive discussions with peers and adults. *Developmental Psychology, 22,* 681–685.

Lane, S., Liu, M., Stone, C. A., & Ankenmann, R. D. (1993, April). *Validity evidence for QUASAR's Mathematics Performance Assessment.* Paper presented at the annual meeting of the American Educational Research Association, Atlanta.

Lane, S., & Parke, C. (1992, April). *Principles for developing performance assessments.* Paper presented at the annual meeting of the American Educational Research Association, San Francisco.

Lane, S., Stone, C. A., Ankenmann, R. D., & Liu, M. (1994). Reliability and validity of a mathematics performance assessment. *International Journal of Educational Research, 21,* 247–266.

Lanier, J., & Little, J. (1986). Research on teacher education. In M. C. Wittrock (Ed.), *Handbook of research on teaching,* (3rd ed., pp. 257–569). New York: Macmillan.

Larsen-Freeman, P. (1976). An explanation for the morpheme acquisition order of second language learners. *Language Learning, 26*(1), 125–134.

Lee, V. (1995). *School context and instructional innovation: The contribution of structure, collaboration and leadership to teachers' implementation.* Unpublished doctoral dissertation, Stanford University.

Leechor, C. (1988). *How high and low achieving students differentially benefit from working together in cooperative small groups.* Unpublished doctoral dissertation, Stanford University.

Light, P., & Glachan, M. (1985). Facilitation of individual problem solving through peer interaction. *Educational Psychology, 5,* 217–225.

Linn, M. C., & Burbules, N. C. (1993). Construction of knowledge and group learning. In K. Tobin (Ed.), *The practice of constructivism in science education* (pp. 91–119). Hillsdale, NJ: Erlbaum.

Linn, R. L. (1979). Validity of inferences based on the proposed Title I evaluation models. *Educational Evaluation and Policy Analysis, 1,* 23–32.

Little, J. W. (1982). Norms of collegiality and experimentation: Workplace conditions of school success. *American Educational Research Journal, 19,* 325–340.

Lockheed, M. E. (1981). *Year one report, classroom interaction, student cooperation, and leadership.* Princeton, NJ: Educational Testing Service.

Lockheed, M. E. (1983). *Sex segregation and male preeminence in elementary classrooms.* Princeton, NJ: Educational Testing Service.

Lockheed, M. E., & Hall, K. P. (1976). Conceptualizing sex as a status characteristic: Application to leadership training strategies. *Journal of Social Issues, 32*(3), 111–124.

Lockheed, M. E., Harris, A. M., & Nemceff, W. P. (1983). Sex and social influence: Does sex function as a status characteristic in mixed-sex groups of children? *Journal of Educational Psychology, 75,* 877–888.

Long, C. (1995). Case studies and a synthesis of three Far West Laboratory regional programs. In *Final Report on the Evaluation of the Far West Laboratory regional programs.* San Francisco: Far West Laboratory for Educational Research and Development.

Lotan, R. A. (1985). *Understanding the theories: Training teachers for implementation of complex instructional technology.* Unpublished doctoral dissertation, Stanford University.

Lotan, R. A. (1989, February). *Collegial feedback: Necessary condition for successful program continuation.* Paper presented at the annual meeting of the Sociology of Education Society, Asilomar, CA.

Lotan, R. A. (1990, March). *Collegial collaboration and program continuation.* Paper presented at the annual meeting of the American Educational Research Association, Boston.

March, J. G., & Simon, H. A. (1958). *Organizations.* New York: Wiley.

Maruyama, G., & Miller, N. (1981). Physical attractiveness and personality. *Progress in Experimental Personality Research, 10,* 203–280.

Mead, G. H. (1934). *Mind, self, and society.* Chicago: University of Chicago Press.

Mercer, J., Iadacola, P., & Moore, H. (1980). Building effective multiethnic schools: Evolving models and paradigms. In W. G. Stephan & J. R. Feagin (Eds.), *School desegregation: Past, present and future* (pp. 281–307). New York: Plenum.

Meyer, J. W., & Rowan, B. (1977). Institutionalized organizations: Formal structure as myth and ceremony. *American Journal of Sociology, 83,* 340–363.

Meyer, J. W., Scott, W. R., & Deal, T. E. (1981). Institutional and technical sources of organizational structure: Explaining the structure of educational organizations. In H. D. Stein (Ed.), *Organization and the human services* (pp. 151–178). Philadelphia: Temple University Press.

Miles, M. B., & Huberman, A. M. (1984). *Qualitative data analysis.* Beverly Hills, CA: Sage.

Morris, R. (1979). *A normative intervention to equalize participation in task-oriented groups.* Unpublished doctoral dissertation, Stanford University.

Morrison, H., & Kuhn, D. (1983). Cognitive aspects of preschoolers' imitation in a play situation. *Child Development, 54,* 1054–1063.

Nash, S. C. (1975). The relationship among sex-role stereotyping, sex-role preference and the sex difference in spatial visualization. *Sex Roles, 1,* 15–32.

National Center for Educational Statistics. (1992). *The condition of education.* Washington, DC: Author.

National Council of Teachers of Mathematics. (1993). *Assessment standards for school mathematics: A working draft.* Reston, VA: Author.

Natriello, G., & Dornbusch, S. M. (1984). *Teacher evaluative standards and student effort.* New York: Longman.

Newman, D., Griffin, P., & Cole, M. (1989). *The construction zone: Working for cognitive change in school.* Cambridge: Cambridge University Press.

Nieto, S. (1992). *Affirming diversity.* New York: Longman.

Noddings, N. (1990). Constructivism in mathematics education. In R. B. Davis, C. A. Maher, & N. Noddings (Eds.), *Constructivist views on the teaching and learning of mathematics.* Washington, DC: National Council of Teachers of Mathematics.

Oakes, J. (1985). *Keeping track: How schools structure inequality.* New Haven: Yale University Press.

Pease-Alvarez, L., Garcia, E., & Espinoza, P. (1991). Effective instruction for language minority students: An early childhood case study. *Early Childhood Research Quarterly, 6*(3), 347–363.

Peng, S. S., Fetters, W. B., & Kolstad, A. (1981). *High school and beyond: A national longitudinal study for the 1980's: A capsule description of high school students.* Washington, DC: U.S. Department of Education, Office of Educational Research and Improvement, National Center for Education Statistics.

Perret-Clermont, A. N. (1980). *Social interaction and cognitive development in children.* London: Academic Press.

Perret-Clermont, A. N., & Schubauer-Leoni, M. L. (1981). Conflict and cooperation as opportunities for learning. In P. Robinson (Ed.), *Communication in development* (pp. 203–233). London: Academic Press.

Perrow, C. (1967). A framework for the comparative analysis of organizations. *American Sociological Review, 32,* 194–208.

Pfeffer, J. (1982). *Organizations and organization theory.* Marshfield, MA: Pitman.

Piaget, J. (1926). *Language and thought of the child.* New York: Harcourt, Brace.

Piaget, J. (1954). *The construction of reality in the child.* New York: Basic Books.

Piaget, J. (1968). *Six psychological studies.* New York: Vintage Press.

Qin, Z., Johnson, D. W., & Johnson, R. T. (1995). Cooperative versus competitive efforts and problem solving. *Review of Educational Research, 65*(2), 129–143.

Ramirez, M., Yuen, S. D., Ramey, D. R., & Pasta, D. J. (1991). *Final report: Longitu-dinal study of structured English immersion strategy, early-exit and late-exit transitional bilingual education programs for language-minority children.* San Mateo, CA: Aguirre International.

Ridgeway, C. L., & Diekema, D. (1992). Are gender differences status differences? In C. L. Ridgeway (Ed.), *Gender, interaction, and inequality* (pp. 157–180). New York: Springer-Verlag.

Risjord, N. K. (1986). *History of the American people.* New York: Holt, Rinehart and Winston.

Rogoff, B. (1990). *Apprenticeship in thinking: Cognitive development in social con-text.* New York: Oxford University Press.

Rosenberg, M., & Simmons, R. G. (1971). *Black and white self esteem: The urban school child.* Washington, DC: American Sociological Association.

Rosenholtz, S. J. (1985). Treating problems of academic status. In J. Berger & M. Zelditch, Jr. (Eds.), *Status, rewards, and influence* (pp. 445–470). San Fran-cisco: Jossey-Bass.

Rosenholtz, S. J. (1989). *Teachers' workplace: The social organization of schools.* New York: Longman.

Rosenholtz, S. J., & Rosenholtz, S. H. (1981). Classroom organization and the per-ception of ability. *Sociology of Education, 54,* 132–140.

Rosenholtz, S. J., & Simpson, C. (1984). The formation of ability conception: Developmental trend or social construction. *Review of Educational Research, 54,* 31–63.

Rosenholtz, S. J., & Wilson, B. (1980). The effect of classroom structure on shared perceptions of ability. *American Educational Research Journal, 17,* 175–182.

Sarbin, T. R., & Allen, V. L. (1968). Role theory. In G. Lindzey & E. Aronson (Eds.), *The handbook of social psychology* (2nd ed.; vol. 1, pp. 488–567). Reading, MA: Addison-Wesley.

Sarkela, T., & Kuusinen, J. (1980). The connection between the instruction given in one's mother tongue and the ability in languages. In C. B. Paulston (Ed.), *Bi-lingual education: Theories and issues.* Rawley, MA: Newbury House.

Schumann, J. H. (1976). Second language acquisition research: Getting a more glo-bal look at the learner. In H. D. Brown (Ed.), *Papers in second language acquisition* (pp. 15–28). Ann Arbor, MI: Language Learning.

Scott, W. R. (1981). *Organizations: Rational, natural, and open systems.* Englewood Cliffs, NJ: Prentice-Hall.

Seliger, H. W. (1977). Does practice make perfect: A story of interaction patterns and L2 competence. *Language Learning, 27*(2), 263–278.

Shepard, L. A. (1989). Why we need better assessments. *Educational Leadership, 46,* 4–9.

Shulman, J. H., Lotan, R. A., & Whitcomb, J. A. (Eds.). (1995). *Groupwork in diverse classrooms: A casebook for educators.* San Francisco: Far West Laboratory for Educational Research and Development.

Shulman, L. S. (1987). Knowledge and teaching: Foundations of the new reform. *Harvard Educational Review, 57,* 1–22.

Silver, E. A., & Lane, S. (1995). Can instructional reform in urban middle schools help students narrow the mathematics performance gap? Some evidence from the QUASAR project. *Research in Middle School Education, 2,* 49–70.

Simpson, C. (1981). Classroom structure and the organization of ability. *Sociology of Education, 54,* 120–132.

Skutnabb-Kangas, T., & Toukomaa, P. (1976). *Teaching migrant children's mother tongue and learning the language of the host country in the context of the sociocultural situation of the migrant family.* Helsinki: Finnish National Commission for UNESCO.

Stanford University Middle Grades Life Science Curriculum Project. (1994). (Field Test Version). Stanford, CA: Author.

Stein, A. H., & Smithells, J. (1969). Age and sex differences in children's sex role standards about achievement. *Developmental Psychology, 1,* 252–259.

Stevenson, B. (1982). *An analysis of the relationship of student–student consultation to academic performance in differentiated classroom settings.* Unpublished doctoral dissertation, Stanford University.

Stone, C. A., Ankenmann, R. D., Lane, S., & Liu, M. (1993, April). *Scaling QUASAR's performance assessment.* Paper presented at the annual meeting of the American Educational Research Association, Atlanta.

Subbotskii, E. V. (1987). Communicative style and the genesis of personality in preschoolers. *Soviet Psychology, 25,* 38–58.

Swanson, P. E. (1993). *Linking theory to practice: Strategies for preservice education.* Unpublished doctoral dissertation, Stanford University.

Tammivaara, J. S. (1982). The effects of task structure on beliefs about competence and participation in small groups. *Sociology of Education, 55,* 212–222.

Thompson, J. D. (1967). *Organizations in action.* New York: McGraw-Hill.

Thorne, B. (1993). *Gender play: Girls and boys in school.* New Brunswick, NJ: Rutgers University Press.

Tobin, K., & Tippins, D. (1993). Constructivism as a referent for teaching and learning. In K. Tobin (Ed.), *The practice of constructivism in science education* (pp. 3–23). Hillsdale, NJ: Erlbaum.

Tudge, J. R. H., & Rogoff, B. (1989). Peer influences on cognitive development: Piagetian and Vygotskian perspectives. In M. Bornstein & J. Bruner (Eds.), *Interaction in human development* (pp. 17–40). Hillsdale, NJ: Erlbaum.

Useem, E. (1992). Middle schools and math groups: Parents' involvement in children's placement. *Sociology of Education, 65,* 263–279.

Van Fossen, B. E., Jones, J. P., & Spade, J. Z. (1987). Curricular tracking and status maintenance. *Sociology of Education, 60,* 104–122.

Villegas, A. M. (1991). *Culturally responsive pedagogy for the 1990's and beyond.* Princeton, NJ: Educational Testing Service.

Vinovskis, M. A. (1993). *Analysis of the quality of research and development at the OERI research and development centers and the OERI regional educational laboratories.* Washington, DC: U.S. Department of Education, Office of Educational Research and Improvement.

von Glasersfeld, E. (1991). Cognition, construction of knowledge and teaching. In

M. R. Matthews (Ed.), *History, philosophy, and science teaching: Selected reading.* New York: OISE Press.

Vygotzky, L. (1962). *Thought and language.* Cambridge, MA: Harvard University Press.

Vygotzky, L. (1978). *Mind in society: The development of higher psychological processes.* Cambridge, MA: Harvard University Press.

Wagner-Gough, J., & Hatch, E. (1975). The importance of input data in second language acquisition studies. *Language Learning, 25*(2), 297–308.

Webb, N. (1982, March). *Interaction patterns: Powerful predictors of achievement in cooperative small groups.* Paper presented at the annual meeting of the American Educational Research Association, New York.

Webb, N. (1983). Predicting learning from student interaction: Defining the interaction variable. *Educational Psychologist, 18,* 33–41.

Webb, N. (1989). Peer interaction and learning in small groups. *International Journal of Educational Research, 13,* 21–40.

Webb, N. (1991). Task-related verbal interaction and mathematics learning in small groups. *Journal of Research in Mathematics Education, 22,* 366–389.

Webb, N., & Kenderski, C. M. (1984). Student interaction and learning in small group and whole-class settings. In P. L. Peterson, L. C. Wilkinson, & M. Hallinan (Eds.), *The social context of instruction: Group organization and group processes* (pp. 153–170). Orlando, FL: Academic Press.

Webster, M., Jr., & Driskell, J. (1983). Beauty as status. *American Journal of Sociology, 89,* 140–165.

Webster, M., Jr., & Foschi, M. (1988). Overview of status generalization. In M. Webster, Jr. & M. Foschi (Eds.), *Status generalization: New theory and research* (pp. 1–20). Stanford: Stanford University Press.

Webster, M., Jr., & Sobieszek, B. (1974). *Sources of self-evaluation: A formal theory of significant others.* New York: Wiley.

Wheatley, G. H. (1991). Constructivist perspectives on science and mathematics learning. *Science Education, 75,* 9–21.

Wilkinson, L. C. (1988). *SYSTAT: The system for statistics.* Evanston, IL: SYSTAT.

Wilson, B. (1979). *Classroom instructional features and conceptions of academic ability.* Unpublished doctoral dissertation, Stanford University.

Wong-Fillmore, L. (1976). *The second time around: Cognitive and social strategies in second language acquisition.* Unpublished doctoral dissertation, Stanford University.

Wong-Fillmore, L., & Valadez, C. (1986). Teaching bilingual learners. In M. C. Wittrock (Ed.), *Handbook on research on teaching* (3rd ed., pp. 648–655). New York: Macmillan.

Zack, M. B. (1988). *Managing the classroom using cooperative groupwork: An assessment.* Unpublished doctoral dissertation, Stanford University.

Zander, A., & Van Egmond, E. (1958). Relationship of intelligence and social power to the interpersonal behavior of children. *Journal of Educational Psychology, 49,* 257–268.

About the Editors and the Contributors

Elizabeth G. Cohen is Professor of Education and Sociology at Stanford University. She has directed the Program for Complex Instruction since its inception. Her sociological research has focused on application of status characteristic theory to the classroom and organization of teaching. She has had a lifelong commitment to increasing the power of applied research in education through the use of strong sociological theory. As a professor in a graduate school of education for more than 30 years, she has chaired over 80 doctoral theses, most of which have been in sociology of education. She also has written a practical book for teachers, applying her ideas to the classroom: *Designing Groupwork: Strategies for Heterogeneous Classrooms* (2nd ed.; Teachers College Press, 1994), Teachers College Press.

Rachel A. Lotan is Co-Director of the Program for Complex Instruction and Senior Research Scholar at Stanford University School of Education. She received a Ph.D. in Education and an M.A. in Sociology from Stanford University. Prior to that, she taught for 10 years and held various administrative positions in junior high and high schools in Israel. Her academic interests are sociology of the classroom, curriculum for heterogeneous classrooms, the social organization of schools, and the professional development of teachers.

Rachel Ben-Ari is Associate Professor in the Department of Psychology and head of the Institute for the Advancement of Social Integration in Schools at Bar-Ilan University, Israel. Her research interests are social psychology, inter-group relations, and heterogeneous classrooms. With the staff of the institute, she trains teachers in implementing educational programs designed to enhance academic and social goals.

Julie A. Bianchini is Assistant Professor of Science Education at California State University, Long Beach. She received both her B.S. in Biological Sciences and her Ph.D. in Curriculum and Teacher Education from Stanford University. Between degree programs, she taught high school biology and physics in San Francisco. While attending graduate school, she participated in a wide range of curriculum development, teacher education, and research activities. She helped create the Human Biology Middle Grades Life Science Curriculum and conducted classroom research in complex instruction. Currently, at CSU Long Beach, she is teaching a science capstone course for liberal studies majors, supervising preservice science teachers, and continuing her research on student learning of science.

Bert Bower is the Executive Director of Teachers' Curriculum Institute. His corporation is dedicated to training and supporting social studies teachers in a series of innovative teaching strategies that allow students with diverse learning styles to "experience" history. He taught social studies for 8 years at Mountain View High School in Mountain View, California, authored several social studies textbooks for D. C. Heath, and received a doctorate in Social Studies Education from Stanford University School of Education.

Ruth Cossey is Assistant Professor of Education at Mills College, where she is currently director of Mathematics and Science Teacher Preparation. Her research interests pertain to the sociology of urban education, with a particular emphasis on issues of communication, assessment, and equity within mathematical education.

Rene Fukuhara Dahl is professor and associate chair in the Department of Recreation and Leisure Studies at San Francisco State University. She received her Ph.D. in Education (Sociology of Education) from Stanford University and has worked with teachers in inner-city elementary schools in the San Francisco Bay Area, Baltimore, and Philadelphia. Since coming to San Francisco State University, she has worked extensively with community-based nonprofit organizations that provide recreation and after-school programs for youth in at-risk environments, helping them to develop assessment and evaluation systems. In addition, she has conducted research on differences in visitor use of national forests by various ethnic groups.

Dey E. Ehrlich received her Ph.D. in Education at Stanford University. She is an educational consultant and researcher. While at the American Institutes for Research, she conducted numerous evaluations of the National Assessment of Educational Progress, as well as assessments of the Armed Services Vocational Aptitude Battery, of school reform for the Hewlett Foundation, and of a number of other educational programs. In her work with the Production Group, she has also co-produced, written, and narrated educational videos for research laboratories, universities, and school districts.

Nancy E. Ellis earned her Ph.D. at Stanford University School of Education. She is an instructor in the graduate program at Trinity College in Burlington, Vermont. Her research interests include teachers' understanding and practice in response to reform in educational policy and pedagogical theory.

Nikola N. Filby is Coordinator of the Regional Laboratory Program at WestEd, where she has worked for the past 20 years on programs linking research and practice. Her area of focus is school change and professional development processes that support teacher and student learning. Since 1990 she has facilitated the dissemination of complex instruction in Arizona, training more than 125 teachers and building district capacity to support and extend the program. She is on the leadership team for the network of 10 regional laboratories, where a key goal is to understand how to support the scaling up of successful reform to have broader and deeper impact. She completed her doctorate at Stanford University in 1975.

Nicole C. Holthuis is currently a doctoral candidate in science education at Stanford University. She received her master's degree in Curriculum and Teacher Education and has a single-subject teaching credential in science. She has taught high school biology, life science, physics, and chemistry. In addition, she has been a research associate for the Program for Complex Instruction and a curriculum writer for the Human Biology Middle Grades Life Science Project. Her dissertation, titled "Scientifically Speaking: Communication, Conceptual Understanding, and Gender Equity in the Constructivist Classroom," focuses on students' science talk as it relates to issues of access and understanding.

Anita Leal-Idrogo has a Ph.D. in Education and an M.A. in Sociology from Stanford University. She also has an M.A. in Rehabilitation Counseling from California State University, Fresno. She is Associate Professor at San Francisco State University in the Department of Counseling, where she teaches courses in rehabilitation counseling, substance abuse counseling, group counseling, and case practices in counseling. She is lead co-editor along with J. Gonzalez-Calvo and V. Krenz of a book titled *Multicultural Women: Health, Disability, and Rehabilitation*, published in 1996 by Kendall-Hunt. For that book, she co-authored a chapter titled "Women of Color in Jeopardy for HIV/AIDS." She is Project Director of a U.S. Department of Education, Rehabilitation Services Administration grant for experimental and innovative training, titled The HEART Project (HIV Education and AIDS Rehabilitation Training), which trains graduate counseling students in counseling people with HIV/AIDS. She is editor of the *Journal of Job Rehabilitation, Journal of Applied Rehabilitation Counseling*, and *Journal of Board of Directors of the National Rehabilitation Counseling Association*.

Christopher C. Morphew is a recent graduate of the doctoral program in Social Sciences in Educational Practices of Stanford University. He is currently Assistant Professor of Professional Studies in Education at Iowa State University, where his teaching and research interests include organizational leadership in higher education, outcomes assessment methods, and comparative research on systems of higher education.

H. Andrea Neves received her Ph.D. in Education from Stanford University in 1983. She is currently Professor of Education at Sonoma State University, California. Her teaching and research interest is the education of language minority and caste minority students. She teaches courses in multicultural education, second language teaching and learning, and research methodologies.

Patricia E. Swanson has been a bilingual teacher in rural and urban schools in both California and Colorado. She used complex instruction with the *Finding Out/Descubrimiento* curriculum extensively in her classes and served as a mentor teacher in complex instruction. In 1987 she began graduate work as a research assistant with the Program for Complex Instruction. She completed her doctorate in 1993 and is currently teaching in the Department of Teacher Education at California State University, Stanislaus. Both her teaching and research continue to reflect her ongoing interest in linking theory to classroom practice and creating more equitable classrooms.

Jennifer A. Whitcomb is currently a doctoral candidate at Stanford University and Project Director of Fostering a Community of Teachers and Learners. With the Program for Complex Instruction, she developed curriculum and assessments for social studies and language arts. She is a secondary English teacher. Her research interests include groupwork, teaching of literature, and teacher education.

Marcia B. Zack wrote her doctoral dissertation on the effects of various types of teacher talk on the implementation of a cooperative groupwork teaching method such as complex instruction. Her academic degrees are a Ph.D. specializing in Language, Literacy, and Culture (Stanford, 1988), an M.A. in Bilingual Education (Stanford, 1986), and an M.Ed. in Counseling Psychology (Boston College, 1980). Her educational interests include cultural adjustment, bilingual teacher training, supervision of student teachers, adult ESL education, international education, and Montessori education in the public schools. She is currently serving as a bilingual elementary school counselor in Yakima, Washington. Her recent work has focused on policies and interventions for managing attention deficit disorders, crisis management in schools and statistical assessment, and public relations for school counseling programs. In addition, she runs a ranch where she breeds German Shepherd dogs, Tennessee Walking horses, and snakes.

Index